SUSAN SALO

Jumping

GRID WORKBOOK

17 Industrial Dr. South Hadley, MA 01075

JUMPING GRID WORKBOOK

To purchase multiple copies of this book, contact:

Clean Run Productions, LLC
17 Industrial Dr.
South Hadley, MA 01075
800-311-6503
Email: info@cleanrun.com
Website: www.cleanrun.com

Edited by Monica Percival

Book design and typesetting by DD Graphix

Cover photo by Doghouse Arts

Interior photos by Susan Salo except where noted

ISBN 978-1-892694-35-5

To contact Susan Salo, visit her website: www.jumpdogs.com

This workbook is dedicated to the dogs, large and small,
who so enrich us all.

Important!

The grids in this workbook are organized in alphabetical order to make it easy to use as a reference book.

If you have never done gridwork before, you should start your training with the foundation grids. Please refer to "Appendix 1: Types of Grids" for a list of the foundation grids and "Appendix 2: Sample Lesson Plans" for a lesson plan designed for dogs with little or no jump education.

TABLE OF CONTENTS

ACKNOWLEDGMENTS

This book is an effort that has taken much time and thought, as I am a bit terrified of the printed word. That said, this would not have been possible without all the seminar participants and lesson takers who have generously allowed me to work with their dogs while my understanding of the dog's mind and athleticism have continued to evolve. I sincerely wish to be of help to the dogs and without the many gracious people who have participated, this understanding would not have been possible. Thank you.

I also need to thank Rachel Sanders who allowed me to work with her dogs as I began this fascinating journey and, of course, a huge thank you to Susan Garrett who single-handedly forced me down people's throats in the beginning and for many years after. I learned a great deal from her and because of her, and for that I am forever grateful.

This and all my efforts would not come to you if not for Monica Percival and Clean Run. It has been for me, a wonderful and enduring collaboration which I have thoroughly enjoyed and hope to continue for many years to come. This is a special time to remember the efforts and friendship of Brad Scott who always helped me feel at ease (if possible) while the making the DVDs; he was always encouraging and he is missed.

Last, but clearly not least, I want to thank all the dogs who offered me insights I will always be mindful of. It has been my pleasure to know all of them.

"Leadership should be born out of the understanding of the needs of those who would be affected by it." —Marian Anderson

INTRODUCTION

The reason most people fail instead of succeed is they trade what they want most for what they want at the moment." —Napoleon

This workbook is designed to be a supplement to my DVDs, with the material offered in a simple, easy-to-use format that you can take onto the practice field. However, you can also use it without the DVDs, although much of the theory behind the grids and jumping methodology will be lost in this case.

For those who have seen the DVDs, you will find some slight changes in spacing or jump height for some of the grids presented here. This is because a great deal of time has elapsed since I made several of the DVDs, and my understanding of biomechanics and proprioception continues to evolve; therefore, I have made some changes. Some of the grids have also been renamed for clarity.

It has always been my training mind-set to make the correct behavior as easy as possible for the dog to perform, while making the incorrect behavior difficult—yet never impossible—thus ensuring freedom of choice for the animal. Dogs try so very hard to please the human; as such, I am a firm believer that a "try" should have value to the dog. After all, we are the only ones who know what success looks like; our dogs are unaware of the outcome we want. So to keep our dogs offering behaviors and to build value for the jumping effort itself, the try should always be rewarded. In the horse world, the rider is attached to the body of the horse and can feel the amount of effort the horse puts into keeping the rails in place, even if on occasion the horse is not successful. When running with our dogs on course, so much of the dog's effort is not seen by the handler since we are simply too busy running and directing our dogs. Gridwork gives you a chance to reward your dog's jumping effort.

German poet Johann Wolfgang von Goethe noted, "There is nothing more frightful than ignorance in action." I find punishing knocked bars abhorrent, primarily because few handlers set out to train the biomechanics of jumping, which are terribly specific and must be completed to perfection in a fraction of a second. An agility dog rarely has the luxury of total focus on a task since he must divide his focus between task (obstacle performance) and handler information (which comes at him in multiple forms simultaneously). And we must all admit that this information is often late, and we are often in our dogs' path obscuring his sight of the obstacle until it's too late for our dogs to respond in the manner we would like. My question is simply, "How can we hold our dogs to a higher performance than we are capable of?

Although we as handlers continually strive to improve our timing, it is nearly impossible to be perfect with our cues for every turn on the course. But in the years since beginning this work, it has become obvious that dogs with a good jumping foundation also have greater mental acuity than dogs that do not. What I mean by this is they have better problem solving skills. Since each grid is a new or different question to our dogs, they have learned from an early age to figure these out as they move, meaning they learn to think quickly on their feet and are more resilient to our handling errors than dogs without this foundation.

The grids in this workbook are intended to give you a means of isolating various aspects of the jumping mechanics and allow time for your dog to practice in a quiet, encouraging environment. The feeling of taking flight, that grace and power when the effort is well performed, is a thing of awesome proportion and I am inspired when I see a dog experience this—I want each dog to "own" that feeling. Practicing gridwork gives your dog an opportunity to focus on his jumping mechanics so you can help him develop understanding and confidence, and ultimately speed.

All of the lines and patterns that are offered in this workbook will ultimately present themselves on agility courses in the form of straight lines, bending lines, and slices. As you teach your dog always to be looking ahead of where he is, he will begin to recognize these patterns no matter how they may be presented in the agility ring, and he will be able to confidently accomplish them. Patience and training time spent on gridwork will pay off in huge dividends later.

You have everything to gain by trying the work and nothing to lose. I am always reminded of one of my favorite quotes of Susan Garrett, "Irritation is motivation. If something bothers you enough, you'll do something about it."

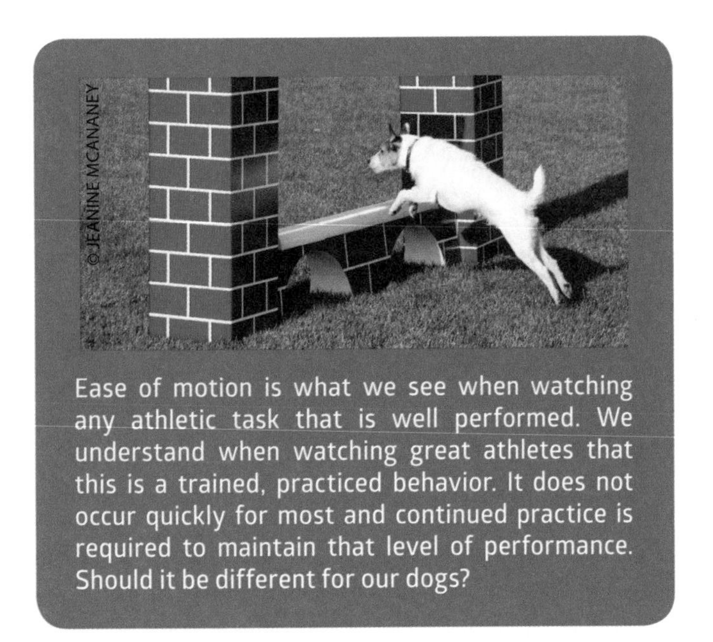

Ease of motion is what we see when watching any athletic task that is well performed. We understand when watching great athletes that this is a trained, practiced behavior. It does not occur quickly for most and continued practice is required to maintain that level of performance. Should it be different for our dogs?

You will notice that many of the grids require a number of jumps and a generous amount of space. While I understand that not everyone has that many jumps or that much room, the reality is the work does take equipment and space. Many of my clients share time at a training facility with friends just for doing their gridwork. This is a wonderful plan on many levels; you have someone to share your interest and a second set of eyes to help you while you are working your dog. As some of you know, I have had a wonderful friend and training partner for 10 years now; in fact, since our first dogs were pups. The training time has been well spent and a true and lasting friendship the result. Another option that training facilities can consider is to offer a monthly class dedicated to gridwork.

When you begin this or any training program, it is important to consider your dog's age, his current physical condition, and his individual needs. Each dog is a different entity; some are more athletic than others, some are quick learners while others take more time, some are more thoughtful, etc. If there was a magic formula for just how much to train gridwork and what to train when, it would make agility handlers happy, but this is simply not the case. You will find as you go through the work that some dogs require a lot of maintenance gridwork to keep them jumping cleanly and confidently. You may also find your dog will go through phases where he holds his jumping skills together for long periods of time and other phases where he needs a great deal of maintenance work—it all ebbs and flows. One of my wonderful mentors in the horse world, Gene Lewis, told me as a young rider always to remember, "If you ride 10 horses a day, each will give you just what you ask of them, but each will do so in their own way—allow for that." Words of wisdom I have never forgotten.

The main thing while training is to be certain your dog maintains joy and excitement for the work. A happy, confident dog is a thrill to run with. I still vividly recall what instantly drew my attention to the sport of agility—the amazing enthusiasm displayed by the dogs. After all, it is the only place where a human is willing to run and play chase with a dog. It is our job to keep our dogs' enthusiasm and joy in the sport going. Set up your dog to be successful and reward him highly for his efforts, and what he offers you as your working partner will amaze even the most skeptical. And, always try to remember that while training is a mechanical skill, the relationship is not. Enjoy the process.

I believe in short, happy training sessions. Don't underestimate the power of latent learning! In my seminars, the dogs do not have long days of training; rather, they have many short working sessions where we are always looking for the quality of the work, not the quantity. Yet, it is always amazing how many people tell me the next day of the seminar how tired their dogs were in the evening, when they really didn't work all that much! Learning new skills and thinking about what they're doing can be as taxing to a dog as physical activity.

Horse people must have horses that are thoughtful toward their work since our bodies, as well as theirs, depend on it. Equestrians live and work in a quiet environment because our work is sensory rather than word-oriented; it is based on "feel" as opposed to sight. I believe that agility enthusiasts would be better served if a bit of that carried over to the sport of agility. Remember that information in the agility partnership is a two-way street. We give our dogs information about what we want with our commands, how we move, where we move to, etc., but because we are busy handling, we often fail to recognize the information our dogs are giving us. Gridwork gives you a chance to "listen" to what your dog is telling you.

The grids in this workbook are in alphabetical order. The description of each grid includes all the information you need to set up the grid and understand the task you are presenting to your dog. In addition, it includes troubleshooting insights to help you solve the various problems that may occur. I strongly encourage people to stick with the training plan for each grid and only become creative with it if you are certain of how to fix a problem should it arise. I think of each grid as a question to the dog; the more simplistic question gets the best answer from the dog.

"Nothing is sweeter than an agility run that begins with my dog at the start line, self-assured and filled with anticipation, and ends without a single footfall out of place. On the other hand, nothing is more disheartening than a run where I can feel my dog measuring his stride, questioning his takeoff spots, and losing his confidence and natural rhythm when presented with a line or series of jumps. Before I started working with Susan Salo, the latter would often leave me discouraged and upset. The frustration had little to do with the outcome of the run, but rather from my lack of understanding and not knowing how to solve the problem. I didn't have the tools to explain to my dog what it was that I wanted, and I didn't know how to instill the confidence back into his performance.

So much of agility jumping education seems to be grossly simplified and narrowly focused on "the bar," it is either left up (good) or brought down (bad). I know that strong, reliable behaviors are not created through punishment but through positive reinforcement. But I didn't know how to set up my dog to be successful—how, for example, to break jumping into its many components and teach, reward, and rebuild the confidence?

Susan is a consummate educator. She is patient, incredibly insightful, and her knowledge seems limitless. Every time I work with her and my understanding grows, I am humbled by the job we have put before our dogs. My current competition dogs are polar opposites, yin and yang. Brite is bold and impetuous; Fearless, ironically, is prone to overthinking and innately cautious. Both were raised from puppyhood on Susan's jump grids and are now entering their prime at five years old.

Susan's gridwork has been instrumental in turning Brite into an extremely efficient jumper. Her efficiency through turns and on straightaways is exceptional and she is a very difficult dog to beat on any Masters Jumpers course. Most importantly, she has also learned to be quick but not hurried. For Brite, getting anywhere fast has always been paramount and that can cause her to rush through her work, leading to mistakes and loss of balance. Susan's gridwork has taught Brite to be balanced both physically and mentally. It is a very powerful combination.

Susan's instruction has also given me the tools to build and maintain Fearless's confidence which could otherwise easily be shaken. His runs are not flashy, yet they are deceptively quick. His speed has come more slowly with understanding, and it is incredibly rewarding to feel him drive a path with resolution.

For Susan's contribution to those perfect runs, where my teammates appear to jump without effort because the task put before them is so well-rehearsed, I am very, very grateful."

—Annie Pyle, 8-time national finalist, 2-time vice-champion, instructor at Clean Run

PHOTOS © CATHI WINKLES PHOTOGRAPHY

"When I first met Susan Salo, I knew a lot about handling and dog training but the knowledge of jumping had eluded me. Over the years, I have learned that jumping is really a complex task that you can break into smaller skills. I now know how to present drills to my dog so that she learns how to balance herself, how to read the distance between obstacles, and where to focus while she jumps.

One of the most valuable things I have learned through all of my dogs' work with Susan's jumping grids is how to interpret what they do, though I have so much more to learn in that department. I have grown to appreciate all that the dog does while we play the sport that we love.

Thanks, Susan, for all that you have taught me and for all that I continue to learn because of the work that you do."

—Jen Pinder, Multiple-time national champion and World Team member, instructor for FiredUp K9s and Highest Hope Dog Sports

BEFORE YOU BEGIN TRAINING

Which Dogs Should Do Gridwork?

- Dogs over one year of age*
- Dogs that have never jumped
- Dogs that are doing agility but have not had isolated jump training
- Dogs rehabilitating from injury or surgery (speak to your veterinarian or canine rehabilitation therapist to determine when it's appropriate to begin)
- Older dogs that are retired from competition but still want (and need) a job that can help them stay in shape and reward them for doing so.

*Note: If you use jump bumps in place of the jumps, dogs younger than one year of age can do the foundation grids as well most of the other grids. Please refer to the *Puppy Jumping* DVD for more information. If a particular grid in this workbook is not recommended for puppies, it is noted in the description.

What "Size" Is My Dog?

In the setup instructions for each grid, there are guidelines for the spacing of the jumps. Although I have used these guidelines with success at seminars and classes, I cannot stress enough these truly are guidelines. A bit of experimenting with spacing may be required to make each grid suitable for your individual dog. But you can use your dog's competition jump height to determine which setup guidelines to use as a *starting point* for each grid:

- Big dogs: Dogs jumping 22" to 26"
- Medium dogs: Dogs jumping 16" to 20"
- Small dogs: Dogs jumping 12" to 14"
- Tiny dogs: Dogs jumping 6" to 8"

Be aware, however, that some tiny dogs, such as a confident Papillon, may have a huge stride for their size while a large dog like a Malinois that carries himself very upright will often have a shorter stride than other dogs his size. So don't be afraid to change the spacing if the grid isn't producing the desired result for your dog.

Targets

With gridwork, we always use a visible target on the ground to show our dogs the path we want them to take. The target becomes an important part of teaching your dog to look ahead and toward his jump rather than at you.

- You should place the target on the landing side of the jump, far enough away that your dog can land and get all four feet on the ground.
- The target must be of high value to your dog so he wants to drive forward to it. If food is used, place the food on a visible target such as a floppy Frisbee or in a small bowl.
- Food should not be offered from your hands because that will raise your dog's focal point up too high; your dog's head position needs to be down and in a natural position.
- If you are using a toy as the target and your dog runs off with toys, add a small piece of rope to the target so you can control it and play *with* your dog after he does the grid.

When using food as a target, place it on a very visible object.

General Guidelines for Gridwork

- Do not set up grids along a fence line or wall; training is about choice. Your dog needs to commit to the path ahead freely and by choice to learn his job.
- Do not allow your dog to back jump through the grids since the performance is rarely good and is not rewarded. We are training the dog to seek work as we move, but not simply to choose the jumps he prefers.
- If you are starting your dog from a sit position, make sure your dog's weight is on his haunches. If your dog starts an exercise in a crouching or "vulture" position, then his weight is on his front and the angle of his shoulders is closed. This is not desirable and can cause knocked bars. An easy way to get a dog to sit upright (which puts his weight on his haunches and opens up the angle of his shoulders) is to ask for a high hand touch after he sits.
- If you are starting your dog from a stand position, make sure your dog is square and nicely balanced.
- Gridwork should be done in short sessions and should always be fun for your dog. If you're making it too difficult for your dog, you're not serving the purpose.
- There are no consequences for errors. Gridwork is not about right or wrong, it is about knowledge and whether your dog understands his job. If the dog fails, he doesn't understand the question.
- Be patient; impatience only slows down your dog's learning.
- Dogs will not all look the same when jumping; they are not cookie cutters. Do not focus too much on form; a dog's jumping form will be good if he is performing the function correctly—form follows function. So focus on teaching your dog to perform the exercise correctly.
- When you are evaluating your dog's performance, it's best to view him from the side. This is a great use for a video camera if you don't have a training partner to help you.

In the photo on the left, the dog's shoulder angle is completely closed and his elbows are abducted. This is an excellent example of a dog that has placed too much weight on the forehand to be allowed to proceed to the jump. In the photo on the right, the dog's sit position has been corrected and he is sitting in a balanced position and ready to jump.

In the photo on the left the dog is square and nicely balanced. In the photo on the right, the dog has reached forward with a foot causing the shoulder to be lower than the hip and leaving the dog off balance.

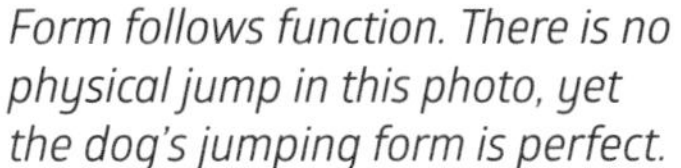

Form follows function. There is no physical jump in this photo, yet the dog's jumping form is perfect.

Here is a dog failing to read the collection necessary for a short distance and landing with one pastern hyperextended. Viewing an isolated moment like this shows how difficult just one poorly performed jump can be on the body of the canine athlete.

How Often Should You Practice Grids?

It is important to realize that gridwork is something you should do throughout your dog's agility career. It is not something you train and then put aside. Your dog will dictate how often you need to work on certain grids. With some dogs, it is relatively easy to maintain their jumping performance, and with others it requires more practice time.

It is never advisable to set up any grid and leave it up for a long period of time. The goal is not to drill one grid until you perfect it—this is a human instinct and does not create the quick understanding you want from your dog. The goal is for your dog to be able to quickly assess each task and perform it with ease, not do it correctly because you've been repeating it over and over again.

You will find it takes longer to set up the grids than it does to school your dog through them. For this reason, if you have the training space and equipment, I advise setting up three or four grids at a time and rotate your dog through them. You can even go back and forth between two grids in a training session rather than working one grid to completion and the next to completion. The goal is a dog that can assess the task quickly; therefore, rotating with each repetition is advisable to begin to build this quality. It also keeps the dog's enthusiasm level high.

The Importance of Good Conditioning, Warm-ups, and Cool Downs

- Conditioning of the canine athlete is of enormous importance in agility and gridwork. Your dog needs to be in good, strong physical condition. When you are working your dog, you are breaking him down at the same rate of speed that you are training him. If you spend an hour a week training your dog, you should spend at least twice that amount of time conditioning him.
- Muscles that are cold should not be stretched. You need to warm up your dog before you stretch him.
- A good cool down after a run or training session is also important.

Reading the Diagrams

The diagrams in this book represent approximations of actual dog and handler interaction. It is impossible to depict precise relationships between the dog and handler with complete accuracy in a two-dimensional image. The diagrams are intended to convey the concepts presented in the text.

In the years since beginning this work, it has become very evident that dogs with a good jumping foundation have greater mental acuity than dogs without a good jumping foundation. What I mean by this is that they have better problem solving skills. Since each type of grid is a new or different question to the dogs, they have learned from an early age to figure these out as they move, meaning they think quickly on their feet without taking extra pats of the ground as they assess the task. This is a major accomplishment when you consider agility is a timed event and speed is an integral part of the dog's job.

Diagram Key

	Bar jump, winged
	Bar jump, nonwinged
	One-bar jump, winged
	One-bar jump, nonwinged
	Parallel spread/double bar jump, winged
	Parallel spread/double bar jump, winged
	Ascending spread jump, winged
	Ascending spread jump, nonwinged
	Triple bar jump/extended spread, winged
	Triple bar jump/extended spread, nonwinged
	Broad jump/long jump
	Panel jump, winged
	Panel jump, nonwinged
	Tire jump
	Wall jump
	Viaduct jump
	Open, pipe, or tube tunnel
	Handler
	Dog sitting
	Dog standing
	Dog lying down
	Dog's path
	Handler's path
	Obstacle plane & other imaginary lines
FC	Front cross
RC	Rear cross
LOP	Lead-out pivot
T	Visible target (a treat on or in an object the dog can see easily or a toy)

ANATOMY OF THE JUMP

Jumping is a difficult and complicated mechanical process, particularly when you consider the rate of speed at which we need our dogs to perform the activity.

Each time your dog completes a stride, his shoulders, head, and neck are weighted heavily as his first forefoot hits the ground to complete the stride. In this instant your dog must also shift the weight off his shoulders and forehand, placing it more heavily over the hips if he's going straight ahead. To load the weight onto his haunches, your dog begins to raise his head slightly. Once weight transfer and load over the haunches is completed, your dog can then drop his head down slightly, rounding his back, and launch into the air. If your dog is watching you at this moment, either your motion or just a hand, he will have limited use of his head and neck, compromising his range of motion in the head through the shoulders. Your dog's shoulders need to elevate *and* move forward as his head bobs down slightly for flight to be successful and provide ease of motion to your dog.

When you see a dog that jerks his head up and back slightly, he is using his shoulder and neck muscles to help create elevation. Correctly done, the biomechanics of jumping require the weight to be carried over the hips, with your dog creating good angles from hip to hock. This is the spring—the tighter the angle, the more power when the spring is released in the form of upward thrust, which creates elevation. If your dog's head stays high, limiting range of motion of the head, neck, and shoulders, his back will suffer from the lack of correct motion and will be slightly inverted (hollow) as opposed to slightly rounded.

When the biomechanics are lacking, your dog will not find the ease of motion that is present in all well-schooled athletes. The body then compensates until it is no longer possible to do so, causing injury or soreness for the athlete.

Some people question the need to teach jumping skills since their dog runs through the woods jumping with ease and grace. Dogs can do this primarily because they have *full focus* on the path they are driving, which allows the body to respond with ease and suppleness. When your dog is doing agility, his focus can be mainly handler focus with task orientation being a last-minute response. True skill is attained with dedicated gridwork training and much practice time. Practicing handling sequences does *not* provide your dog with the time and focus necessary to acquire the biomechanics necessary for good jumping skills.

In this sequence, the dog lands and gathers with head, neck, and shoulders rising as the weight is shifted to the dog's hindquarters. The dog's hind feet are placed closely and tightly together, which allows equal distribution of weight. As the dog begins to elevate, the shoulders and head rise for liftoff. Once the dog creates elevation, the dog's head drops down and reaches forward to allow a comfortable stretch through the air. This sequence shows proper biomechanics, allowing for ease of motion for the dog.

PHOTOS © JEANINE MCANANEY

In this sequence, we see a young dog just learning the biomechanics of jumping. In the first photo, he arrives at the takeoff spot unprepared and unorganized to leave the ground. Note how separated the hind feet are, leaving the dog with limited balance, while the shoulders have yet to snap up, making the attempt fragile at best. In the next photo, the attempt is slightly better because the hindquarters have come together to provide greater balance, yet the shoulder and forelegs have not improved. In the last shot, the young dog has figured out how to make this jump work. The dog has landed and gathered nicely, elevating his shoulders and back with nice form. His head begins to drop and reach forward. This demonstrates the process of learning the dog needs to experience in a calm and relaxed manner to produce reliable biomechanics at speed and with repetition.

© JEANINE MCANANEY

This photo is one of my very favorites for demonstrating the complexity of weight shift and shoulder elevation. Note that both dogs have made good angles with their hindquarters to allow maximum power off the ground; however, the dog on the left is very late to elevate his shoulders and although the dog on the right is more correct, he is still a little late with one shoulder. Putting it all together in a timely manner takes practice for the dog.

ADJUSTABLE STRIDE GRID #1 (FOUNDATION)

Overview

This is a grid of huge importance for your dog. Agility courses require your dog to adjust his stride by compressing or lengthening it as appropriate for any given distance between obstacles. Your dog needs to learn to look ahead and adjust himself to accommodate these changes in distances throughout the agility course. I want my dogs to continue to drive at speed through the course unless I am cueing deceleration. To do this, your dog needs to understand where his takeoff place is. Then he can change the location of that takeoff place as necessary. An adjustable stride allows your dog to cover ground efficiently and jump cleanly.

The concept of an adjustable stride seems simple enough, but although all dogs can adjust their stride while running, many cannot do it when it comes to the biomechanics of jumping. In this grid we not only deal with our dogs' ability to adjust his stride, but also with the problem of where that perfect takeoff place is for each dog. While working on the adjustability of the stride, by nature of the exercise, we are also driving our dogs to an appropriate takeoff place.

The foundation adjustable stride grid offers your dog only one stride to a jump that is set at full height (or close to it); therefore, your dog does not have to know from very far back where his takeoff spot is or how to find it, this grid shows him. Once your dog has an understanding of where he is driving to, he will begin to look for that takeoff spot from greater distances.

We have all seen dogs on any given weekend that are careful, clean jumpers, *but* they are seldom very fast. These dogs have figured out that when their stride is shorter, their balance is greater because their feet are always underneath them and weight shift to come off the ground is relatively easy to perform. These dogs have not learned that they can adjust their stride to gain greater speed and still perform the all-important weight shift to make the necessary angle of elevation. This short stride is the dog's "comfort zone," and many are not convinced that giving it up is a good idea. If knocked bars have ever been met with displeasure, even if it was just a sigh from the handler, the dog's need to stay in his comfort zone may be even stronger. The distance grid can help these dogs become more operant in the sense that they begin to get comfortable experimenting with adjusting their stride. But no one can predict how fast or slow this process will be. This is truly one of those grids where only you know the desired result, and your dog does not. It is your job to be patient while your dog figures out this game, meaning that as you are walking out to your position, your dog is looking down the line to assess what needs to take place in the given distance. The target is imperative for this to work.

A frequent issue in training this grid is that many handlers do not understand what a stride is, let alone how to adjust it, so there are many layers that go into understanding this exercise for both dogs and handlers. If you have the DVD, it is worthwhile to spend the time watching some of the dogs performing this grid.

A stride is defined as the cycle of body movements that begins when your dog touches a front foot on the ground and ends when that foot touches the ground again. So for the one-stride portion of this grid, we are looking for two "pats" of the ground: the first being the landing from the three-part "bounce" or ladder/plyometric grid and the second being the completion of the stride. So if there are three pats of the ground, your dog has added an extra stride.

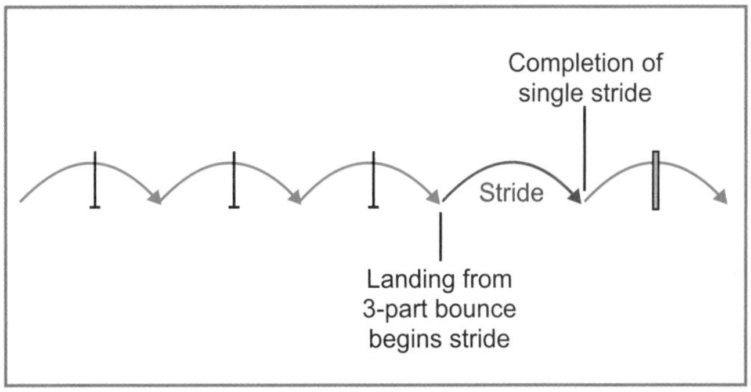

Completion of single stride

Stride

Landing from 3-part bounce begins stride

Caution: The goal of this exercise is *never* to test how long a stride your dog can produce. There is no need to try to overextend your dog's stride. The idea is to produce an adjustable stride within a reasonable distance. Stretching your dog out too far will only make weight transfer and angle of elevation more difficult to achieve, and serves no useful purpose. You are looking for ease of motion; your dog should use only as much energy as is necessary for clearing the jump and he should change his stride fluidly (whether lengthening or compressing it) as suitable for the distance.

Reference DVD

See Distance Grid on the *Foundation Jumping* DVD.

Setting Up the Grid

This grid requires four jumps, three of which can be non-winged. The jumps are placed in a straight line.

The grid begins with a three-part "bounce" or ladder/plyometric grid. This is familiar to your dog and it also creates the compression necessary to propel your dog into the larger space where he must land and take one stride to drive to the proper takeoff spot for the fourth jump. These jumps have little height and are *never* raised.

Jump #4 will have height and should be the winged jump so it is the dominant focal point for your dog, helping draw his eye and attention to the end of the line of jumps. This jump will be moved in or out with each repetition so the distance between jumps #3 and #4 is never the same. If you do not move the jump, your dog will simply pattern the exercise, which is not the goal.

Jump #4 should be changed out often to school your dog through different types of hurdles in this picture: ascending double, parallel double, triple, extended spread, tire, wall jump, viaduct, and panel. I do not use the broad jump or long jump in this exercise; this obstacle should be isolated and schooled separately.

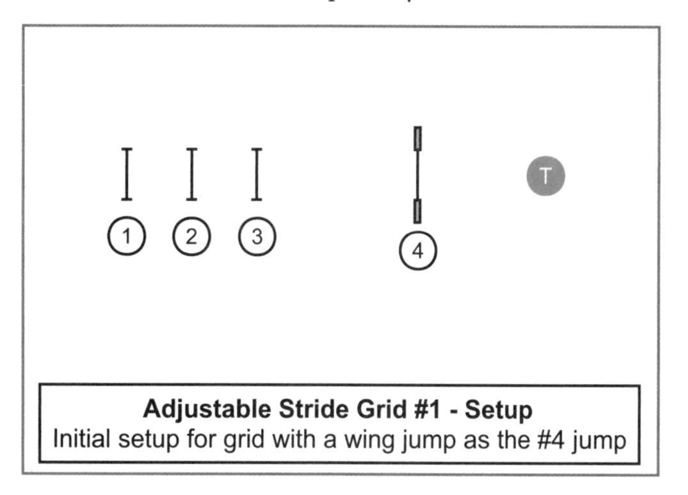

Adjustable Stride Grid #1 - Setup
Initial setup for grid with a wing jump as the #4 jump

Jump Spacing and Height

Use the information below to determine the jump spacing and jump heights for the grid. Although I have used these distances with success at seminars, they are only guidelines and you may need to adjust them for your dog. Spacing between the jumps is measured from the center of one jump to the center of the next.

Note: A bit of experimenting with spacing may be required to gain the one stride to jump #4.

Big Dogs

- *Jumps #1–#3 (bounce/ladder grid):* Space these jumps 6' apart and set at a maximum of 6"–8" in height. The height of these jumps never increases during the exercise.
- *Jump #4:* The starting position of jump #4 is 15'–17' from jump #3. Jump #4 can be set at your dog's competition height; however, when introducing the exercise, set the bar at least one height lower until you are certain your dog can do the exercise with success.
- *Moving jump #4:* This jump moves for each repetition your dog performs. Do four reps moving jump #4 away from jump #3 by about 1' each time. For example, if you begin with jump #4 spaced 15' from jump #3, then jump #4 will be 19' away after four reps. Then do three more repetitions moving jump #4 closer to jump #3 by 1' each time so jump #4 returns to its starting position.

Medium Dogs

- *Jumps #1–#3 (bounce/ladder grid):* Space these jumps 5' apart and set at a maximum of 6" in height. The height of these jumps never increases during the exercise.
- *Jump #4:* The starting position of jump #4 is 14'–15' from jump #3. Jump #4 can be set at your dog's competition height; however, when introducing the exercise, set the bar at least one height lower until you are certain your dog can do the exercise with success.
- *Moving jump #4:* This jump moves for each repetition your dog performs. Do four reps moving jump #4 away from jump #3 by 1' each time. For example, if you begin with jump #4 spaced 14' from jump #3, then jump #4 will be 18' away after four reps. Then do three more repetitions moving jump #4 closer to jump #3 by 1' each time so jump #4 returns to its starting position.

Small Dogs

- *Jumps #1–#3 (bounce/ladder grid):* Space these jumps 4' apart and set at a maximum of 4" in height. The height of these jumps never increases during the exercise.
- *Jump #4:* The starting position of jump #4 is 10'–12' from jump #3. Jump #4 can be set at your dog's competition height; however, when introducing the exercise, set the bar at least one height lower until you are certain your dog can do the exercise with success.

- *Moving jump #4:* This jump moves for each repetition your dog performs. Do three reps moving jump #4 away from jump #3 by 6"–8" each time. For example, if you begin with jump #4 spaced 10' from jump #3, then jump #4 will be 11.5'–12' away after three reps. Then do two more repetitions moving jump #4 closer to jump #3 by 6"–8" each time so jump #4 returns to its starting position.

Tiny Dogs

- *Jumps #1–#3 (bounce/ladder grid):* Space these jumps 3' apart and set at a maximum of 4" in height. The height of these jumps never increases during the exercise.
- *Jump #4:* The starting position of jump #4 is 8'–9' from jump #3. Jump #4 can be set at your dog's competition height; however, when introducing the exercise, set the bar at least one height lower until you are certain your dog can do the exercise with success.
- *Moving jump #4:* This jump moves for each repetition your dog performs. Do three reps moving jump #4 away from jump #3 by 6" each time. For example, if you begin with jump #4 spaced 8' from jump #3, then jump #4 will be 9.5' away after three reps. Then do two more repetitions moving jump #4 closer to jump #3 by 6" each time so jump #4 returns to its starting position.

Target

The target should be clearly visible to your dog from his starting position. Place it about 10' from the last jump *before* you take your dog to the start line. Because the position of the last jump in this grid distance changes for each repetition, be certain the target moves farther out as the grid expands and moves closer in as the grid shrinks in size.

Dog's Starting Position

- Line up your dog so he is facing the center of the first jump.
- The distance between your dog and the jump should be half the distance of the first space in the grid. For example, if jumps #1 and #2 are 6' apart, then start your dog 3' from the first jump.
- Your dog can be in a sit, stand, or down.
- Your dog should be looking forward at the jump or target before you release him. If you do not have a start-line stay, have a training partner restrain your dog.

Handler's Position

- Lead out and stand one step ahead of the target and one step laterally off the target. This allows your dog to get to the target without passing the plane of your body.
- Face the direction your dog is traveling, looking over your shoulder to watch him.
- Sometimes stand to the left of the target and sometimes stand to the right to work your dog on both sides.

Note: This is not a grid that I would do as a send-away, at least at first, since dogs will carry their head a bit higher when traveling away from the handler if they are not confident they are correct. When your dog raises his head, his stride will always be shorter, causing extra strides.

This dog is making a nice effort over the viaduct with a slightly long takeoff spot, which tends to be the natural preference of this dog. Since this dog is always successful with jumping, I do not modify his jumping effort.

Progressions

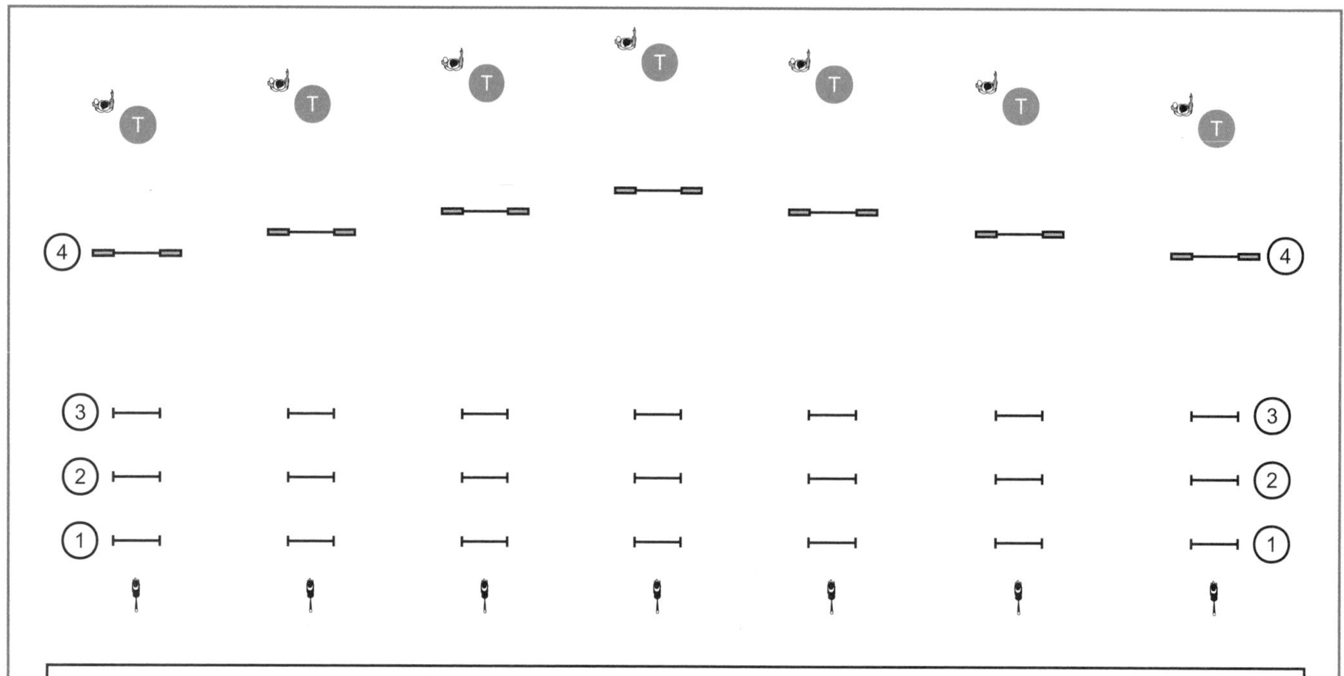

Problem Solving

Problem: Your dog runs from his start-line position directly to the target without entering the grid.

Solution: When dogs run around a grid, it is their way of saying, "This is just too much and I don't understand what I am to do here." Simplify the question to your dog by breaking the task down into smaller parts. Step 1: Target and reward your dog for doing just the three-part bounce grid. Step 2: Place the target right before the last jump. Step 3: Place the target after the jump. Finally, offer your dog one more repetition to make certain he is comfortable with the process before you begin to move the jump.

Problem: Your dog enters and completes the three-part bounce/ladder grid and then exits before the last jump.

Solution: This is a common response as your dog does not perceive the last jump as part of the line due to the larger spacing between jumps #3 and #4. Place the target right before the last jump and do one or two repetitions to correct your dog's path. Then move the target so it's after the last jump.

If your dog goes around the last jump again, shorten the distance between jumps #3 and #4 by 1'–2' and lower the height of the last jump. Repeat the grid until your dog stays on the correct path and then increase the jump height.

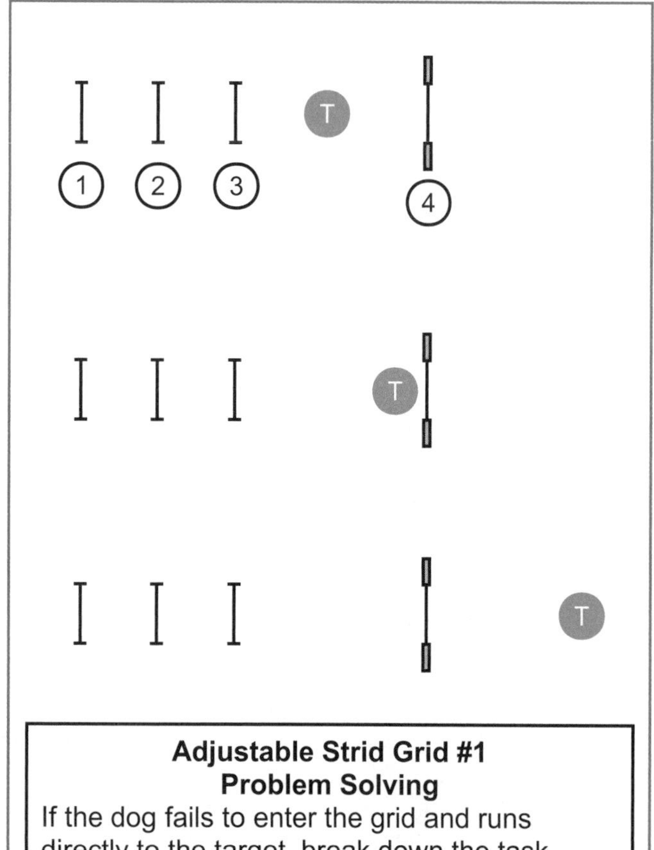

Problem: Your dog adds a second stride in the one-stride distance between jumps #3 and #4.

Solution: Shorten the beginning distance between jumps #3 and #4 by 1' to encourage your dog to come forward and try using just one stride. If your dog still adds a stride, lower the jump height (often significantly) to encourage your dog to drive forward. Remember, first and foremost, this grid is a distance question! If this fixes the distance question for your dog, then you can gradually add height back to jump #4.

Problem: Your dog bounces between jumps #3 and #4.

Solution: If your dog has bounced the distance once, give him a second try; many dogs will be startled by the distance and offer a bounce once, but when given a second opportunity at the same distance they will adapt their striding and add the stride. Other dogs, particularly young ones, love the power and feeling of bouncing the jumps. Before you can try to vary his stride, you need to find the distance where your dog will offer one stride. Lengthen the beginning distance between jumps #3 and #4 by 1'–2' and then repeat the grid. This part of the process always fascinates me as you are having a conversation with your dog—he is telling you how he feels about a given space.

Problem: No matter how you move jump #4 your dog offers multiple strides.

Solution: Find where your dog is comfortable by shortening the distance between jumps #3 and #4 to drive your dog to a good takeoff spot for the last jump. Play with the distance by increasing it by only 4"–6". If your dog does not add extra strides with this small amount of added distance, immediately move the jump back in to the shorter distance and repeat the grid. This is a reward for your dog's effort to extend his stride and helps build your dog's confidence. Confidence is critical, so your dog's perception of difficulty must be honored. Then, instead of continuing to extend the distance, simply play with increasing or decreasing the distance by 8"–10" until your dog is comfortable with the exercise.

For a great many dogs, the question of what to do with space offered is really one they do not understand independently; they only know how to handle the space depending on how their handler is moving. This is not desirable as it puts the burden on you to always be fast and correct.

How Much to Practice?

When starting gridwork your dog, this grid requires a good deal of practice—just not all at once! Big and medium dogs can do seven successful repetitions in a session, four reps moving the jump out and then three moving it back in. Small and tiny dogs can do five successful repetitions in a session, three reps moving the jump out and then two moving it back in.

If your dog is successful at reading the space and producing a nice single stride at the various distances, and has worked through all the different types of jumps, then this is an excellent tune-up grid to do during the week before a trial to remind your dog to work with some independence and not base his stride based solely on how fast or slow you are moving.

For trained dogs that are not having any problems with their jumping, I generally offer this grid once a month.

Proofing

- You can gradually increase your lateral distance from the target to a distance that reflects the normal working space between you and your dog.
- Once your dog is confidently and successfully reading the space and producing a nice single stride at the various distances offered, begin a training session with jump #4 at the longest distance from jump #3 to see if your dog can read the space correctly on the first try; for example, if you have been moving jump #4 incrementally from 14'–18', then start with jumps #3 and #4 spaced at 18'. If your dog reads that space well, move the jump to your shortest distance on the next repetition; 14' in our example. If your dog reads that distance, move the jump to the intermediate distance; 16' in our example. In short, once your dog has tuned into what this grid is about and can perform it reliably, then you can play with the distances, being mindful that the goal is a one-stride distance, not multiple strides, and that you don't want to attempt to overextend your dog's stride.
- Proofing this grid also means working it with all the different hurdles you will see on courses inserted into the last jump spot (except for the broad jump or long jump as previously noted).
- It is also a good idea to add visual distractions to jump #4, such as flower pots or other decorations, to proof your dog's confidence with jumps that look different.

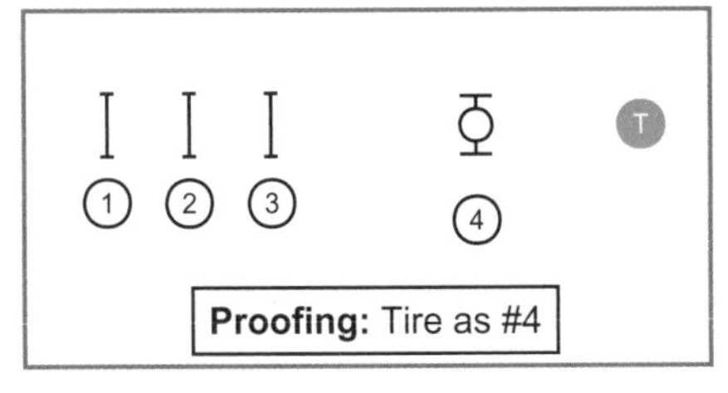

Proofing: Tire as #4

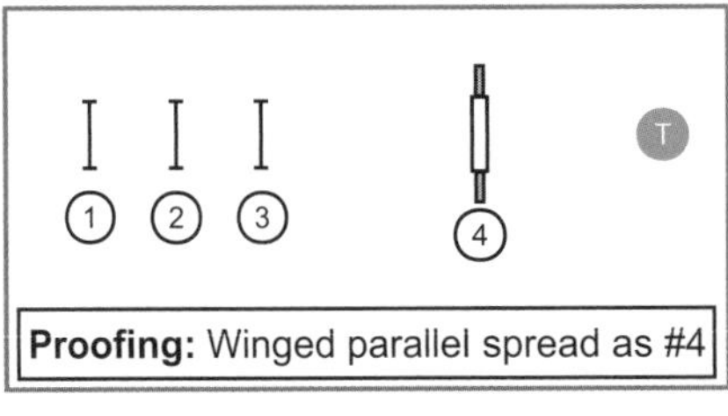

Proofing: Winged parallel spread as #4

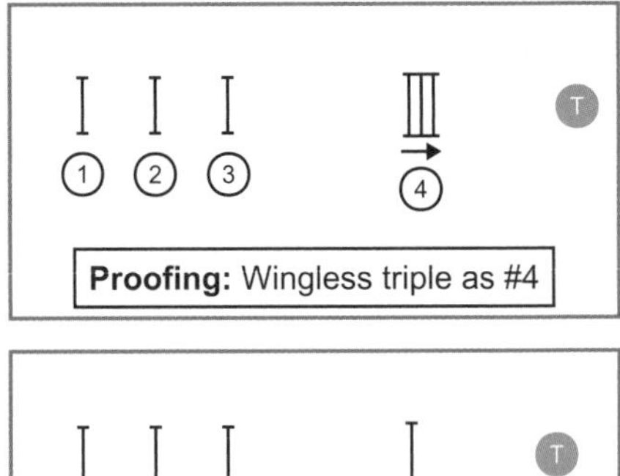

Proofing: Wingless triple as #4

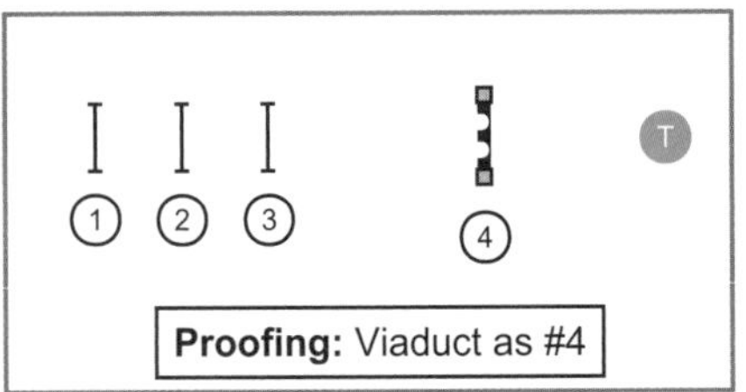

Proofing: Viaduct as #4

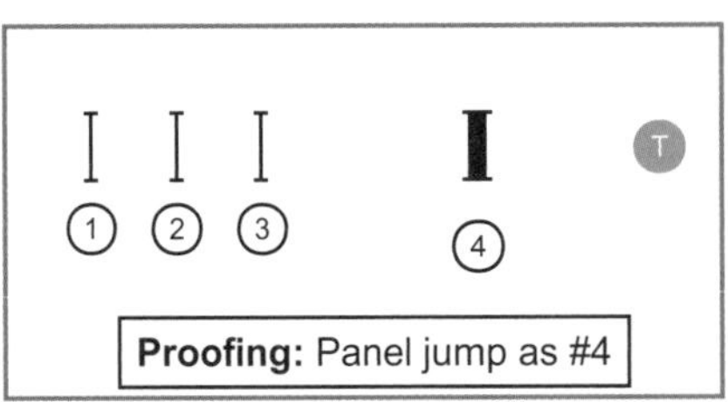

Proofing: Panel jump as #4

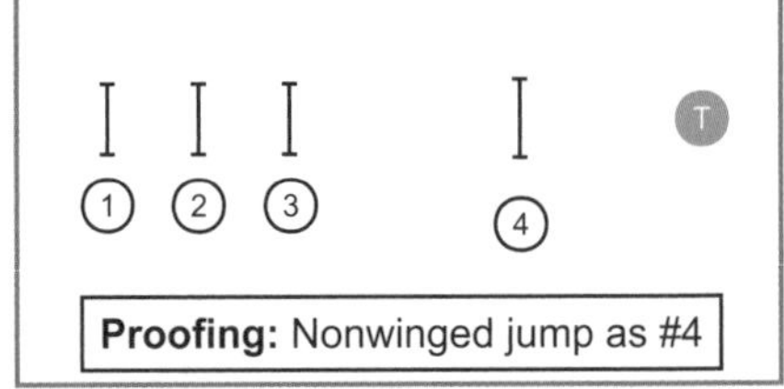

Proofing: Nonwinged jump as #4

Adding Handler Motion

Most handlers rush into running with their dogs before the dog understands the mechanical effort needed to do the task with precision. There is much work needed to get your dog to the point where he's ready for you to be in motion. Adding handler motion should only begin after you have completed the proofing work above, and your dog is producing a reliable one stride for all different types of jumps at varying distances.

As always, remember to work your dog on both your left and right side.

1. Lead out halfway through the grid, release your dog, and move forward at a walk. Your dog should complete the grid correctly and continue driving forward toward the target. As you walk, your dog will pass you so it's a good idea to have a trained "Go On" cue that you can give as your dog catches up with you.
2. Lead out halfway through the grid, release your dog, and move forward at a jog.
3. Lead out halfway through the grid, release your dog, and move forward at a run.
4. Run with your dog from the start.

These steps should be done incrementally so your dog's performance doesn't change. If your dog starts to have difficulty with your motion, you are increasing your speed too quickly. Your dog needs an opportunity to become comfortable with motion while still focusing on his job.

When you add motion, you need to be mindful of the spacing between the jumps, so proofing can be successful and your motion is reinforcing the behavior you want from your dog. If jump #4 is at the shortest distance from #3, for example, you do not want to indicate full speed ahead to your dog unless a bounce might be the desired result.

Once you are running with your dog, your dog may start to leave out the stride and bounce. In this case, more space is required. Adjust the spacing between jumps #3 and #4 as necessary, being mindful the purpose of the exercise is a one-stride distance. This grid should be a fun and informative grid to proof with motion since you will begin to sense what your motion cues mean to your dog and find the balance of motion that tells your dog whether you want a short, medium, or long stride.

Do not lead out to the last jump in the grid and stand there as your dog approaches unless you want your dog to add another (second) stride, since this position cues a turn.

Adding Handling

There is no change of sides in this exercise so crosses are not necessary.

Grid Variations

The foundation adjustable stride grid can be worked with a different one-stride distance at each end so you don't have to move the jumps. You do not work the grid from one end to the other; rather, you always begin by setting your dog up to start with the three-part bounce.

Also see "Adjustable Stride Grid #2" in the next section.

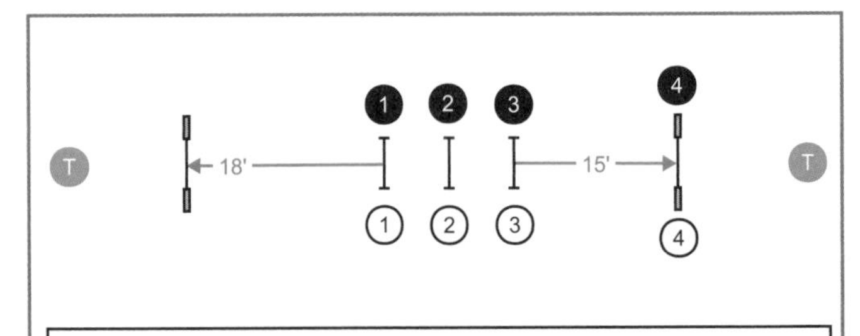

Adjustable Stride Grid #1 - Variation
This setup for the foundation adjustable stride grid allows you to work two different distances without moving the jumps. The dog always starts the exercise with the three-part bounce part of the grid.

ADJUSTABLE STRIDE GRID #2

Overview

This version of the adjustable stride grid offers a distance at each end of the "bounce" or ladder/plyometric portion plus a bend for your dog to perform as well. The interesting thing about offering the adjustable stride grid in this way is that dogs will usually demonstrate just how much they prefer a straight line over a bend. When doing this grid in seminars, many dogs will take the jump that's straight ahead even when the handler and the target are clearly presenting the turning jump. The dog has a preference!

You'll also notice that the jumps in the bounce/ladder section of this version of the grid are zigzagged. This has a visual impact on the dogs and forces them to pay attention to that portion of the work. We want our dogs to be looking ahead, yet we don't want them to ignore what may appear trivial to them. By angling the jumps in the ladder, it is saying to your dog, "First, take care of this."

Handling can be incorporated into this version of the grid or you can be stationary at the target with a less experienced dog. But when adding handling, remember that the point of this exercise is still to give your dog practice at reading distances and producing a nice single stride to various types of jumps.

Reference DVD

See Exercise #2 on the *Tuning Up for Competition* DVD.

Setting Up the Grid

This version of the adjustable stride grid requires a few more jumps than version #1. But if you are limited on space and/or jumps, setting up just one half of the grid is more than ample for schooling. If you are doing the complete grid, you will need four nonwinged jumps and six winged jumps; to do half of the grid, you will need four nonwinged jumps and three winged jumps.

Center the bounce portion of the grid in the middle of your work area and then walk off your dog's one-stride distance to the straight-on jump from each end of the ladder. You'll notice the guidelines provided below allow for a slightly longer one stride to the straight jump than in adjustable stride grid #1. This is because dogs are happy to come forward to take the straight jump after doing the left and right bend; the straight jump becomes a reward for the bend work.

Next, walk off the distance to the left and right bend jump from the end of the ladder. At first each jump on the bend should be placed at the *shortest* distance in the range recommended below, since when your dog is turning, his spine is bent and his stride will always be shorter than when he is traveling straight.

The three jumps on the left and right ends of the grid should be changed out often to school your dog through different types of hurdles in this picture (see "Proofing"): ascending double, parallel double, triple, extended spread, tire, wall jump, viaduct, and panel. I do not use the broad jump or long jump in this exercise; this obstacle should be isolated and schooled separately.

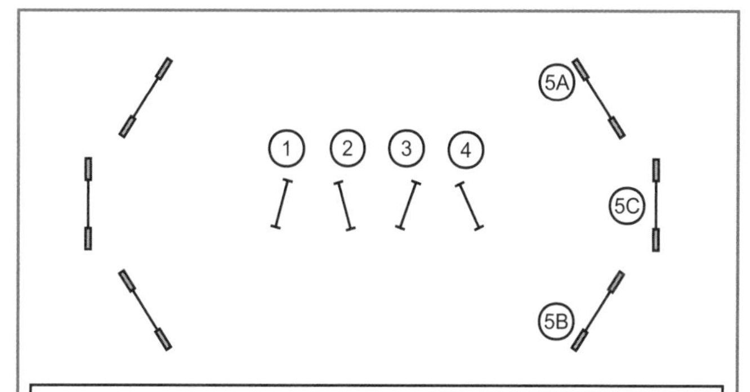

Adjustable Stride Grid #2 - Setup
This is the initial setup for this grid. But if you don't have enough space or equipment, you can set up the three winged jumps on just one side of the ladder.

Jump Spacing and Height

Use the information below to determine the jump spacing and jump heights for the grid. Although I have used these distances with success at seminars, they are only guidelines and you may need to adjust them for your dog. Spacing between the jumps is measured from the center of one jump to the center of the next.

Big Dogs

- *Jumps #1–#4 (bounce/ladder):* Space these jumps 6' apart and set at a maximum of 6"–8" in height. The height of these jumps never increases during the exercise.
- *Jumps #5A and #5B:* Position these jumps so they are 15'–17' from jump #4, beginning work at the low end of the range. The jumps can be set at your dog's competition height.

- *Jump #5C:* Position this jump so it is 16'–18' from jump #4. The jump can be set at your dog's competition height.

Medium Dogs

- *Jumps #1–#4 (bounce/ladder):* Space these jumps 5' apart and set at a maximum of 6" in height. The height of these jumps never increases during the exercise.
- *Jumps #5A and #5B:* Position these jumps so they are 14'–15' from jump #4, beginning work at the low end of the range. The jumps can be set at your dog's competition height.
- *Jump #5C:* Position this jump so it is 15'–16' from jump #4. The jump can be set at your dog's competition height.

Small Dogs

- *Jumps #1–#4 (bounce/ladder):* Space these jumps 4' apart and set at a maximum of 4" in height. The height of these jumps never increases during the exercise.
- *Jumps #5A and #5B:* Position these jumps so they are 10'–12' from jump #4, beginning work at the low end of the range. The jumps can be set at your dog's competition height.
- *Jump #5C:* Position this jump so it is 12'–13' from jump #4. The jump can be set at your dog's competition height.

Tiny Dogs

- *Jumps #1–#4 (bounce/ladder):* Space these jumps 3' apart and set at a maximum of 4" in height. The height of these jumps never increases during the exercise.
- *Jumps #5A and #5B:* Position these jumps so they are 8'–9' from jump #4, beginning work at the low end of the range. The jumps can be set at your dog's competition height.
- *Jump #5C:* Position this jump so it is 10'–11' from jump #4. The jump can be set at your dog's competition height.

Target

The target should be clearly visible to your dog from his starting position. Place the target about 10' from the jump you are planning to take at #5 *before* you take your dog to the start line.

Dog's Starting Position

When starting with the ladder grid:

- Line up your dog so he is facing the center of the first jump.
- The distance between your dog and the jump should be half the distance of the first space in the grid. For example, if jumps #1 and #2 are 6' apart, then start your dog 3' from the first jump.
- Your dog can be in a sit, stand, or down.
- Your dog should be looking forward at the jump or target before you release him.

With more experienced dogs, you can work your dog both into and out of compression by starting at the center jump on one end of the grid and going straight through the ladder grid to the center jump on the other side of the grid. When doing this advanced progression, the distance between your dog and the first jump should equal one steady, short stride for your dog:

- Big dogs: 9'–11'
- Medium dogs: 7'–9'
- Small dogs: 5'–6'
- Tiny dogs: 4'–5'

This will allow your dog to begin with the most power and greatest balance. Starting your dog farther from the jump may cause even a well-educated jumping dog to want to flatten out or become frenetic.

If you do not have a start-line stay, have a training partner restrain your dog.

Handler's Position

- Lead out and stand one step ahead of the target and one step laterally off the target. This allows your dog to get to the target without passing the plane of your body.
- Face the direction your dog is traveling, looking over your shoulder to watch him.
- Sometimes stand to the left of the target and sometimes stand to the right to work your dog on both sides.

Progressions

Stage 1

Whenever a ladder grid is mixed with real distance, I always begin the training session by doing several repetitions of just the ladder grid to help your dog come forward with good, clean footwork.

Stage 2

Starting with the four-jump bounce for each repetition, I then work a left bend, a right bend, and then the straight-on jump. The straight-on jump is done last as a reward for the bend work. Repeat for the jumps at the opposite end of the ladder.

Stage 3 (Advanced)

With more experienced dogs, you can work your dog both into and out of compression by starting at one end of the grid and going straight through the ladder grid to the center jump on the other side of the grid.

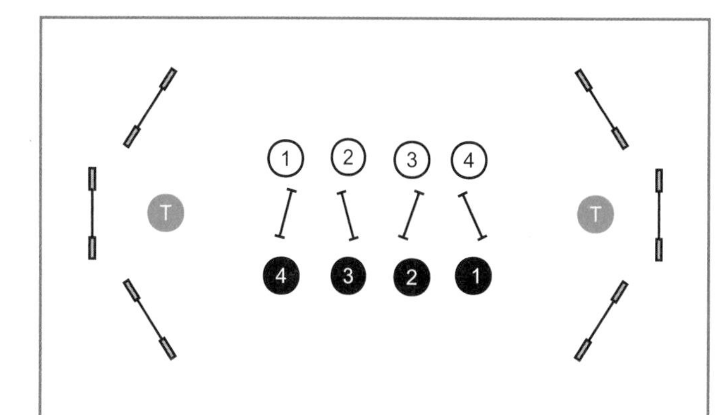

Adjustable Stride Grid #2 - Stage 1
Begin the session by doing several repetitions of just the bounce/ladder portion of the grid.

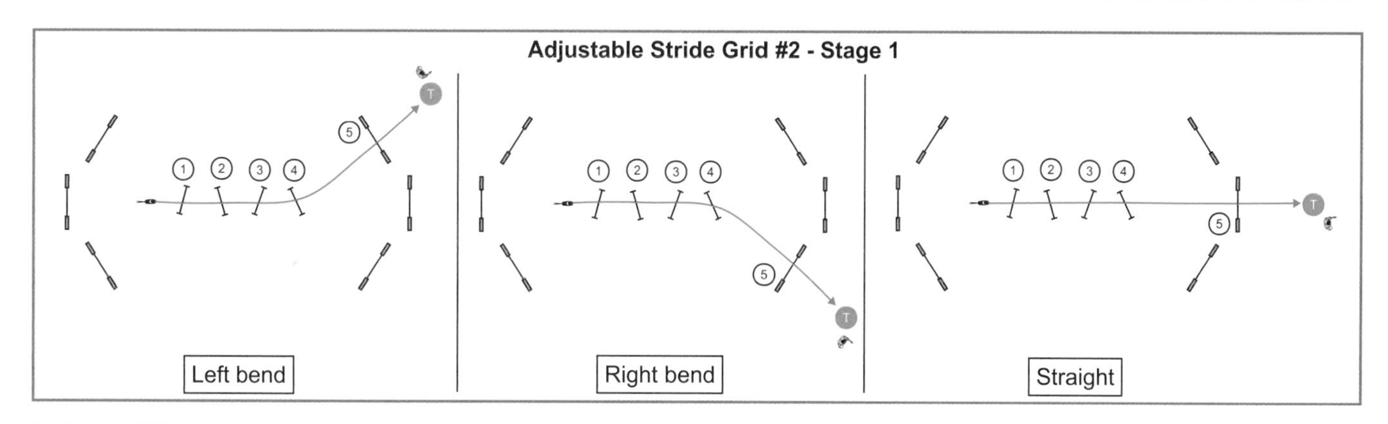

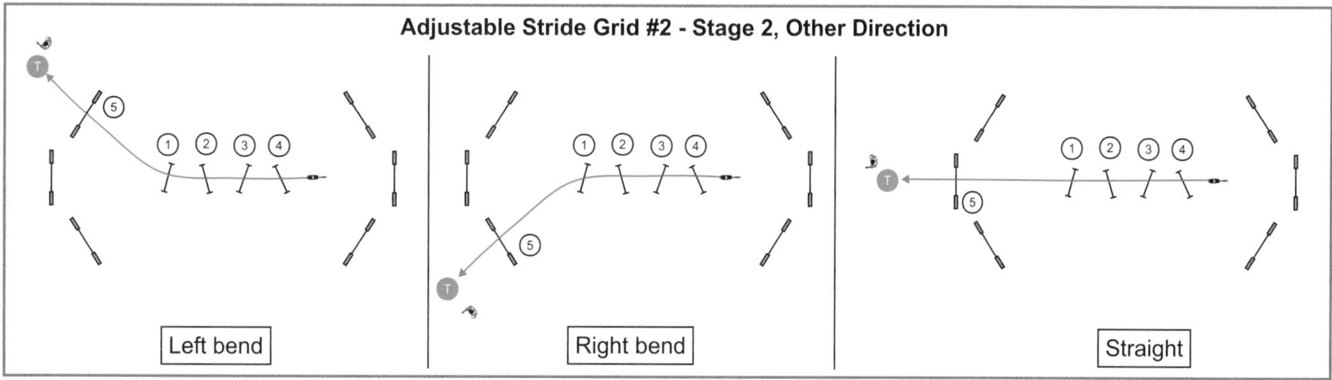

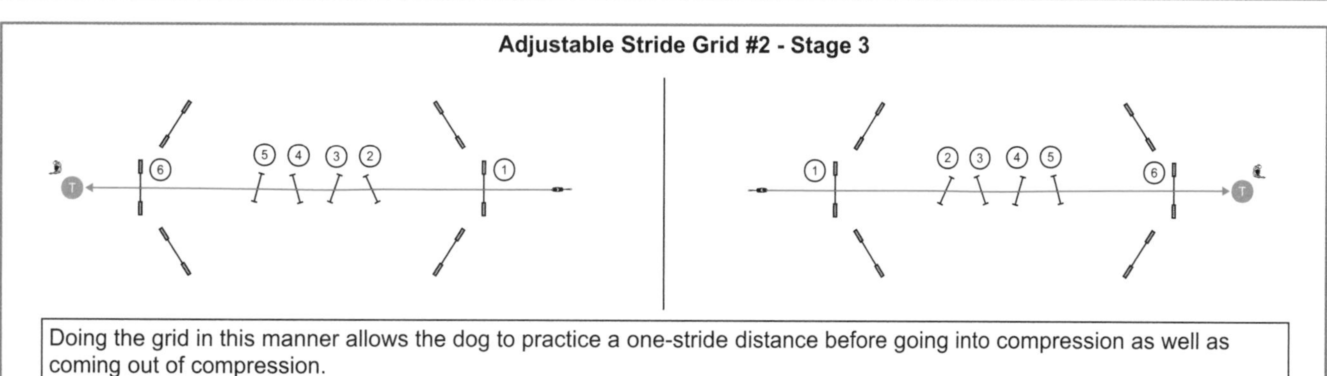

Doing the grid in this manner allows the dog to practice a one-stride distance before going into compression as well as coming out of compression.

Problem Solving

Problem: Your dog chooses to go straight even though you and the target are indicating one of the jumps on the bend.

Solution: Put the target in front of the jump on the bend and do one repetition. Then move the target back to the landing side of the jump and try again. I have to chuckle when a dog chooses the straight line even with all the information telling him he is wrong; the dog says, "But I so want that one!"

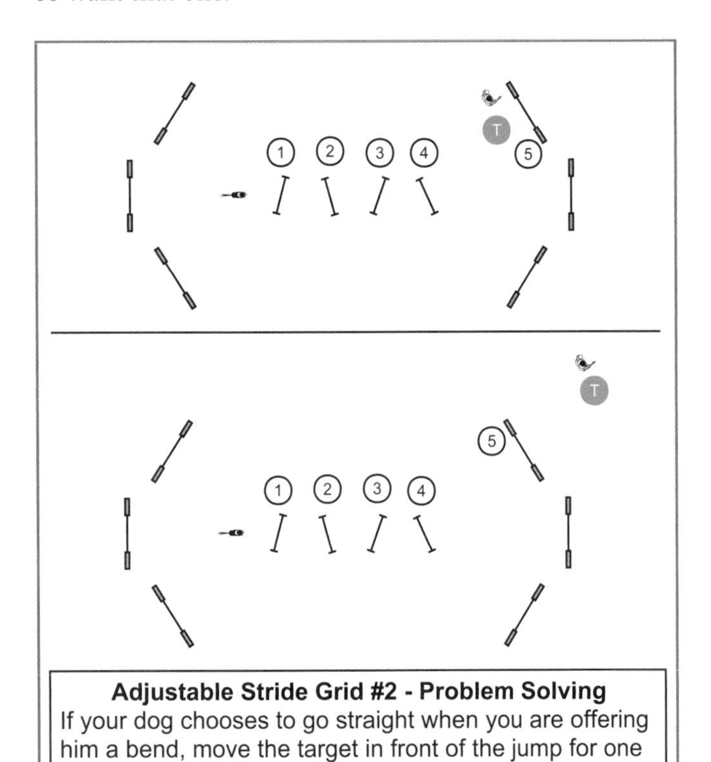

Adjustable Stride Grid #2 - Problem Solving
If your dog chooses to go straight when you are offering him a bend, move the target in front of the jump for one repetition and then move it back to the landing side.

Problem: Your dog runs from his start-line position straight to the end of the grid without entering the grid.

Solution: When dogs run around a grid it is their way of saying, "This is just too much and I don't understand what I am to do here." Simplify the question by breaking the task down into smaller parts. Step 1: Target and reward your dog for doing just the four-part bounce grid. Step 2: Place the target right before jump #5. Step 3: Place the target after the jump.

Problem: Dog enters and completes the four-part bounce grid and then exits before the last jump.

Solution: This is a common response because your dog does not perceive the last jump as part of the line due to the larger spacing between jumps #4 and #5. Place the target right before jump #5 and do one or two repetitions to correct your dog's path. Then move the target so it's after jump #5.

If your dog goes around the last jump again, shorten the distance between jumps #4 and #5 by 1'–2' and lower the height of the last jump. Repeat the grid until your dog stays on the correct path and then increase the jump height.

Problem: Your dog adds a second stride in the one-stride distance between jumps #4 and #5.

Solution: Shorten the beginning distance between jumps #4 and #5 by 1' to encourage your dog to come forward and try using just one stride. If your dog still adds a stride, lower the jump height (often significantly) to encourage your dog to drive forward. Remember, first and foremost, this grid is a distance question! If lowering the jump height answers the distance question for your dog, then you can gradually add height back to jump #5.

Problem: Your dog bounces between jumps #4 and #5.

Solution: If your dog has bounced the distance once, give him a second try; many dogs will be startled by the distance and offer a bounce once, but when given a second opportunity at the same distance they will change their striding and add the stride. Other dogs, particularly young ones, love the power and feeling of bouncing the jumps. Before you can try to vary his stride, you need to find the distance where your dog will offer one stride. So lengthen the beginning distance between jumps #4 and #5 by 1'–2' and then repeat the grid. This part of the process always fascinates me as you are having a conversation with your dog—he is telling you how he feels about a given space.

Problem: No matter how you move jump #5 your dog offers multiple strides.

Solution: Find where your dog is comfortable by shortening the distance between jumps #4 and #5 to drive your dog to a good takeoff spot for jump #5. If your dog is successful, increase the distance by 4"–6". If your dog does not add extra strides with this small amount of added distance, immediately move the jump back to the shorter distance and repeat the grid. This is a reward for your dog's effort to extend his stride and helps build your dog's confidence. Confidence is critical, so your dog's perception of difficulty must be honored. As your dog develops confidence you can incrementally increase the distance, always offering a decreased distance to your dog as a reward for opening up his stride. However, if your dog is struggling with this grid, it is a good idea to go back to the adjustable stride grid #1 and practice foundation work.

How Much to Practice?

As with many of the grids, this one offers many options, but I recommend doing only one repetition of each option in a single session.

This is an advanced grid that can be offered as part of your dog's maintenance training.

Proofing

- You can gradually increase your lateral distance from the target to a distance that reflects the normal working space between you and your dog.
- Once your dog is confidently and successfully reading the space and producing a nice single stride, you can proof the grid by beginning the session with jump #5 at your dog's largest one-stride distance to see if he can read the space correctly on the first try. If your dog reads that space well, move jump #5 to his shortest one-stride distance on the next repetition. In short, once your dog has determined what this grid is about and can perform it reliably, you can play with the distances, being mindful that the goal is a one-stride distance, not multiple strides, and that you don't want to overextend your dog's stride.
- Proofing this grid also means working it with all the different hurdles you will see on courses inserted into the jump #5A, #5B, and #5C spots (except for the broad jump or long jump as previously explained).
- It is also a good idea to add a few visual distractions to jump 5A, #5B, or #5C, such as flower pots or other decorations, to proof your dog's confidence with jumps that look different.
- If you have the full grid set up with three jumps at each end, and you are going straight through the grid from one end to the other, you can vary each one-stride distance offered. For example, if you have a medium dog, you might have one distance spaced at 14' and the other at 16'.

Adding Handler Motion

Most handlers rush into running with their dogs before the dog understands the mechanical effort required to do the task with precision. There is much work needed to get your dog to the point where he's ready for you to be in motion. Adding handler motion should only begin after you have completed the proofing work above, and your dog is producing a reliable one stride for all different types of jumps at varying distances.

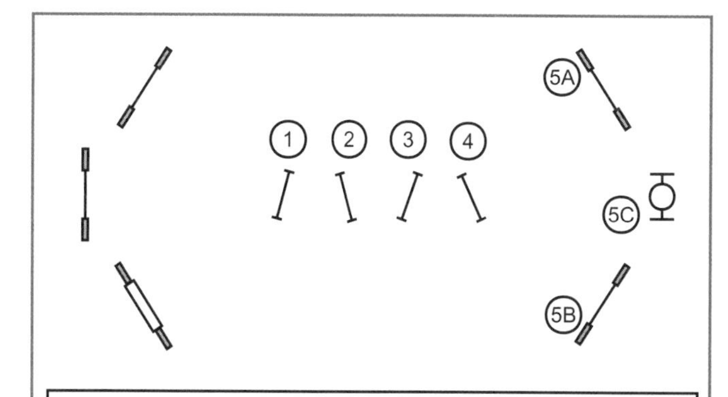

Adjustable Stride Grid #2 - Proofing Different Hurdles
Proofing this grid means working it with all the various hurdles you will be seeing on courses inserted into the jump #5A, #5B, and #5C spots.

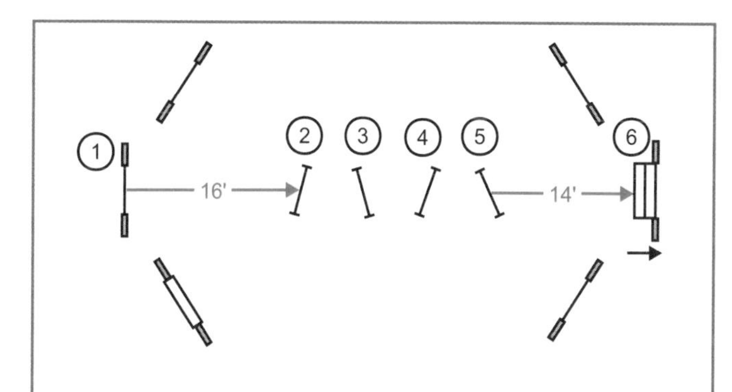

Adjustable Stride Grid #2
Proofing Different One-Stride Distances
If you are working with the full grid, you can use two different one-stride distances for proofing.

As always, remember to work your dog on both your left and right side.

1. Lead out halfway through the grid, release your dog, and move forward at a walk. Your dog should complete the grid correctly and continue driving forward toward the target. As you walk, your dog will pass you so it's a good idea to have a trained "Go On" cue that you can give as your dog catches up with you.
2. Lead out halfway through the grid, release your dog, and move forward at a jog.
3. Lead out halfway through the grid, release your dog, and move forward at a run.
4. Run with your dog from the start.

These steps are done incrementally so your dog's performance does not change. If your dog starts to have difficulty with your motion, you are increasing your speed too quickly. Your dog needs the opportunity to become comfortable with motion while still focusing on his job.

When you add motion you need to be mindful of the spacing between the jumps so proofing can be successful and your motion is reinforcing the behavior you want from your dog. If jump #5 is at the shortest one-stride distance for your dog, for example, you do not want to indicate full speed ahead to your dog unless a bounce might be the desired outcome.

Once you are running with your dog, your dog may start to leave out the stride and bounce. In this case, more space is required. Adjust the spacing between jumps #4 and #5 as necessary, being mindful the purpose of the exercise is a one-stride distance. This grid should actually be a fun and informative grid to proof with motion since you will begin to sense what your motion cues mean to your dog and find the balance of motion that tells your dog whether you desire a short, medium, or long stride.

Do not lead out to the last jump in the grid and stand there as your dog approaches unless you want your dog to add another (second) stride, since this position cues a turn.

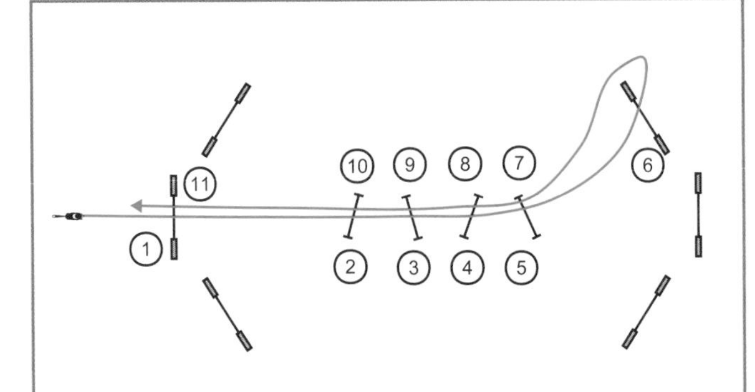

Adjustable Stride Grid #2
Adding Handling
If you are working with the full grid, you can add handling. For example, do a front or rear cross to turn the dog to one of the bend jumps and then go back the way you came.

Adding Handling

This is a grid that has many options for introducing some basic handling once your dog is proficient with the primary job of reading a space and adjusting his stride. Instead of driving straight through the grid, for example, you can do a front or rear cross to take one of the bend jumps and then turn your dog back into the ladder to go back the other way.

Make up your own sequences. But when you're getting creative with the handling options and adding more handler speed to the exercise, keep in mind you should not do more than five or six repetitions. It's easy to get carried away by the fact we now get to "play" and we then push our dog until mistakes begin to show up. Learn to quit while you are ahead and your dog has success. Also, if your dog is having a problem with more handler motion, don't be afraid to break the exercise down into parts or reduce your speed until you have success. You can then build gradually on that success.

Grid Variations

None.

Nice execution of a triple jump. Note the different striping used on the center bar of the triple. This can be problematic for some dogs.

BEND WORK FOUNDATION GRID

Overview

All handlers in my seminars would like their dogs to bend tighter on turns so they can negotiate the line faster and more efficiently, but they haven't given much thought to just how difficult it is for dogs to bend while jumping. Bend work is one of the most important skill sets in jumping, but it is also one of the most difficult aspects of jump training. Dogs seek straight lines because it makes the set point easier to find and perform correctly. There are many talented dogs that can power into a turn and jump well and there are many that can jump well and power out of a turn, but there are few dogs that can do both at speed while keeping the bars up.

To smoothly and efficiently jump on a turn, your dog must know that he is supposed to take the jump and that he must turn through the jump to get to the next obstacle. Ideally, he must get this information in time for him to begin the turn *prior* to leaving the ground. If your dog is aware of the jump and the turn, your dog's head will turn toward the new direction and his body will follow. If, however, your dog's focus is mainly on you and secondly on the jump, or if your dog doesn't get the necessary cues in a timely enough manner to be of help, the result will often be a straight jump. In this case, your dog cannot turn until he lands, which puts more torque on his shoulders and usually creates extra strides as well.

Bending requires your dog to produce either a right lead or left lead, referring to which foreleg your dog is using to take him to the jump and away from the jump as he lands. If your dog is on the correct lead for the turn, he can turn tightly and smoothly. But if this task is not completed in the way that your dog's body is intended to work (that is, your dog performs the jump on the wrong lead), your dog will not be as balanced as he should be for the jumping effort. This is a very complex process, so it's understandable that when the conversation turns to leads, most seminar participants begin to feel a bit out of their element. The truth is that when we're running with our dog on course, most of us are unaware of which lead our dog is on, let alone know how to influence his choice of lead. The bottom line is that if we give our dogs the correct information in a timely manner, they will take care of any necessary lead changes. You will know that you've been successful if the spine of your dog is in the shape of a comma when he's jumping on a turn; he should not be swinging his hips wide to counterbalance himself and he should not be landing straight ahead and then turning.

Biomechanics change drastically when your dog is asked to bend and jump. When your dog is gathering to come off the ground and jump in a straight line, he carries his weight off both legs equally; his hips and legs work together to produce the weight transfer, angle of elevation,

The dog's spine is in the shape of a comma when bend work is done correctly; he should not be swinging his hips wide to counterbalance himself. The dog should be comfortable and balanced while powering into a turn, jumping, and powering out of a turn without adding strides.

When a dog is jumping on a turn, each hind limb has a different task and his weight is not equally distributed. The inside hind leg is taking the shorter path, but it is the primary weight-bearing and lifting leg.

and takeoff. When your dog is jumping on a turn, each hind limb has a different task and his weight is not equally distributed. The inside hind leg is taking the shorter path, but it is the primary weight-bearing and lifting leg. The outside hind leg is providing some stability, but is only partially weight-bearing. Your dog must then gather himself and load his weight onto the weight-bearing leg to push off the ground, supporting his body precariously on that one hind leg. Working on the ladder (plyometric) grids is an excellent way to help develop the necessary strength.

It is difficult work for a dog to produce, sustain, and jump off a given lead. Your dog must have excellent strength in his core and haunches to produce bend work efficiently and consistently. So, be sure your dog is in condition to start this work and be sure the running surface is suitable.

Bend work is one of the places in training where the dynamic of motion is so precise and so difficult that you must set aside time to allow your dog to work through the process at his own speed until he becomes skillful. There is nothing you can do to speed up your dog's understanding or ability to do the work, except be patient, supportive, and reward the try itself. Once your dog is comfortable with the mechanics of the task, he will begin to produce speed while performing it. Don't push your dog for speed; let him offer it.

If we allow enough time for bend work in practice, our dogs can become fairly ambidextrous and not have a dominant lead or side issue that prevents them from turning and jumping nicely in both directions.

I also feel that it is essential to end each bend work session with a few repetitions of a straight line to insure your dog has the opportunity to extend his muscles again.

"Infinite patience produces immediate results."
—Chinese proverb

PHOTOS © JEANINE MCANANEY

This photo shows the difficulty involved with loading the weight to lift off the ground. When the dog begins the turn off the ground and through the air, his weight is not borne equally off both hind legs. Here you can see the main weight-bearing leg is the inside hind leg. The outside hind leg is the drive leg; at set point, this leg is stabilizing but not fully weight-bearing. This is the main reason dogs have such difficulty turning through the air.

Here the dog is landing hard after a jump where he failed to initiate the turn before liftoff. Note the hyperextension of the dog's pasterns.

Our first dog has landed turning tightly with great balance and he is powering out of the turn beautifully. Note the collection the dog has offered in order to power out of the turn; the front legs are behind the dog at this point.

Our second dog has completed the jump and is also making a good turn with balance and forward power; however, this dog did not provide quite as much collection as the first dog offered, making the turn slightly slower than the first dog's turn.

Our third dog is in the same position as the second dog; but, look closely and you'll see that due to a bit less core strength, this dog's hocks are lying on the ground and he's on the top of his pasterns on the front. Despite these problems, the jump and turn were successful.

Reference DVD

See Bend Work on the *Foundation Jumping* DVD.

Setting Up the Grid

This grid requires five jumps, one of which must be a winged jump. The foundation bend work grid begins with a triangle, then adds an arc on each side of the triangle so the finished product looks like the letter W.

It may seem like the bend work grids don't allow your dog enough room, but a dog's strides will always be shorter when bending, so in reality there is ample space. Bend work grids are the most forgiving to set up. Because your dog will always be bent in the shape of a comma, the spacing between the jumps does not need to be quite as precise as one might think. Your dog can also drive his own line through the turns giving himself a bit more room (or less) if needed. But it *is* very important when setting up bend work grids to be certain the inside jump standards are all on the same curved line (imagine drawing a chalk line in a circle).

At first I angle the bars of each jump so the tightest (also the more difficult) path is clearly presented to your dog. If you were to draw a circle through the tightest path, the inside of the bar is set lower and the outside of the bar is set higher. This disparity helps your dog to take the path of least resistance even though it is the harder path to perform. Because your dog's eye is drawn to the lowest part of the jump his body will follow.

PHOTOS © JEANINE MCANANEY

The initial foundation bend grid (left) looks like a triangle. Notice the jump bars are angled to make the tight line easier for the dog to perform. The complete foundation bend grid (right) looks like the letter W. The bars are set normally, not at an angle.

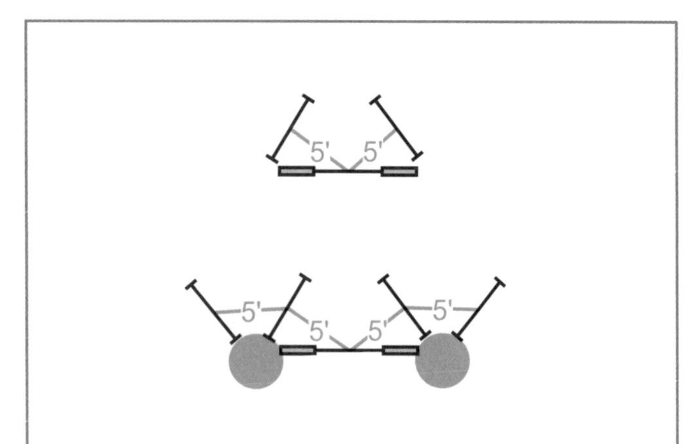

Bend Work Grid Initial Setup
Bend work starts with the 3-jump triangle grid. After the initial work, a jump is added to each side of the triangle to form a W. Notice how the inside standards of the W line up if you draw an imaginary circle. The distances shown here are only examples. See "Jump Spacing and Height" to set up the grid for your dog.

Jump Spacing and Height

Use the information below to determine the jump spacing and jump heights for the grid. Although I have used these distances with success at seminars, they are only guidelines and you may need to adjust them for your dog. Spacing between the jumps is measured from the center of one jump to the center of the next.

Big Dogs

Space the jumps 5'–6' apart. For the triangle grid, the inside end of the jump bars are set at 8" and the outside end at 16". For the W grid, the bars are set horizontally at no more than 8".

Medium Dogs

Space the jumps 5'–5.5' apart. For the triangle grid, the inside end of the jump bars are set at 6" and the outside end at 16". For the W grid, the bars are set horizontally at no more than 6".

Small Dogs

Space the jumps 3'–4' apart. For the triangle grid, the inside end of the jump bars are set at 4" and the outside end at 12". For the W grid, the bars are set horizontally at no more than 4".

Tiny Dogs

Space the jumps 2'–3'. For the triangle grid, the inside end of the jump bars are set at 4" and the outside end at 8". For the W grid, the bars are set horizontally at no more than 4".

Target

Place the target on the tight line of the circle at the end of the bend, giving your dog room to get to it without landing on it.

Dog's Starting Position

For the bending repetitions:

- We do not want a sit or a stay for bend work; remember, your dog would prefer not to bend. You need to begin with forward motion into the grid. You will put your hand in your dog's collar, move forward with your dog, release him into the grid, and then rotate into the turn.
- Position your dog so he is centered on the first jump, facing straight ahead, and looking at the jump; do *not* place your dog on an angle to the first jump.
- Give yourself room to take several steps forward with your dog to guarantee he takes jump #2. Many handlers take only one step forward, say "Go," release their dog, and then abruptly stop motion. At that point their dog looks immediately for an exit from the grid to get back to the handler. This happens because motion overrides everything else, so leave yourself enough distance from the first jump of the grid to move forward and get your dog going.

For the straight-line repetitions:

- The distance between your dog and the first jump should be half the distance of the space in the grid. Setting up your dog too far back will cause him to enter the grid with more speed than he will be able to handle.

Handler's Position

This is one foundation exercise where you are handling your dog. You need to move forward with your dog into the grid while *not* pushing your dog off the tight line. Think of this exercise as a wheel; you, the handler, are the hub of the wheel and the rotation of your hips and shoulders influences your dog's turn.

You will put your hand in your dog's collar, move forward with your dog, release him into the grid, and then rotate into the turn. Your shoulders and hips, not an extended hand or arm, should rotate to support your dog through each piece of the grid. An arm supports distance and for foundation bend work there is no distance from your dog; you are right next to him. Try hard to keep your arm/hand "quiet" because it's essential for your dog to focus forward on the task while he "feels" you moving with him—if it has nothing to say, put it away.

It's important to turn while your dog is in the grid or you will push your dog off the tight line. Be careful not to race to intersect with the target or again you will be pushing your dog off the tight line that we want him to find and drive. If you're using a toy, your dog should drive to the target, get it, and then come in to you for play. If your dog runs off with toys, you will want to "leash" your toy for this exercise with a rope or a leash with the snap cut off.

Note: For those of you interested in leads, if you have your dog on your left, it's a right-lead bend for him. If you have your dog on your right, it's a left-lead bend for him.

Progressions

Using the triangle setup, do three successful circles in one direction. Reward your dog at the end of each circle. Then switch sides and do three successful circles in the other direction, rewarding each try. This is one of the few cases in gridwork where we allow our dogs to pattern the behavior we want. Break the pattern by doing one circle in each direction. End the session with a straight line in each direction.

At an early stage it will become clear that your dog is more comfortable going either right or left through the grid. To avoid creating anxiety, begin each training session going in the direction that your dog does with the most ease, then do the more difficult direction, then end the training session by repeating the easier direction. The human part of the team always wants to address the problem-side with great diligence, but you don't want to stress your dog about it. Training the "good side" first and last helps maintain your dog's confidence.

Once your dog is comfortable going in both directions in the basic bend grid (this will take multiple training sessions!), you can put the next piece of the puzzle in place by adding a jump at each end of the triangle. This is the complete foundation bend work grid. I use the same three jumps to make a triangle as before, but now I add two more jumps to make an inverted triangle at each end of the grid, forming the letter W. The spacing between jumps is the same as before, but now you will set the jump bars to a horizontal position.

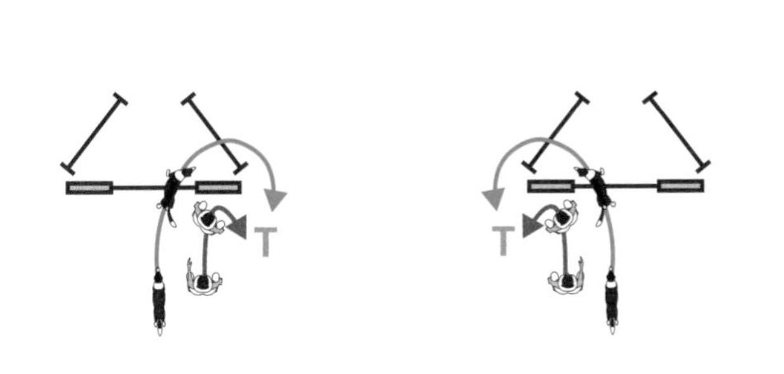

Bend Work Triangle Setup
Progressions
Do three circles in one direction and then three in the other. Use a target to keep your dog on a tight line and reward after each circle. Finish with one circle in each direction. Remember to take several steps with the dog straight forward into the grid, and to turn your shoulders and hips while your dog is turning.

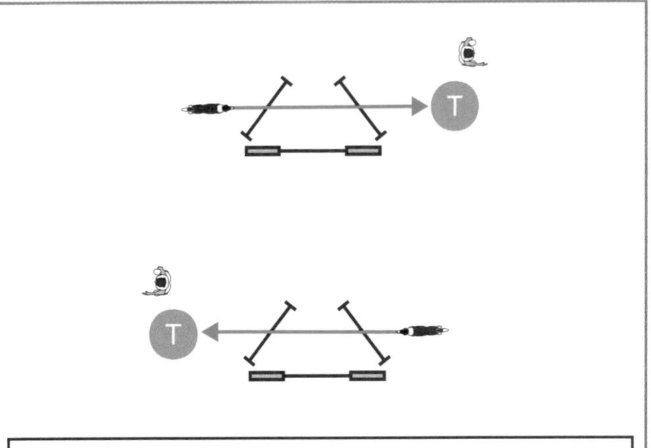

Bend Work Triangle Setup
Progressions
End each and every bend work session with a few repetitions of a straight line to insure your dog has the opportunity to elongate his muscles again.

When doing the complete bendwork foundation grid, a session consists of the following eight repetitions:

1. Dog is on your left side and goes from the center jump of the W to the right side. This is a right-lead turn for your dog.
2. Dog is on your right side and goes straight across the four jumps at the back of the grid. Although this is a straight line, it is one of the tightest straight lines offered in gridwork, so use caution if you are adding motion.
3. Dog is on your left side and goes from the end jump to the center jump. This is another right-lead turn for your dog.
4. Dog is on your right side and goes from the center jump of the W to the left side. This is a left-lead turn for your dog.
5. Dog is on your left side and goes straight across the four jumps at the back of the grid.
6. Dog is on your right side and goes from the end jump to the center jump. This is another left-lead turn for your dog.
7. Dog is on your right side and goes straight across the four jumps at the back of the grid.
8. Dog is on your left side and goes straight across the four jumps at the back of the grid.

Full Bend Grid Setup - Progressions
Working two right-lead turns and a straight line in between.

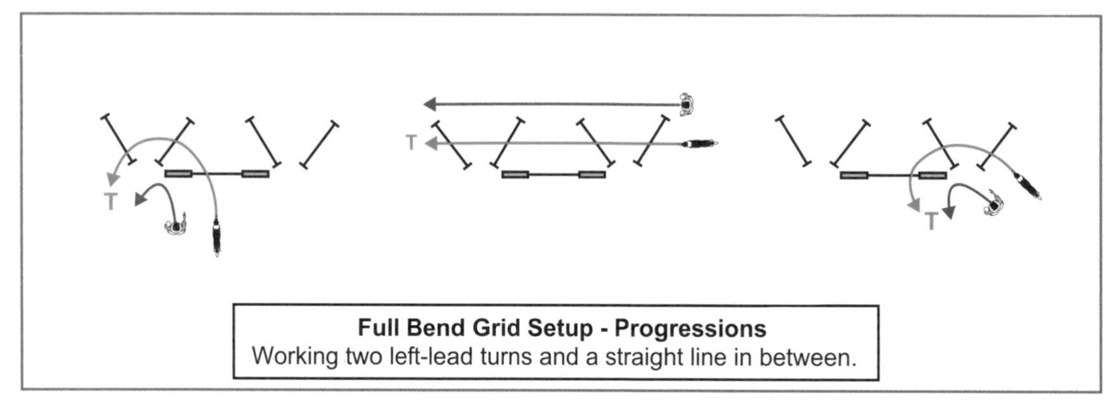

Full Bend Grid Setup - Progressions
Working two left-lead turns and a straight line in between.

Full Bend Grid Setup - Progressions
Finish the session with a straight line in each direction.

Problem Solving

Problem: Your dog cuts across your feet and goes directly to the target without entering the grid.

Solution: This is something that happens often. Your dog must learn that he has to do the work to get the target. Make sure that you are holding your dog by his collar and moving forward with your dog. Keep a light hold on the collar until your dog begins to step away from you and into the grid.

Problem: Your dog begins to enter the grid, stops forward motion, and then finds the fastest way out of the grid.

Solution: You need to send your dog forward and into the grid with enough forward speed to guarantee that your dog takes jump #2. Motion overrides everything else, so your dog wants to stop going forward if you abruptly stop moving forward. This is the main reason bend work always begins in motion. If the problem persists for more than one or two repetitions, put a freestanding wing in place to help block your dog's exit. This aid must be faded as quickly as possible once understanding of the task begins.

Problem: Your dog takes a wide path between jumps #1 and #2 and exits the grid without taking jump #3.

Solution: This can occur if: 1) your dog has too much forward momentum into the grid and he fails to see jump #3 until it's too late or 2) you have too much forward motion, which drives your dog too far forward to be able to turn and bend. The more reactive to movement your dog, the less handler motion is required to guarantee jump #2. You may need to experiment with the dog to find the right amount of motion required for him to successfully take jump #2 on a tight line.

Problem: Your dog jumps the wrong bend moving away from you rather than the correct bend moving toward you or your dog jumps toward the wrong bend creating a wide turn.

Solution: Make certain your dog is entering the grid perpendicular to the first jump. Do not try to "spin" your dog into the grid at an angle because the first line your dog will see is the wrong bend.

Problem: When doing the four-jump straight line in the W bend grid, your dog takes the last two jumps as one.

Solution: This is one of the tightest lines used in gridwork and the option to take the last two jumps as one is simply easier for your dog than interacting with the space. To ensure that your dog understands, you need to slow everything down. You can initially perform the line as a recall to the target and then gradually add motion starting at a walk, progressing to a jog, and then eventually running. Another alternative is to move the target and place it in front of the last jump in the line. Do one repetition with the target there, and then move it back to the landing side of the jump and try again.

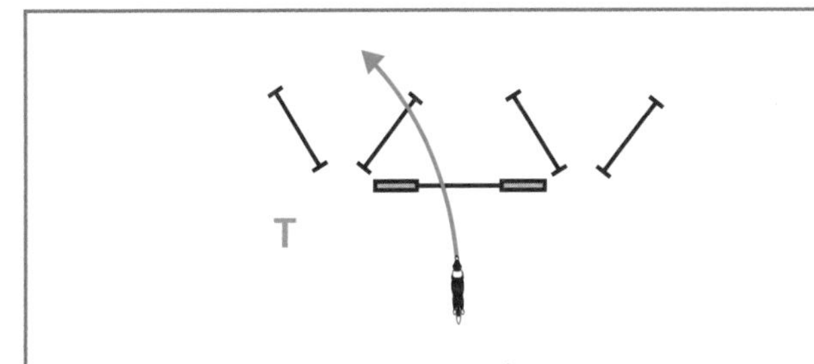

Bend Work - Problem Solving
If there is too much forward speed into the grid, your dog may go wide and exit the grid without taking jump #3.

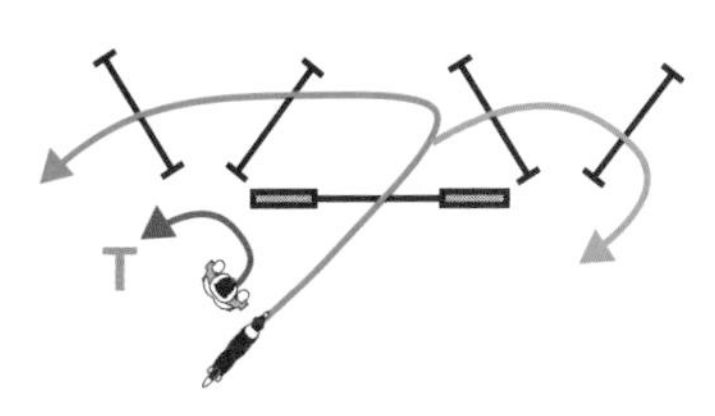

Bend Work - Problem Solving
Do not "spin" your dog into the grid because the first thing he will see is the incorrect bend, which will cause him to take the wrong jump or turn widely.

How Much to Practice?

It is important for your dog to be comfortable with the foundation bend work before progressing to more advanced bend work grids. Success with bend work requires a good bit of practice, but each dog has different needs and progresses at a different rate. Conditioning also comes into play during bend work training. Our dogs give us all the answers, so pay attention to your dog during training sessions to judge the ease with which he is performing the task. If his performance seems labored, visit bend work a bit more often in your training plan, but cut down on the number of repetitions during each session.

With a trained dog, bend work is a skill that you need to practice monthly. It can be offered through the bend work foundation grid as well as other bending grids.

Proofing

You can gradually increase your lateral distance from your dog. As you begin to proof some distance from the grid, an extended hand or arm is suitable. When you add distance, be sure to continue supporting your dog by turning your hips and shoulders.

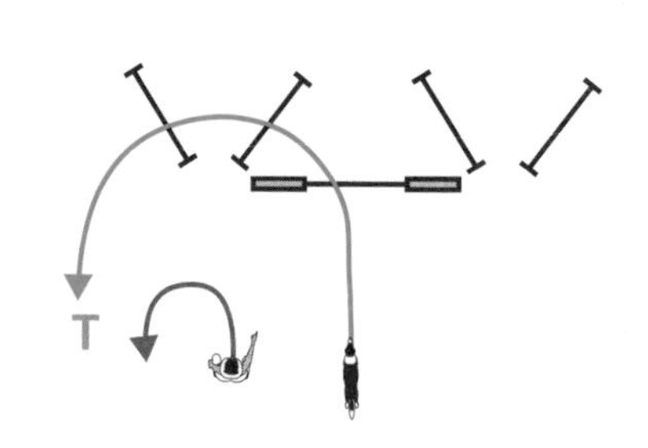

Bend Work
Proofing
When you proof distance with the grid, be sure to continue supporting your dog by turning your hips and shoulders.

Adding Handler Motion

This is one of the few grids where handler motion is included from the start. Bend work offers a wonderful opportunity to fine tune communication with your dog. When stepping forward with your dog to start the grid, it will be an experiment to see just how much motion is enough to guarantee jump #2 and what is too much to give you the performance you seek. Your rotation supporting each jump is also critical. You should be rotating so your hip and shoulder are moving *with* your dog. You'll find that if you rotate too quickly and get ahead of your dog, you will cause him to make errors.

Adding Handling

Once your dog has mastered the complete foundation bend work grid, performing it with speed and ease, you can turn the basic grid into a front cross drill where your dog is performing the grid as a figure-eight with continuous motion. Rather than placing the target, carry it with you and drop it at your feet as you break off the exercise. You are encouraging more speed with this exercise so be mindful that your dog's footwork for the bends is still "clean." Your goal is always to rehearse correct footwork, so don't be afraid of putting the target back out and breaking down the exercise.

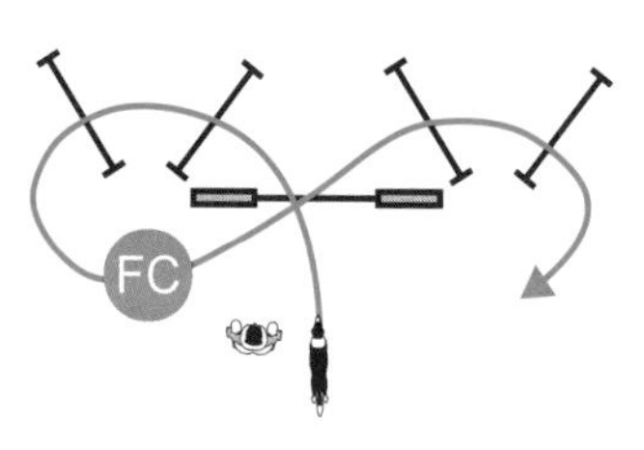

Bend Work
Adding Handling
This is a front cross drill. Your dog is performing the grid as a figure-eight with continuous motion. Rather than placing the target, drop it on the ground as you break off the exercise.

Pay attention to whether your dog is smoother going one direction than the other. If this is the case, it is likely that your dog hasn't yet mastered the footwork for that given lead, and he needs more time doing the basic foundation bend work.

Remember, you cannot proof what you don't have! So if you begin to sequence through this grid as a figure-eight and your dog immediately begins turning his head to check in with you, rather than driving forward and looking for work, you have gone too far too fast. We want to create success, not pattern failure.

Grid Variations

You can turn the W-shaped bend grid into a five-jump arc grid using the winged jump as the center of the arc. The winged jump then represents a handler-restriction line to avoid crossing so your dog is encouraged to hold the tight line. It seems like a more simplistic bend grid than the W; however, it can be more difficult for some dogs as there are now five jumps through which to balance footwork whereas on the W grid your dog must maintain footwork for only three jumps. For your dog this *is* a difference and care should be given once again to make certain your dog can perform the task with ease. The jump height remains low for this grid as well.

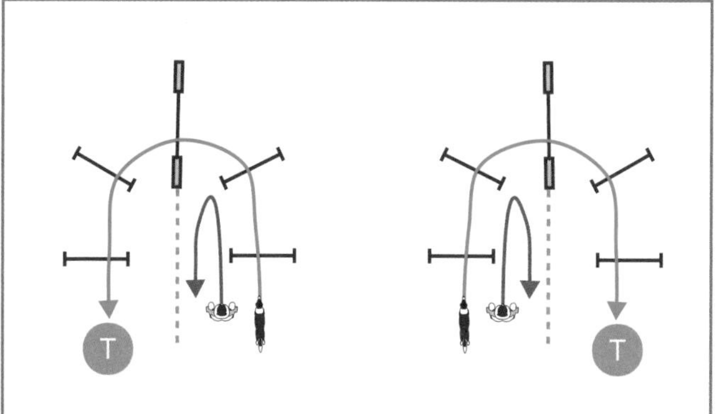

Bend Work Grid Variation
Turn the five jumps into an arc. Don't go past the dashed green line or you will push your dog off the tight line.

Everyone knows that dogs can jump; however, jumping 20 obstacles at full speed, while also paying attention to the handler, raises that task to a new level of difficulty that requires time and training for success to be consistently duplicated.

"I had the luxury of working with Susan on a consistent basis with two of my dogs. At the age of 5 1/2 years, one of my dogs successfully changed her jumping patterns from being a fairly consistent bar knocker to a dog that rarely drops a bar. I think what made the difference with this dog is that Susan helped her realize that there is a thought process involved with jumping and negotiating an agility course. She actually learned to think about what she was doing rather than just running fast and rocketing over the bars. When a dog puts themselves on the sidelines after doing one grid a few times, you know they are mentally tired. Speed is not the end all, but speed with some thoughtful jumping is a wonderful thing in our sport.

I have had the good fortune to bring up my young dog working under Susan's tutelage using her jump program. I am the proud partner to a beautiful jumping dog that will look for his lines and then confidently flow through them. He is able to look ahead and adjust his stride according to what is in front of him, whether it be a straight line or a curve. I don't have to "babysit" him; he has the schooling to take on the task at hand. I am so grateful to Susan for her help. I look forward to raising my baby puppy with her!"

—Susan Cochran, National champion and multiple-time World Team member

CIRCLE GRID

Overview

This four-jump circle appears deceptively simple, but it is not simple, nor is it easy for your dog to complete the grid smoothly. In the bend work foundation grid, your dog is bouncing between the jumps so he is constantly in compression, meaning that he is gathered and prepared to leave the ground; whereas in the circle grid, your dog must produce a given lead, sustain the lead as he takes a stride, and then jump from that lead around the circle of four jumps.

The process seems simple to us because we don't have to do it. This grid is done with horses as well, and any rider can tell you that how the animal steps in to the first jump is crucial and then that exact rhythm and tempo must be sustained for three more jumps for the performance to be smooth and look effortless. Horse people often "lovingly" refer to this grid as the circle of death. If the horse and rider can't maintain their rhythm, the performance gets messy very quickly. The same applies to dogs; if the dog cannot sustain a given lead, the turns will not be tight or comfortable for him.

The circle grid is offered with some height, mainly because the arc of the jumping effort will help your dog use the space offered. This is still a plyometric grid, however, and should never be offered at full height. When the grid is done correctly, your dog's performance will look smooth and fluid without any added steps or strides.

Important: Do not introduce this grid until you have completed the bend work foundation grid, since your dog is meant to be producing a given lead here.

Reference DVD

See Exercise #2 on the *Advanced Jumping* DVD.

Setting Up the Grid

You will need four jumps for this grid: two nonwinged jumps and two winged jumps. The jumps are set like hands on a clock; the two winged jumps are at 3:00 and 9:00 and the two nonwinged jumps are at 6:00 and 12:00.

Jump Spacing and Height

Use the information below to determine the jump spacing and jump heights for the grid. Although I have used these distances with success at seminars, they are only

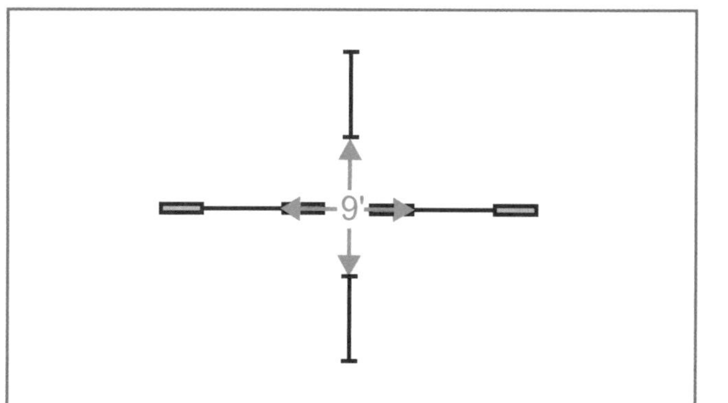

Circle Grid - Measuring the Spacing
The spacing for this grid is measured from jump standard to jump standard, **not** wing to wing. The distance shown here is only an example. See "Jump Spacing and Height" to set up the grid for your dog.

guidelines and you may need to adjust them for your dog. Remember the spine of your dog is constantly bent during performance of this exercise; therefore, his stride will always be shorter than it is on a straight path.

Note: The spacing between the jumps for this grid is measured from jump standard to jump standard.

Big Dogs

Space the jumps 9' apart from standard to standard and set at 16" in height.

Medium Dogs

Space the jumps 8' apart from standard to standard and set at 14" in height.

Small Dogs

Space the jumps 6' apart from standard to standard and set at 8" in height.

Tiny Dogs

Space the jumps 5' apart from standard to standard and set at 4"–6" in height.

Target

Before you start, place the target in front of the wing of jump #1 to ensure that you are giving your dog room to land from jump #4 and keep him driving on a bend through the last jump.

Dog's Starting Position

We do not want a sit or a stay for bend work; remember, your dog would prefer not to bend. You need to begin with forward motion into the grid. This grid will be a stride for your dog rather than a bounce so the distance between your dog and the first jump should equal one steady, short stride for your dog:

- Big dogs: 9'–11'
- Medium dogs: 7'–9'
- Small dogs: 5'–6'
- Tiny dogs: 4'–5'

Position your dog so he is centered on the first jump, facing straight ahead, and looking at the jump; do *not* place your dog on an angle to the first jump.

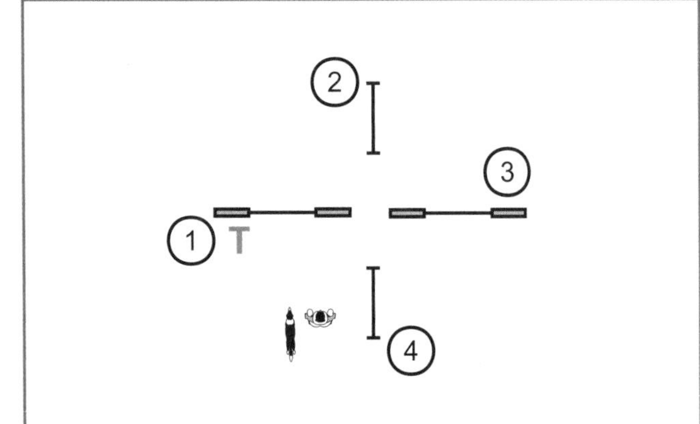

Circle Grid - Positioning the Dog & the Target
Position your dog so he can take one steady, short stride to jump #1. Position the target so that he has room to land from jump #4 and so that you are encouraging him to bend over jump #4.

Handler's Position

Move forward with your dog to start the grid while *not* pushing him off the tight line. Think of this exercise as a wheel; you, the handler, are the hub of the wheel and the rotation of your hips and shoulders influences the dog's turn. You will step forward with your dog, slip into the hub position, and then rotate your shoulders and hips to support your dog through each piece of the grid. This is a tight circle, so you don't want to use an extended hand or arm. An arm supports distance, and for this grid there is no distance from your dog; you are right next to him. Try hard to keep your arm/hand "quiet" because it's essential for your dog to focus forward on the task while he "feels" you moving with him—if it has nothing to say, put it away.

It's important to turn while your dog is in the grid or you will push your dog off the tight line. Be careful not to race to intersect with the target or again you will push your dog off the tight line that we want him to find and drive. If you're using a toy, your dog should drive to the target, get it, and then come in to you for play. If your dog runs off with toys, you will want to "leash" your toy for this exercise with a rope or a leash with the snap cut off.

Note: For those of you interested in leads, if you have your dog on your left, it's a right-lead bend for him. If you have your dog on your right, it's a left-lead bend for him.

Progressions

I begin training this grid with only one repetition in each direction in a session. When your dog is performing the grid well, do two repetitions in each direction rewarding your dog after *each* circle. Because of the degree of difficulty, I would do no more than four consecutive repetitions.

Many dogs are more comfortable going either right or left through the grid. To avoid creating anxiety, begin each training session going in the direction that your dog does with the most ease. Then, do the more difficult direction, and end the training session by repeating the easier direction. The human part of the team always wants to address the problem side with great diligence, but you don't want to stress your dog about it. Training the "good side" first and last helps maintain your dog's confidence.

Note: Although we show the dog and handler starting with the winged jump, you can choose to start at *any* jump in the circle.

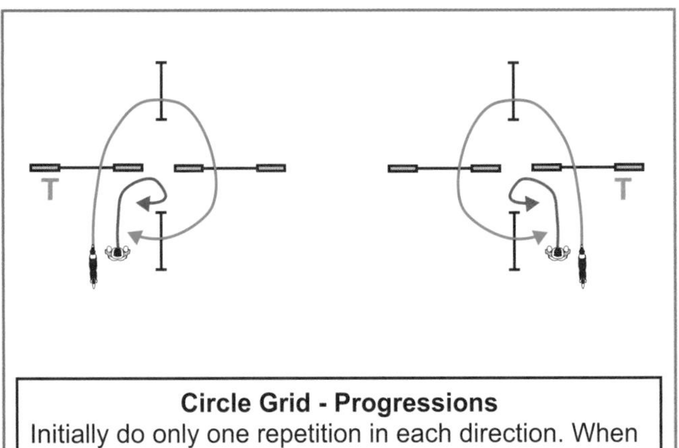

Circle Grid - Progressions
Initially do only one repetition in each direction. When your dog is performing the grid well, you can do a total of four reps.

Problem Solving

Problem: Your dog adds an extra stride in one of the spaces.

Solution: Rather than altering the grid right away, allow your dog some time to try to work through it. Many dogs, if not most, take an extra stride in a space simply because they cannot sustain the given lead; therefore, they will land on the wrong lead and have to change leads for the next jump, which causes them to add the extra stride. Most often, dogs learn to do this grid in the given distance and become comfortable with practice.

Problem: After some practice your dog is still consistently adding an extra stride in the space offered.

Solution: Shorten the distance between the standards by 6"–12".

Problem: Your dog bounces one of the spaces rather than providing a stride.

Solution: Allow your dog some practice time. Your dog may well have overpowered the prior jump causing him to land too deep to include a stride in the given space; therefore, a bounce was the only option left for your dog to continue the path.

Problem: Your dog cuts across your feet and goes directly to the target without entering the grid.

Solution: If necessary, hold your dog by his collar as you move forward with him. Keep a light hold on the collar until your dog begins to step away from you and into the grid. Your dog simply must learn that he has to do the work to get the target.

How Much to Practice?

The circle grid is physically demanding for the dog. Practice this grid with regularity but not with too many repetitions at a time, always being mindful of your dog's physical condition, age, and weight. Bend work *is* hard on your dog's body. It requires a high degree of balance and core strength, which many dogs lack, so work it slowly.

Make sure your dog is comfortable with the circle grid before trying the circle to extension grid or the circle to figure-8 grid.

Proofing

When your dog is doing the circle grid with smoothness and apparent ease, you can proof this grid by doing continuous repetitions (no reward until the last rep) in one direction, which requires your dog to sustain the lead for a longer period of time. Start with two repetitions in one direction and gradually build up to four. Rather than placing the target, carry it with you and drop it at your feet as you break off the exercise.

Pay attention to whether your dog is smoother going one direction than the other. If this is the case, it is likely that your dog hasn't yet mastered the footwork for that given lead and he needs more time doing the basic foundation bend work.

Adding Handler Motion

Because the handling area in this grid is so restricted, handler motion is minimized to standing in the hub position and rotating with your dog.

Adding Handling

There is no change of side in this exercise so crosses are not necessary.

Grid Variations

See Circle to Extension Grid.

An agility dog rarely has the luxury of total focus on task since he must divide his focus between task (obstacle performance) and handler information.

© RICH KNECHT PHOTOGRAPHY

"My dog TangoBango is 12 years old and just finished her MACH7 (full jump height) yesterday. Of course, she is no longer as fast as she used to be, but last summer she began knocking bars, something she had never done before. For a while, I thought she was losing her strength to jump. However, she could still do the A-frame, dogwalk, teeter, and table with little effort. After being at Susan's seminar and watching her work with an Irish Wolfhound on the simple plyometric grids, then reading her article on the grids in Clean Run, I decided that maybe what TangoBango really needed was to work on that brain-muscle connection.

I set up the simple grid in my back yard and worked her on it every few days. What I would typically see is that she would improve her ability to come forward to an appropriate takeoff spot with each repetition. Once I saw her power forward through each and every space (usually 4-5 reps), I would stop the session.

The impact of this grid on her jumping has been really amazing. Yes, she still continued to knock a few bars (jumping into the sun or coming out of a chute into a close triple jump), but her improved confidence and willingness to power over the jumps has been quite obvious. I have also seen this "bleed" over in other activities requiring quick muscle response such as running up and down stairs and doing the thing that spaniels love to do—leaping around with joy.

I do believe TangoBango owes that MACH7 (and it will be her last one) to Susan!"

—Mary Mandish-Steigerwald, Running Welsh Springer Spaniels in agility for 15 years

CIRCLE TO EXTENSION GRID

Overview

In this grid, I am looking for the dogs to drive out of a circle to a jump at a distance with smooth, fluid striding. You build this grid incrementally over time. Each addition to the grid adds to the difficulty level. Once all the pieces of this grid are set, there are several lines for your dog to perform other than just the circle. Each line offers its own question to your dog and adds to the complexity of problem solving required. Take time to build an understanding of the task, not simply do the exercise.

When you get to the final setup of the grid, there will be change of side required, so be sure to walk the setup until you are certain of your handling and positioning. Of course the danger here is that when the jump grids allow for handling, people often forget the point is to school your dog on jumping. This is *not* a handling exercise to drill until *we* get it right.

Your dog's success with this grid will be greatly influenced by the timing of the information we provide. Rewarding each and every try is more important than ever.

Important: Do not introduce this grid until your dog can perform the basic circle grid smoothly and consistently.

Reference DVD

None.

Setting Up the Grid

Initially you will need four jumps to set up the circle: two nonwinged jumps and two winged jumps. These jumps are set like hands on a clock; the two winged jumps are at 3:00 and 9:00 and the two nonwinged jumps are at 6:00 and 12:00.

When you build the extension portion of the grid, you will need an additional four jumps; these can be winged or nonwinged. I prefer to offer dogs a winged jump as the first jump out of the circle because it gives them a more powerful visual to drive toward. I would then place a nonwinged jump as the second jump since this jump requires that your dog work a bit harder to find the jump and drive to it. In addition, the nonwinged jump will be easier for your dog to turn around when we add that into the exercise.

I position the first jump after the circle (#1A and #1B) using the common competition distance of 15', measured center to center, to allow for acceleration from your dog and to provide ample handling room. This distance should be an easy one stride for the medium to big dogs, provided they are looking ahead for the next logical piece of work and their target. For the tiny to small dogs, this 15' space will generally be a two-stride distance, and even three strides for the tinier dogs. I use a jump on each side of the circle so the exercise can be performed with your dog on your right or left without having to move equipment.

The second jump after the circle (#2A and #2B) is positioned 45° from the winged jump at a distance of 15'. However, I do *not* add another jump on each side of the circle until your dog is driving out of the circle looking for the next obstacle without offering head checks toward you.

Jump Spacing and Height

Use the information below to determine the jump spacing and jump heights for the grid. Although I have used these distances with success at seminars, they are only guidelines and you may need to adjust them for your dog.

Note: The spacing for the circle portion of the grid is measured from jump standard to jump standard.

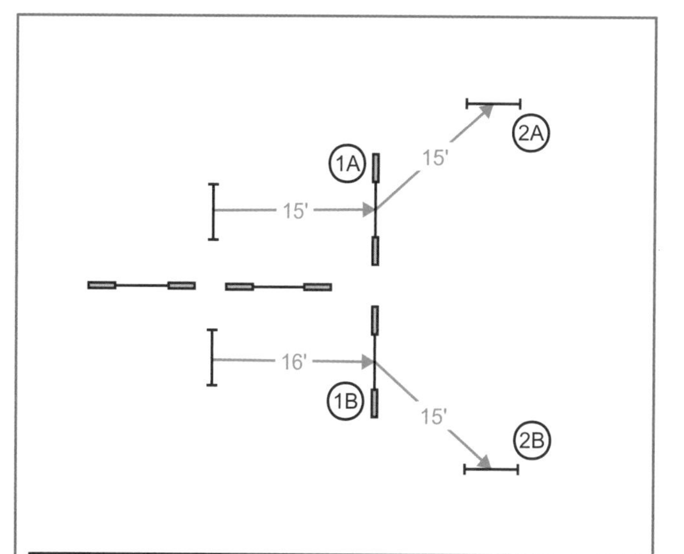

Circle to Extension Grid - Setup
This is the full setup for the circle to extension grid. Start with just the circle, then add a jump after the circle on each side (#1A and #1B). Do not add another jump (#2A and #2B) until your dog is driving out of the circle to jump #1 smoothly and with consistency.

Big Dogs

- *Circle:* Space the jumps 9' apart from standard to standard and set at 16" in height.
- *Jumps #1 and #2:* These may be set at your dog's competition height.

Medium Dogs

- *Circle:* Space the jumps 8' apart from standard to standard and set at 14" in height.
- *Jumps #1 and #2:* These may be set at your dog's competition height.

Small Dogs

- *Circle:* Space the jumps 6' apart from standard to standard and set at 8" in height.
- *Jumps #1 and #2:* These may be set at your dog's competition height.

Tiny Dogs

- *Circle:* Space the jumps 5' apart from standard to standard and set at 4"–6" in height.
- *Jumps #1 and #2:* These may be set at your dog's competition height.

Target

When your dog is driving out of the circle to jump #1, placed the target 10' after jump #1 on a line that makes it visible to your dog once he begins to drive straight out of the circle.

When adding jump #2, the target is placed 10' past that jump so it's visible on your dog's path from jump #1.

Dog's Starting Position

We do not want a sit or a stay for bend work. You need to begin with forward motion into the grid. Remember the circle portion of this grid will be a stride for your dog rather than a bounce so the distance between your dog and the first jump should equal one steady, short stride for your dog:

- Big dogs: 9'–11'
- Medium dogs: 7'–9'
- Small dogs: 5'–6'
- Tiny dogs: 4'–5'.

Position your dog so he is centered on the first jump, facing straight ahead, and looking at the jump; do *not* place your dog on an angle to the first jump.

Handler's Position

Move forward with your dog to start the circle portion of the grid while *not* pushing him off the tight line. Think of this exercise as a wheel; you, the handler, are the hub of the wheel and the rotation of your hips and shoulders influences your dog's turn. You will step forward with your dog, slip into the hub position, and then rotate your shoulders and hips to support your dog through each piece of the grid.

As your dog is approaching the second jump of the circle, you will begin to move from the hub position toward the first jump leading out of the grid. Once you add the second jump out of the grid, you will need to do either a front or rear cross to get to that jump.

Progressions

This grid is built up progressively over multiple training sessions.

Stage 1

Initially set up just the circle portion of the grid and do one repetition in each direction. Since your dog should have already done lots of work with the circle grid before trying the circle to extension grid, you should just need a warm-up.

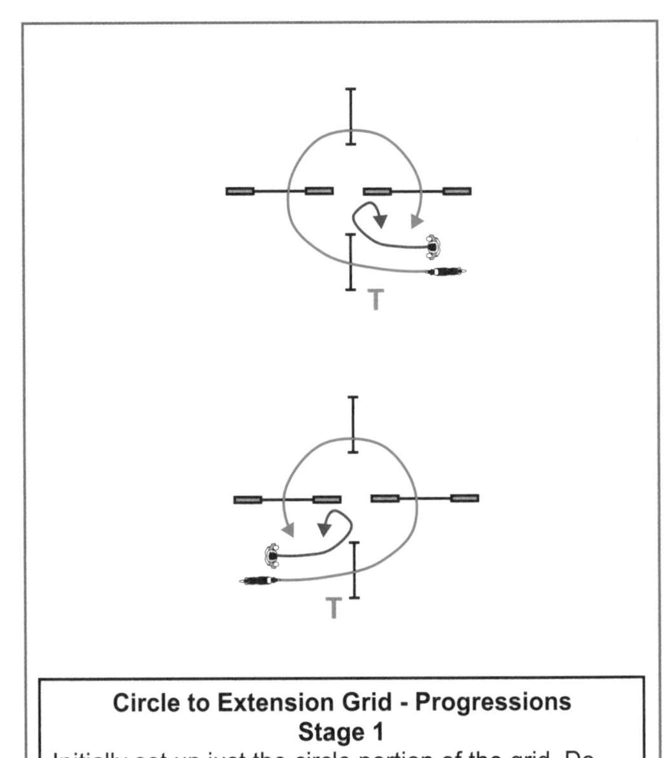

Circle to Extension Grid - Progressions
Stage 1
Initially set up just the circle portion of the grid. Do one repetition of the circle grid in each direction.

Stage 2

Add one jump after the circle on each side. Do two repetitions in each direction. With this grid there is a straight line that should be offered to your dog after completing the bend work to straighten out his spine and extend the muscles. Do one repetition in each direction to end the session.

When your dog is doing the straight line *from compression* to extension, you can run with your dog, use a leadout, or use a recall. However, when your dog is doing the straight line from extension *to compression,* you need to do the exercise as a recall so you are stationary.

Do not progress to the next stage until your dog can complete the grid smoothly and with consistent success.

Stage 3

Add a second jump after the circle on each side. At this point a front or rear cross is required to get to jump #5.

Do two repetitions in each direction. Again, there is a straight line that should be offered to your dog after completing the bend work. Do one repetition in each direction to end the session.

When your dog is doing the straight line *from compression* to extension, you can run with your dog, use a leadout, or use a recall. However, when your dog is doing the straight line from extension *to compression,* you need to do the exercise as a recall so you are stationary.

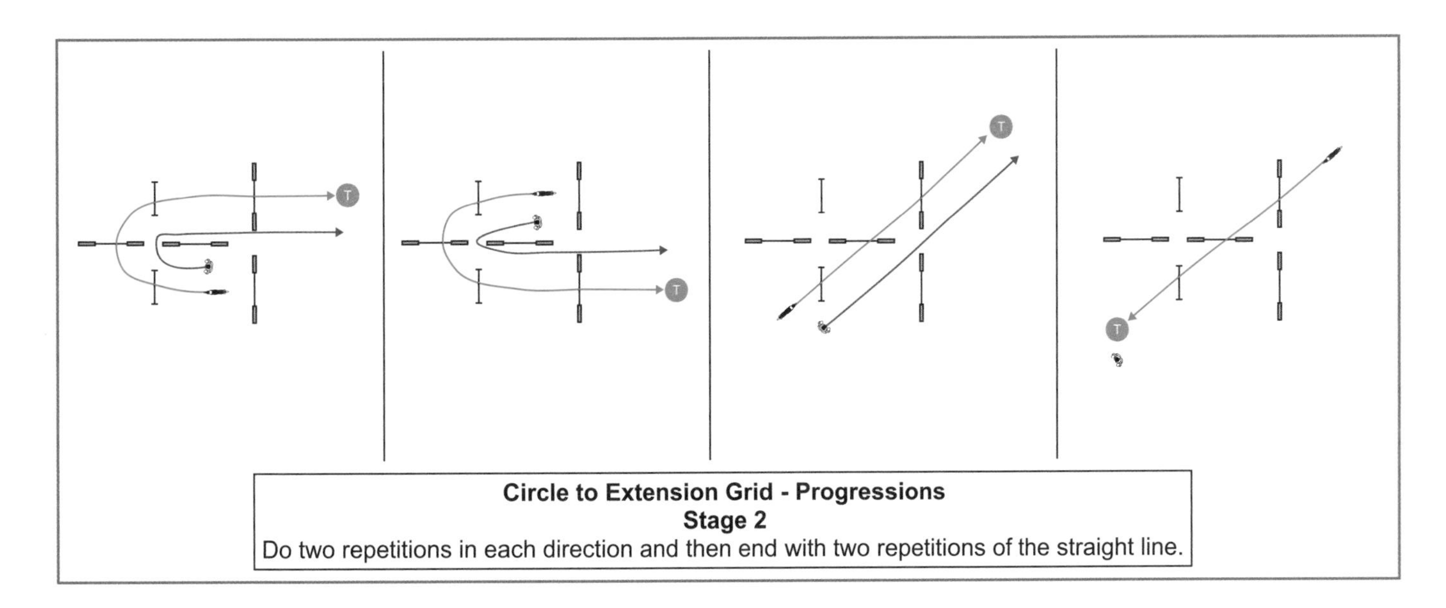

Circle to Extension Grid - Progressions
Stage 2
Do two repetitions in each direction and then end with two repetitions of the straight line.

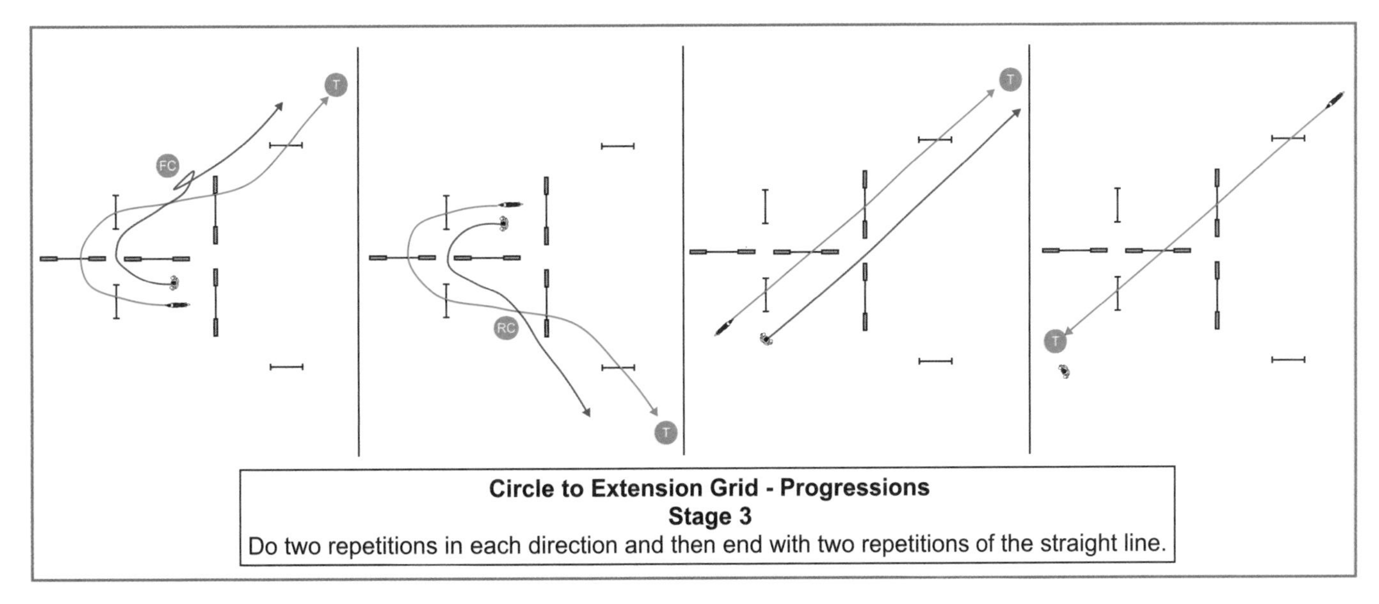

Circle to Extension Grid - Progressions
Stage 3
Do two repetitions in each direction and then end with two repetitions of the straight line.

Problem Solving

Problem: After jumps #1A and #1B have been added, your dog fails to drive ahead to jump #1, getting "stuck" on you.

Solution: Place the target in front of jump #1 for a repetition or two to encourage your dog to drive forward. Then move the target back to its original position after the jump. The problem may also be that you're not providing timely forward motion.

Problem: When you add jumps #2A and #2B, your dog sights the target as he is coming out of the circle, leaving the grid and running for the target.

Solution: Build the correct path for your dog by "backchaining" the target. First place the target in front of jump #1 on your dog's path and do one or two repetitions. Next place the target in front of jump #2 on your dog's path and do one or two repetitions. Finally, place the target in its original position, and see if your dog now understands that he must follow the work to get to the target.

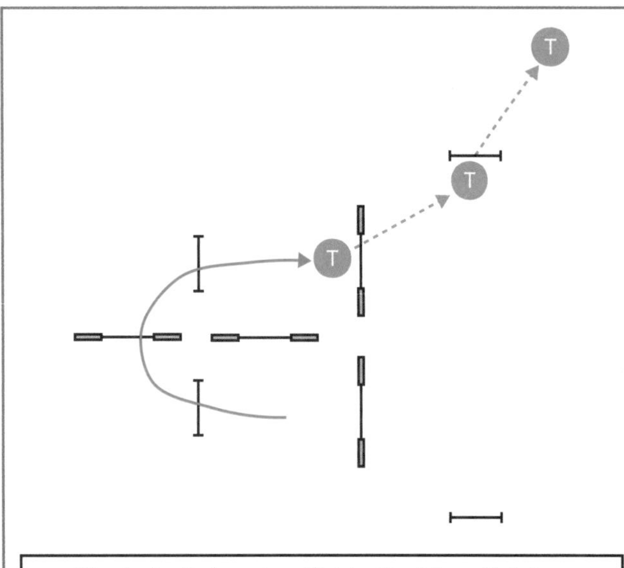

Circle to Extension Grid - Problem Solving
If your dog leaves the grid for the target as he's coming out of the circle, backchain the exercise by moving the target.

How Much to Practice?

Once you get to stage 3, I recommend doing no more than six repetitions in one session.

This is an advanced grid that can be offered as part of your dog's maintenance training.

Proofing

You are proofing your dog as you gradually increase the difficulty of this grid. With each change there are several lines for your dog to perform other than just the circle.

Adding Handler Motion

When doing just the circle by itself, the handling area in this grid is so restricted that handler motion is minimized to standing in the hub position and rotating with your dog. But once you add jump #1, you will need to move forward out of the hub of the circle, which will cue acceleration to your dog. If your dog has problems performing the exit jump smoothly, it is helpful to have a video camera or training partner so you can assess how your position and/or speed is affecting your dog's line and movement.

Adding Handling

Once you add jump #2 to the grid, you need to use a front or rear cross to get your dog from jump #1 to jump #2. If your dog is now uncertain of his path, then you need to go back to the previous stage and build understanding as you go.

Grid Variations

For the more advanced dogs, you can ask your dog to perform the full grid in the opposite direction, starting with the straight line and then going into the circle. When doing this, start with just one jump into the circle and gradually build to both jumps. You are preparing your dog for the big weight shift necessary for going from extension back into compression.

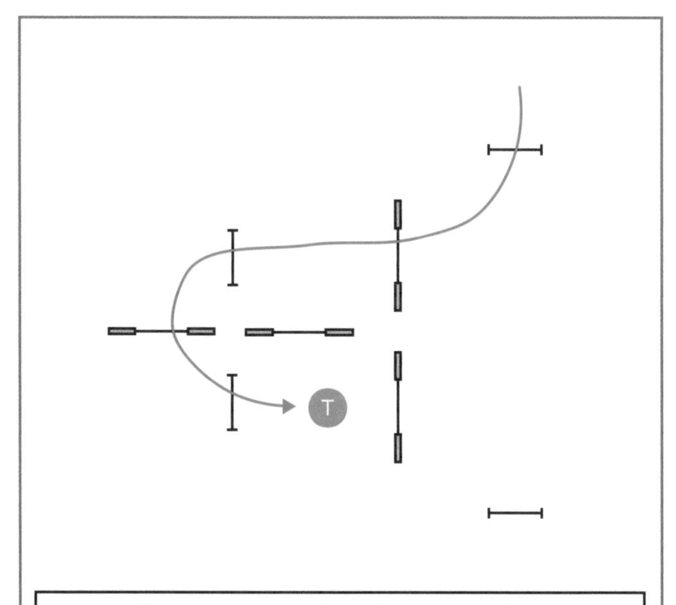

Circle to Extension Grid - Variation
With this advanced variation of the grid, your dog is going from extension into compression. Start by doing just one jump going into the grid and then add the second one.

CIRCLE TO FIGURE-8 GRID

Overview

The circle to figure-8 grid is one of my favorite grids, because it covers so many skill sets in one grid. The grid requires your dog to produce, sustain, and jump off a given lead with repetition, which is difficult for him to perform. We're looking for smoothness and footwork as your dog's stride carries him from jump to jump. The grid allows your dog to get into flow and find his rhythm, something that can be elusive for dogs on today's agility courses. This is the place where your dog finds a rhythm that simply feels good to him and he has a chance to actually pattern how that feels. My criteria for my own dogs is that at least 75% of their jumps feel good to them while they're jumping as I handle them. If I fall short of that goal in a training session, this is the type of grid I would offer the next day to allow that good feeling to be put back into place for them. The act of flight, correctly performed, is an exhilarating feeling like none other; on the other hand, flight insecurely performed can be a frightening experience for your dog. We never really know how many jumps of a frightening nature our dogs will tolerate until their performance begins to erode into something less confident. It is my sincere intent that I never find that place with any dog I deal with.

If you build the stages of this grid with care, not only does it offer many skills for your dog to practice, it allows you to incorporate motion information, thereby isolating specific skills and coordinating timing and handling. This grid is fun for you and your dog if approached properly.

Adding handler motion should only improve your dog's performance, never degrade his performance. All of this grid can and should be performed with no motion or limited motion to begin with. Handler motion is then carefully built in through the stages. It is never wise to simply rush into handling sequences just because you can. I once got a fortune cookie that I kept for years as the saying was so true: "It is never crowded on the extra mile." Take the time to build the steps that provide your dog with ease of motion and confidence, so he feels good about his work. You will see it in your dog's speed and enthusiasm toward jumping, and that will be your reward for showing patience and allowing your dog time to practice his jumping skills, not always as they relate to handling.

Important: Do not introduce this grid until your dog can perform the basic circle grid smoothly and consistently.

Reference DVD

See Exercise #1 on the *Proofing Jump Work with Motion* DVD.

Setting Up the Grid

This grid requires 12 jumps (more if you use the shortest recommended distances between jumps). I like to use a combination of winged and nonwinged jumps to build the grid.

Set the center jump in the middle of your work area. I often use a double for the center jump. If you don't have a double, depending on the specific construction of your jumps, you may be able to make one by placing two single jumps close together. Place a facilitator jump on one side of the center jump to create a set point.

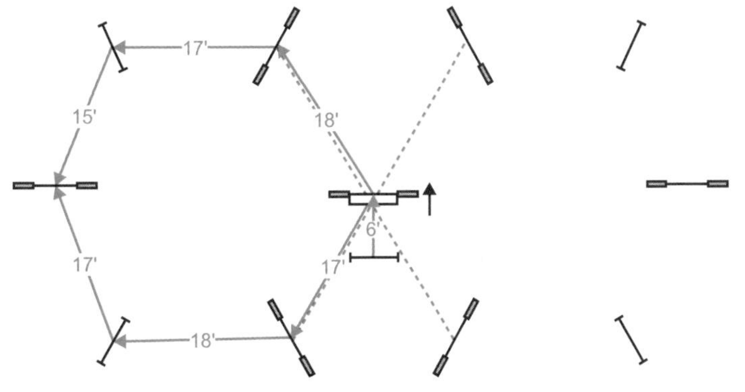

Next, set four jumps, two off each side of the center jump, to form an "X" as shown in the diagram. You can use a mix of 15'–18' between jumps, measured from the center of one jump to the center of the next jump. The spacing does *not* have to be the same on each of the circles.

Place the remaining jumps to complete the circle. Intersperse winged and nonwinged jumps, again using a mix of spa-

Circle to Figure-8 Grid - Setup
First, place the center jump in the middle of your work area with a set point faciliator on one side. Then place four jumps, two on each side, to form an X (red dashed lines). Finally, place the remaining jumps to create a soft, arcing circle on each side. You can use a mix of 15'-18' of spacing between jumps.

cing between 15'–18'. The goal is to create a soft, arcing circle on each side of the set point.

Go to each end of the "X" and look through the jumps to make sure your dog has a clear path on each slice; however, don't worry about the facilitator jump being on the slice path because it will be removed for the slice exercise. Also, check that there is a clear path across the top of the setup. Don't worry if it's not a perfect straight line, as long as it's a reasonable line for your dog to perform. I encourage dogs to find these lines, because they do appear on courses.

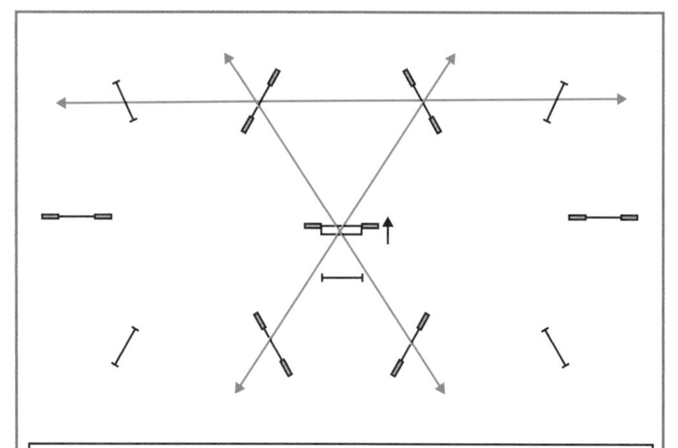

Circle to Figure-8 Grid - Setup Check
Look through the jumps to make sure your dog has a clear path on each slice of the X; do not worry about the facilitator jump being on this path. Also check that there is a clear path across the jumps at the top of the grid.

Notes:

- Remember that when your dog is bending, his stride will always be shorter than when he's traveling on a straight line because his spine is constantly curved through the bend. The 15'-18' distance will be one or two strides for the bigger dogs and two or three strides for the smaller dogs. If working a very tiny dog, you could tighten up the spacing to 12'–14'; however, because this grid is meant to allow your dog to flow, I would not decrease the spacing more than that, because the limited space then impedes handler motion.
- While the grid looks perfect in the diagram, it never looks the same for me when I set it up! I have built this grid many times and it always seems to be slightly different each time. In reality this is a good thing, as long as your "X" is in place and you have a basic circle for your dog to work.

Jump Spacing and Height

Use the information below to determine the jump spacing and jump heights for the grid. Although I have used these distances with success at seminars, they are only guidelines and you may need to adjust them for your dog. Spacing between the jumps is measured from the center of one jump to the center of the next.

Big Dogs

- *Set point:* Space the facilitator jump 6' from the center jump. Set the center jump at your dog's competition jump height and set the facilitator jump at a maximum of 6" in height.
- *Circles:* All jumps on the circle should be at your dog's competition jump height or close to that height. Space the jumps 15'–18' apart.

Medium Dogs

- *Set point:* Space the facilitator jump 5' from the center jump. Set the center jump at your dog's competition jump height and set the facilitator jump at a maximum of 4"–6" in height.
- *Circles:* All jumps on the circle should be at your dog's competition jump height or close to that height. Space the jumps 15'–18' apart.

Small Dogs

- *Set point:* Space the facilitator jump 4' from the center jump. Set the center jump at your dog's competition jump height and set the facilitator jump at a maximum of 4" in height.
- *Circles:* All jumps on the circle should be at your dog's competition jump height or close to that height. Space the jumps 15'–18' apart.

Tiny Dogs

- *Set point:* Space the facilitator jump 2'–3' from the center jump. Set the center jump at your dog's competition jump height and set the facilitator jump at a maximum of 4" in height.
- *Circles:* All jumps on the circle should be at your dog's competition jump height or close to that height. Space the jumps 15'–18' apart.

Target

The target moves for each stage of this grid as described in "Progressions."

Dog's Starting Position

For stages 1–4:

- Line up your dog so he is facing the center of the facilitator jump.
- The distance between your dog and the facilitator jump should be half the distance of the space in the set point grid. For example, if the facilitator jump and the center jump are spaced 6' apart, then start your dog 3' from the facilitator jump.
- Your dog can be in a sit, stand, or down.
- Your dog should be looking forward at the jump or target before you release him.

If you do not have a start-line stay, have a training partner restrain your dog.

Once the initial stages of the grid have been performed and the circle becomes the figure-8 in stage 5, the facilitator jump is removed from the grid. At this point your dog needs to start at a distance from jump #1 that is equal to one steady, short stride for him:

- Big dogs: 9'–11'
- Medium dogs: 7'–9'
- Small dogs: 5'–6'
- Tiny dogs: 4'–5'

Remember, the shorter the stride, the greater the balance and power. So find a good distance for your dog and then become consistent with walking off that distance for your dog.

Handler's Position

Your position changes for each stage of this grid as described in "Progressions."

Progressions

This grid is built up progressively *each time* you do it. Even when your dog is performing the complete figure-8 with ease in both directions, you will always start the training session by building the grid up from stage 1 through stage 7. Consider stages 1 through 3 to be a warm-up for stages 4 and 5, and think of stages 6 and 7 as a "cool down" from the pressure of handler movement.

Stage 1

Place the target 10' past the jump in the set point exercise in the center and on a slight arc that leads your dog toward jump #2. The target should be visible to your dog. Lead out and stand one step ahead of the target and one step laterally off the target. This allows your dog to get to the target without passing the plane of your body.

Do the exercise several times and then move the target to jump #2 on the opposite circle and repeat.

If your dog is successful and comfortable with the exercise, move on to stage 2.

Stage 2

Place the target 10' past jump #2. Your dog is performing the set point to a jump. The target should be placed so it's visible to your dog when he's taking jump #1. Lead out and stand one step ahead of the target and one step laterally off the target.

Do the exercise several times and then move the target so it's 10' past jump #2 on the opposite circle and repeat.

If your dog is successful and comfortable with the exercise, move on to stage 3.

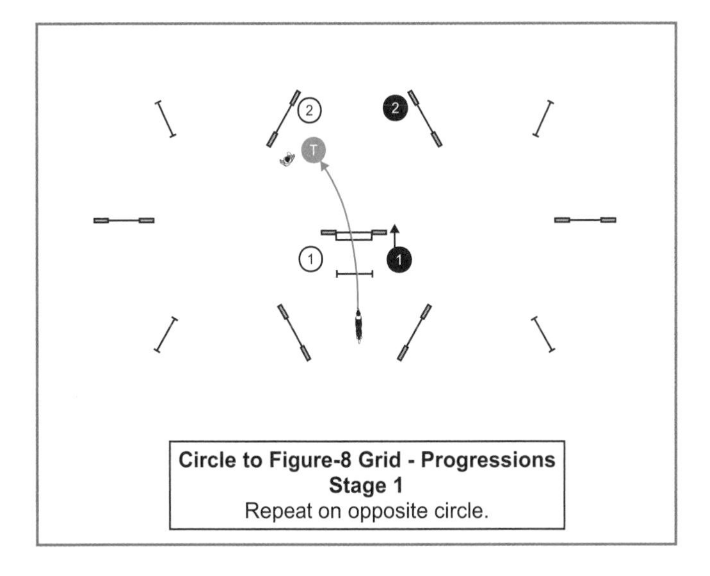

Circle to Figure-8 Grid - Progressions
Stage 1
Repeat on opposite circle.

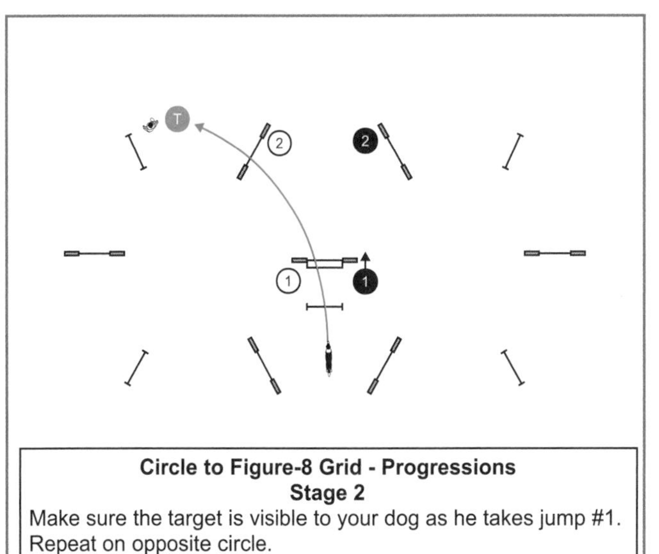

Circle to Figure-8 Grid - Progressions
Stage 2
Make sure the target is visible to your dog as he takes jump #1.
Repeat on opposite circle.

Stage 3

Place the target 10' past jump #3. Your dog is performing the set point to two jumps on the arc. The target should be placed so it's visible to your dog when he's taking jump #2. Lead out and stand one step ahead of the target and one step laterally off the target.

Do the exercise several times and then move the target so it's 10' past jump #3 on the opposite circle and repeat.

If your dog is successful and comfortable with the exercise, move on to stage 4.

Stage 4

Drop the target directly behind your dog at the start line. Your dog now will drive from the set point and continue around the circle of jumps back to his target.

At this stage you are increasing your lateral distance from your dog and you will need to introduce some minimal motion. Preferably you can lead out to the center "hub" position of the circle and move slowly in a small circle, supporting your dog by turning your shoulders and hips as your dog performs the jumps. If it's necessary for you to be closer to the jumps to support your dog while he does the circle, then work on gradually adding more lateral distance until you can handle from the center of the circle.

Do two or three repetitions and repeat the exercise on the opposite circle.

Do not progress to the next stage until your dog can complete the circle smoothly and with consistent success *in both directions.*

Stage 5

Remove the facilitator jump.

In this stage you are going to do a complete figure-8, which means you will need to use a front or rear cross at #7 to change sides. Be certain to walk both options before running your dog through the exercise.

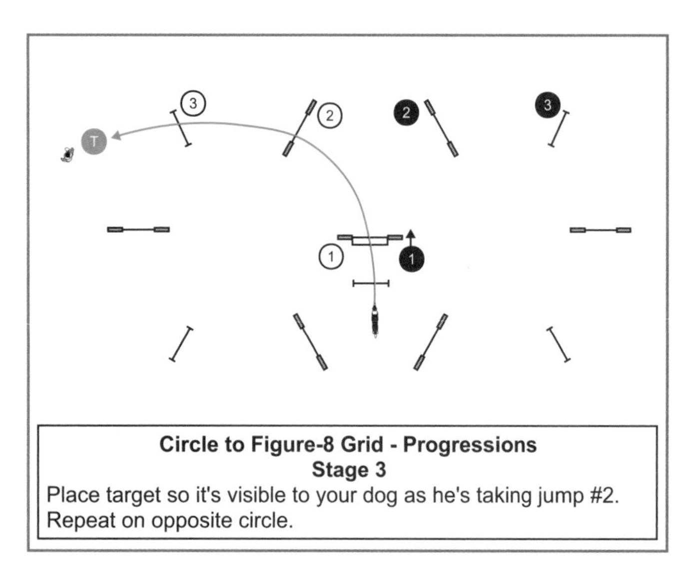

Circle to Figure-8 Grid - Progressions
Stage 3
Place target so it's visible to your dog as he's taking jump #2. Repeat on opposite circle.

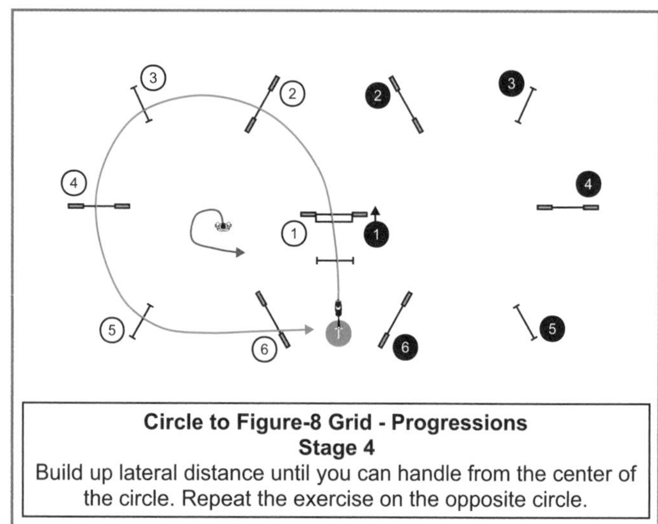

Circle to Figure-8 Grid - Progressions
Stage 4
Build up lateral distance until you can handle from the center of the circle. Repeat the exercise on the opposite circle.

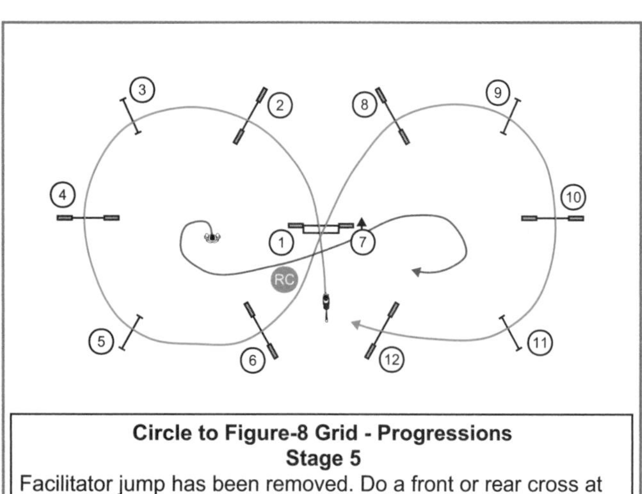

Circle to Figure-8 Grid - Progressions
Stage 5
Facilitator jump has been removed. Do a front or rear cross at jump #7. Repeat the exercise in opposite direction.

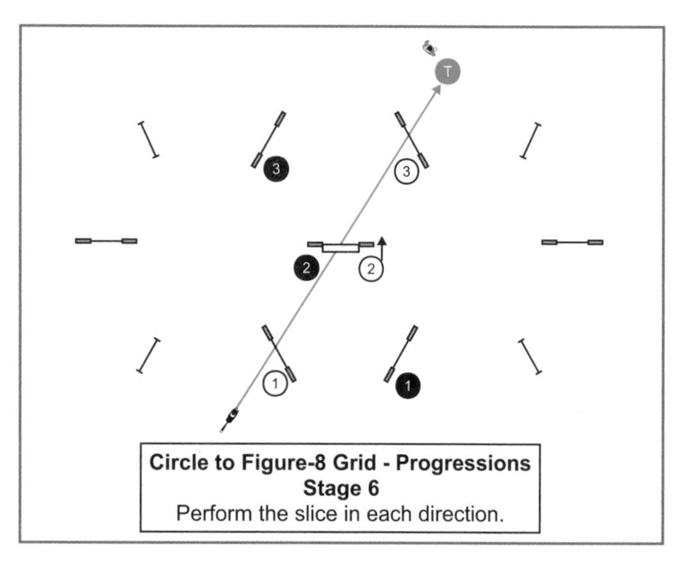

Circle to Figure-8 Grid - Progressions
Stage 6
Perform the slice in each direction.

To start the exercise, set up your dog in front of jump #1 at a steady, short one-stride distance. Rather than placing the target, carry it with you and drop it at your feet as you break off the exercise after jump #12.

Do two or three repetitions and then repeat the exercise starting with your dog on your left and traveling into the circle on the right side to start.

Once you have built up to stage 5, always do stages 6 and 7 before you end the training session.

Stage 6

After the handling stage it is important to back off the handling and offer your dog the chance to perform the slices through the center of the grid (the "X") and the line across the top of the grid quietly and without the pressure of handler motion. I believe that our dogs need the chance to settle and think again after motion, followed by more motion, or when faster motion is offered. Offering motion signals "game on" and can easily push many young dogs over the top with arousal. Some give and take of that pressure becomes increasingly important for the young, motion-reactive dogs so they are reminded they must still execute their job with thought and care—even once it becomes "game on." In addition, your dog has worked through many repetitions of circle work with this drill; therefore, the straight lines allow your dog to lengthen his spine and relax the muscles before ending a session of bend work.

Also, the use of the target at the end of the training session provides balance. Once we are handling and the target is no longer on the ground, we become the dominant information to our dogs. By bringing the target back into the picture, we help encourage our dogs to be looking ahead and task oriented again.

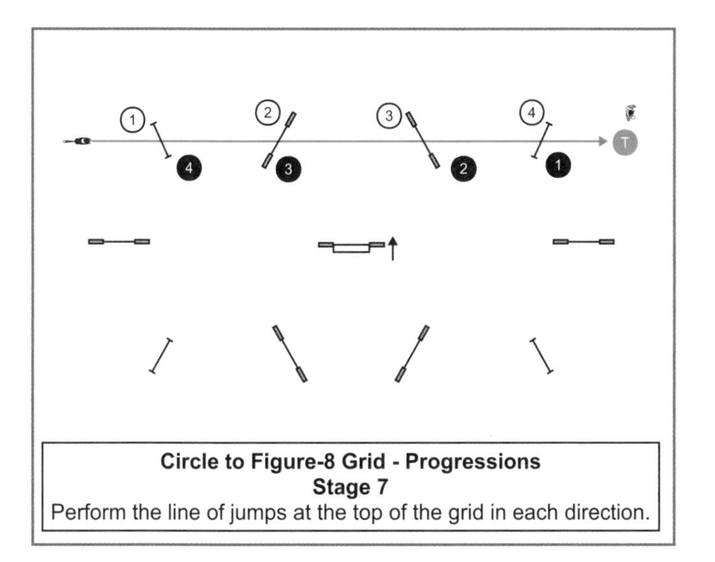

Circle to Figure-8 Grid - Progressions
Stage 7
Perform the line of jumps at the top of the grid in each direction.

Place the target 10' past jump #3. Lead out and stand one step ahead of the target and one step laterally off the target.

Do the exercise once and then move the target so it's 10' past jump #3 on the opposite circle and repeat.

Stage 7

Place the target 10' past jump #4. Lead out and stand one step ahead of the target and one step laterally off the target.

Do the exercise once and then move the target and repeat going in the opposite direction.

Problem Solving

Problem: Your dog pulls off the line of jumps and comes into you.

Solution: This can often happen when the mix of jumps includes a nonwinged jump. After the dog takes several winged jumps (greater visual impact), the nonwinged jump can be insignificant to him unless it is supported by you. If this is the problem, place the target in front of the nonwinged jump your dog pulled off and repeat the exercise, ending at the target. Do this once or twice and then retry the entire exercise.

This problem is also common if your lateral distance from your dog is greater than he is comfortable with so he aborts the jump and comes with you. Your dog is correct, so reward him! On the next repetition, decrease your lateral distance from your dog to where he can be successful. Then work on slowly building up more lateral distance in small increments. This exercise provides valuable information, showing you just how much support your dog needs from you to take the jumps.

Problem: Your dog begins dropping bars once handling motion increases.

Solution: Reduce your motion until your dog settles into his work. Handler motion is a *huge* stimulant to your dog and should not be rushed into before your dog has the skills to deal with it. Go back to the step where your dog was consistent, which could be motion but less speed; for example, instead of running you can jog or instead of jogging you can walk. Work that step a bit longer and then try gradually increasing your speed.

"There are no shortcuts to any place worth going." —Beverly Sills

Problem: Your dog aborts the third jump on the center slice.

Solution: Place the target in front of jump #3 and do jumps #1 and #2 to the target once and then retry the entire slice. If your dog still refuses the jump, repeat the targeting exercise and lower the height of jump #3. Slice jumps are an acquired skill for many dogs. Even though we see the slice as a straight line, most dogs do not and many struggle with it. Meet your dog where he "thinks he can" and build from there. Remember, it is only your dog's perception of the difficulty that counts here, since he is the one performing the task.

Problem: Your dog cannot find the straight line across the top of the grid.

Solution: This is a common problem depending on the difficulty of that line. Often when this grid is set up, your dog does not see the obvious path until he has committed to the prior jump. If your dog needs help, I would offer assistance with the target, as opposed to handling. Build the line by offering the target in front of jump #3, then move the target so it is in front of jump #4, and then finally move the target 10' after jump #4. It is much easier to handle a dog that is always looking ahead for the next logical obstacle supported by your motion, as opposed to a dog that requires you to be at each jump. If the latter is your dog, you are likely slowing him down. Handling a dog that is schooled, skilled, and has sharp mental acuity is a supporting role, not a dominant role. Take the time to train your dog to look ahead for obstacles and then enjoy the ride!

How Much to Practice?

Build this grid starting at stage 1 *every* time you offer it to your dog, though you can reduce the number of repetitions in stages 1–3 so you aren't doing as many set points. As I said before, the grid setup always comes out a bit different and the use of different jumps can be of influence. So take the time to target your dog's path in stages 1 through 3 before you start the stages that require handler movement. Think of it this way: stages 1 through 3 are a warm-up for stages 4 and 5, and stages 6 and 7 are a "cool down" from the pressure of handler movement.

With a trained dog, bend work is a skill that you need to practice monthly. It can be offered through the circle to figure-8 grid as well as other bending grids.

Proofing

You are systematically proofing your dog as you gradually add to the difficulty of this grid and introduce handler motion.

You can also work on increasing your lateral distance from your dog as you work in the hub position.

Adding Handler Motion

Handler motion is built into this grid when you get to stages 4 and 5, but only go as far and as fast as determined by your dog's success. With some dogs you will need to start the exercise with you at a walk and then slowly increase handler motion over time.

Remember that an extended hand/arm is intended to support distance. If you are in the hub position of the circle or laterally off your dog's path, then the hand/arm is suitable. But if you are running alongside your dog as he jumps, the hand can distract your dog from focusing forward on the task.

Adding Handling

Once you are doing the full figure-8, you will need to use a front or rear cross at the center jump to change sides. Try both to determine which option is the smoothest and fastest for your dog. The eventual goal is to have your dog's jumping form constant regardless of which cross you use.

Grid Variations

Oval to figure-8 grid

"There is no substitute for work. Worthwhile results come from hard work and careful planning. Failing to prepare is preparing to fail." —Coach John Wooden

FIGURE-8 GRID

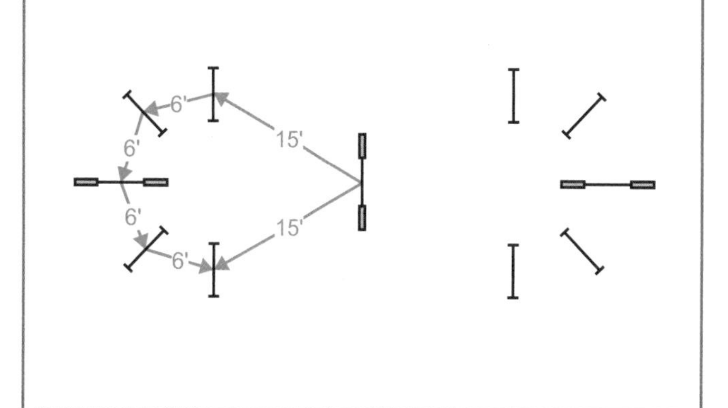

Figure-8 Grid - Setup
The distances shown here are only examples. See "Jump Spacing and Height" to set up the grid for your dog.

Overview

The figure-8 grid is another lead-change exercise that generates a lot of speed and enthusiasm from dogs. It contains a plyometric element, which requires speed, balance, and footwork. It also tests your dog's ability to read his line and understand the coming lead change. Your dog also has an opportunity to practice offering the lead change in the air over the transition jump rather than adding an additional stride prior to the jump. You will get a chance to work on giving smooth and timely information that allows your dog to continue to drive the line without being distracted by unnecessary information or having to ask questions because he's not being given enough support. I find these simple grids are a wonderful way to perfect the feel and timing of providing handling information to your dog, because you are not required to race to a spot to deliver the information. The work is quiet and allows your dog to begin trusting quiet, subtle information that encourages him to seek his task and continue to look for the next logical piece of work that your motion indicates.

Once introduced, this grid is one of the less complicated jump grids so it's wonderful for allowing your dog to "blow off some steam" after doing a difficult handling sequence or after doing a more complicated grid or a grid your dog struggled with. The figure-8 grid is meant to be fast and fun for you and your dog. It offers a happy solution for a dog that is stressed and in need of a speed circle to brighten him.

Important: Do not introduce this grid until your dog can perform the basic circle grid smoothly and consistently.

Reference DVD

See Exercise #3 on the *Tuning Up for Competition* DVD.

Setting Up the Grid

This grid requires eight nonwinged jumps and three winged jumps. I use a winged jump for the center of each of the arcs as a reference point. With the wing as a strong focal point, it will help you remember that you should not cross the plane of that jump when you set up for a rear cross, so as not to push your dog off the tight line through the arc. You will cross the plane of the jump only if you are performing a front cross. The third winged jump is placed between the two arcs. This is the jump your dog drives to out of the arc, and it is offered at your dog's competition height.

Jump Spacing and Height

Use the information below to determine the jump spacing and jump heights for the grid. Although I have used these distances with success at seminars, they are only guidelines and you may need to adjust them for your dog. Spacing between the jumps is measured from the center of one jump to the center of the next.

Big Dogs

- *Arcs:* Space the jumps 6' apart and set at 6" in height. Because each arc is a plyometric exercise, the jump height should not be increased.
- *Center Jump:* The center jump should be 15' away from the ends of the arc. Set the jump at your dog's competition jump height. (Note: 15' out of the bend for the big dogs should be a single stride.)

Medium Dogs

- *Arcs:* Space the jumps 5' apart and set at 6" in height. The height of these jumps never increases during the exercise.
- *Center Jump:* The center jump should be 15' away from the ends of the arc. Set the jump at your dog's competition jump height. (Note: 15' out of the bend for the medium dogs will most likely be two strides.)

Small Dogs

- *Arcs:* Space the jumps 4' apart and set at 4" in height. The height of these jumps never increases during the exercise.
- *Center Jump:* The center jump should be 12' away from the ends of the arc. Set the jump at your dog's competition jump height. (Note: 12' out of the bend for the small dogs will most likely be one stride, but will be two strides for some.)

Tiny Dogs

- *Arcs:* Space the jumps 1.5' to 2' apart and set at 4" in height. The height of these jumps never increases during the exercise.
- *Center Jump:* The center jump should be 12' away from the ends of the arc. Set the jump at your dog's competition jump height. (Note: 12' out of the bend for the tiny dogs will most likely be two strides.)

Target

The target moves for each stage of this grid as described in "Progressions."

Dog's Starting Position

We do not want a sit or a stay for bend work; remember, your dog would prefer not to bend. You need to begin with forward motion into the grid. The arcs in this grid are set up to be a plyometric exercise for your dog; they are *not* spaced at a one-stride distance as in the circle grid. Set up your dog in front of the first jump, giving yourself just enough room to take several steps forward with your dog to guarantee he takes jump #2.

Position your dog so he is centered on the first jump, facing straight ahead, and looking at the jump; do *not* place your dog on an angle to the first jump.

Handler's Position

You need to move forward with your dog to start the arc portion of the grid while *not* pushing him off the tight line. Think of this exercise as a wheel; you, the handler, are the hub of the wheel and the rotation of your hips and shoulders influences the turn of your dog. You will step forward with your dog, slip into the hub position, and then rotate your shoulders and hips to support your dog through the arc.

As your dog is approaching the third jump of the arc (the winged jump), you will begin to move from the hub position toward the winged jump in the center. Continue moving toward the target smoothly.

Once you are ready to do the complete figure-8, you will need to do either a front or rear cross to change sides. Be certain to walk both options prior to running your dog through the exercise. Determine which option is the smoothest and fastest for your dog.

Progressions

This grid is built up progressively during a training session every time you do it.

Stage 1

Place the target on the tight line after jump #5. Make sure you give your dog enough room to land from jump #5 while still keeping him driving on a bend through the last jump.

Do one repetition of the arc in each direction.

Stage 2

Now you are going to train your dog to start looking for the next arc. Move the full-height winged jump in the middle as shown in the diagram so there is a jump after the arc. Place the target in front of the jump and do the sequence shown once. Then move the target to the landing side of the jump and repeat the sequence once.

Move the jump to the other side of the arc and follow the same process working in the opposite direction.

Stage 3

Move the full-height winged jump back to the center of the grid.

Place the target in front of jump #7 and do the sequence once or twice. Pay attention not only to your dog's path but to where his head is pointing. Before you progress to the next stage you want to make certain he is looking for the next logical jump to take.

Repeat this process working in the opposite direction.

Stage 4

In this stage you are going to do a complete figure-8, which means you will need to use a front or rear cross at #6 to change sides. Rather than placing the target, carry it with you and drop it at your feet as you break off the exercise after jump #11. Do three repetitions.

Repeat three times working in the opposite direction.

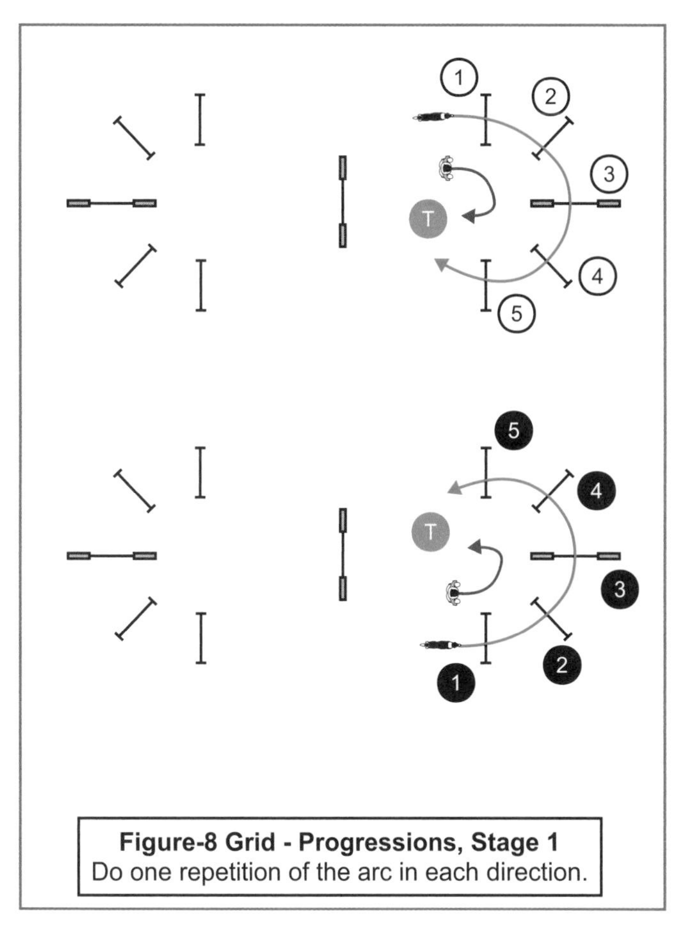

Figure-8 Grid - Progressions, Stage 1
Do one repetition of the arc in each direction.

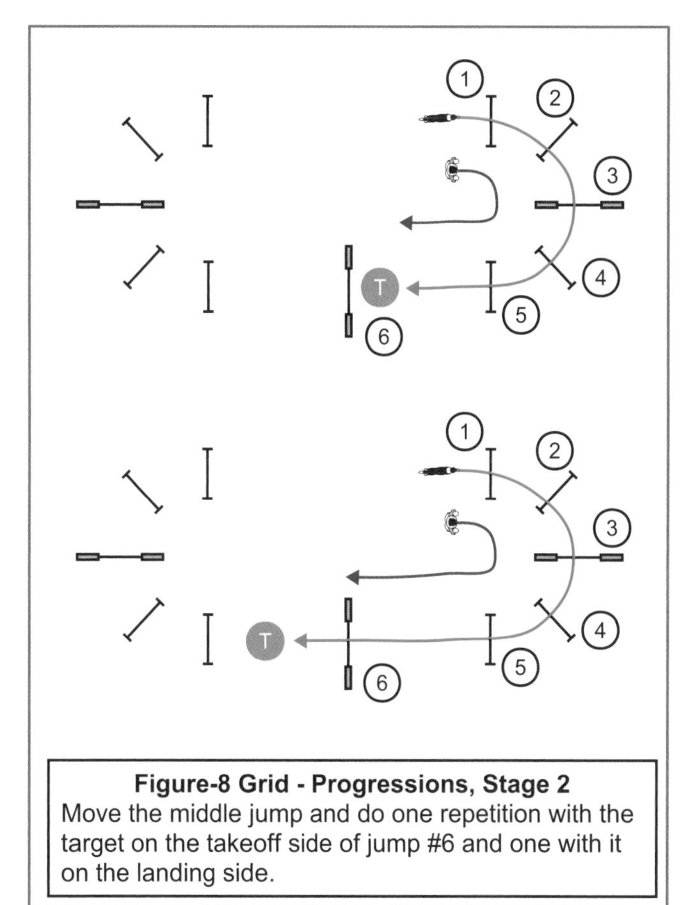

Figure-8 Grid - Progressions, Stage 2
Move the middle jump and do one repetition with the target on the takeoff side of jump #6 and one with it on the landing side.

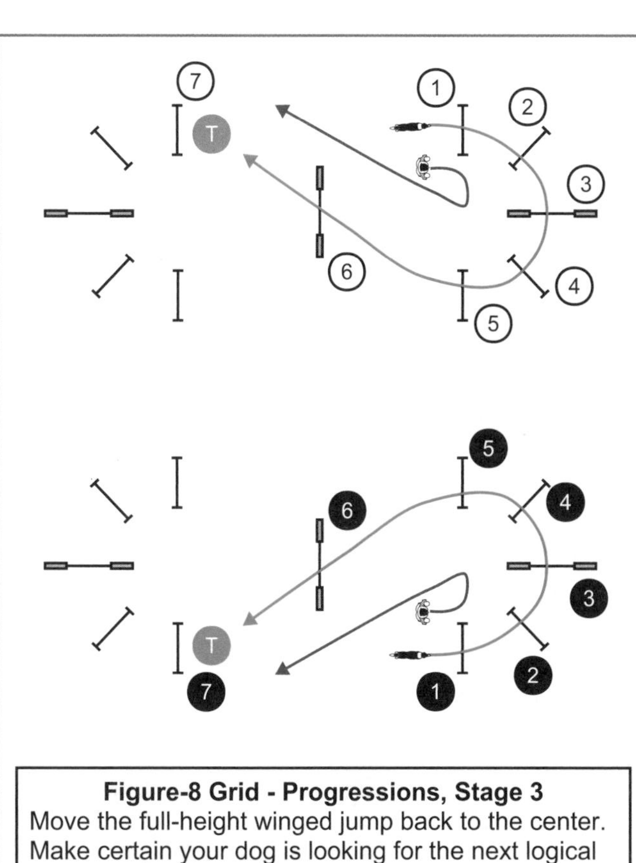

Figure-8 Grid - Progressions, Stage 3
Move the full-height winged jump back to the center. Make certain your dog is looking for the next logical jump to take before progressing.

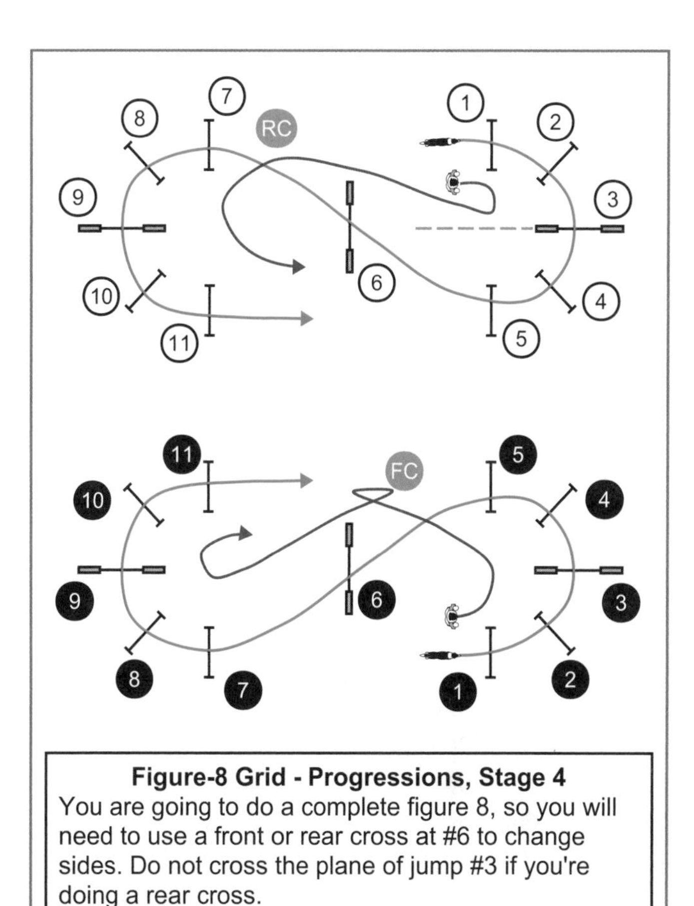

Figure-8 Grid - Progressions, Stage 4
You are going to do a complete figure 8, so you will need to use a front or rear cross at #6 to change sides. Do not cross the plane of jump #3 if you're doing a rear cross.

Problem Solving

Problem: Your dog fails to sight and drive to the jump out of the arc (jump #6) because he does not perceive it as part of the line.

Solution: Place the target in front of jump #6 to correct your dog's path and keep him looking forward. Do this exercise once and then place the target on the other side of the jump and repeat. Also, make sure that you are moving forward toward the jump.

Problem: Once the whole figure-8 is introduced, your dog "stalls out" and fails to drive to the next obstacle.

Solution: Revisit the stages of progression as you may have gone too fast through the steps. The goal is to build understanding so your dog is always looking for the next logical obstacle to execute as long as your path supports it.

How Much to Practice?

You build this grid starting at stage 1 *every* time you offer it to your dog, though you can reduce the number of repetitions in stage 4.

With a trained dog, bend work is a skill that you need to practice monthly. It can be offered through the figure-8 grid as well as other bending grids.

Proofing

You are proofing your dog as you gradually increase handler motion. You can also work on increasing your lateral distance from your dog.

Adding Handler Motion

Handler motion is built into this grid as you work through the progression, but only go as far and as fast as determined by your dog's success. With some dogs, you will need to start the exercise at a walk and then slowly increase your motion as your dog's understanding improves.

Adding Handling

Once you are doing the full figure-8, you will need to use a front or rear cross at the center jump to change sides. Try both to determine which option is the smoothest and fastest for your dog. The eventual goal is to have your dog's jumping form constant regardless of which cross you use.

Even though this is a fast and furious grid, it is *still* a jumping lesson for your dog. Do not rehearse failure for your dog just because handling is allowed. Also, be aware that once your dog gets rolling along through this grid he will often be having so much fun that he is willing to keep going without you—do not allow this because it will encourage sloppy handling on your part.

Grid Variations

None.

Gridwork is widely dismissed by many agility handlers as a nonessential portion of the dog's athletic training. This is due mainly to handlers thinking that "any dog can jump; therefore, why would one need to dedicate time to training it?" Fair enough! But the difference is night and day. A dog jumping fallen branches and ditches while running free in the woods can navigate these obstacles with great ease, primarily due to two major factors: 1) The dog running free has total focus forward on his path, and 2) because of this focus the dog's body responds quickly and appropriately. This is, however, not the dog we run with for agility.

JUMPS AND TUNNELS GRID

Overview

When we introduce tunnels into jump work, there will be significantly more speed attached to the exercise, since most dogs enjoy tunnels quite a bit. In the jumps and tunnels grid, we offer our dogs a bounce/plyometric portion for practicing weight shift, speed, balance, and footwork over a distance to the tunnel. Out of the tunnel there is a single jump centered in the space between the two tunnels. So there is a "striding distance" into the tunnel from the single jump and out of the tunnel to the single jump.

What I look for is smooth, fluid footwork, which tells me the dog knows where he is in relation to his takeoff spot for either the grid or the single jump. Additional "pats" of the ground tell me the dog has questions. Surprisingly, the dog's questions are typically related to the grid rather than the single jump since the grid requires a bigger weight shift because of the amount of collection needed. When space is offered that allows the dog to stride rather than to bounce, I really want to see him being decisive.

As your dog exits a tunnel he has three things to determine:

1. Where are you?
2. What path are you presenting?
3. What obstacle is to be taken next?

Generally your dog considers these things in that order. If your dog is slow to assess the task, the fallout will be added strides that are unnecessary until your dog has the chance to work through this problem.

We also must deal with our dogs' dominant thought, which can undermine an otherwise brilliant agility round. As the dog approaches the jump is he thinking, "Do I lower myself to get into the tunnel?" *or* "Do I first perform this jump and then lower myself for the tunnel?" I am a firm believer that the jump itself can help teach a dog what we want. If we want our dogs to pay more attention to the jump than to the tunnel, the jump needs to state that to the dogs. So I use a prominent double, a panel jump, a wall jump, or any jump that says, "First, deal with me," as opposed to an unimportant-looking nonwinged jump that is better saved for when you are ready to proof the behavior.

For dogs that lack thought and care in their jump execution when faced with a tunnel, I often recommend a using 3' jump bar with one big stripe centered on it. Place the short bar on a winged jump before a tunnel. The narrow "opening" of the jump causes dogs to pay more attention to the task at hand. This is just another way of offering the dog correct information so you don't feel the need to "manage bars."

This is a fast, fun exercise for dog and handler and one that reminds me of a quote from race car legend, Mario Andretti: "If everything seems under control, you are not going fast enough." This is apt for agility and a good reminder for us to keep the fun in our training sessions.

Reference DVD

See Exercise #5 on the *Tuning Up for Competition* DVD.

Setting Up the Grid

This grid requires two tunnels, four nonwinged jumps, and a winged jump. The obstacles can be arranged to form either a circle or an oval. You should practice with both setups, since the handling changes from one to the other.

I use nonwinged jumps for the four-part "bounce" or ladder/plyometric grid. I angle the jumps in a zig-zag formation because it causes your dog to give the setup a harder look than he would if the jumps were straight like the rungs of a ladder. With his attention called to these jumps, your dog will offer the appropriate weight shift necessary to enter the grid.

Use a winged jump, parallel double (so it can be taken from both directions), panel jump, tire, or wall jump for the single jump between the two tunnels.

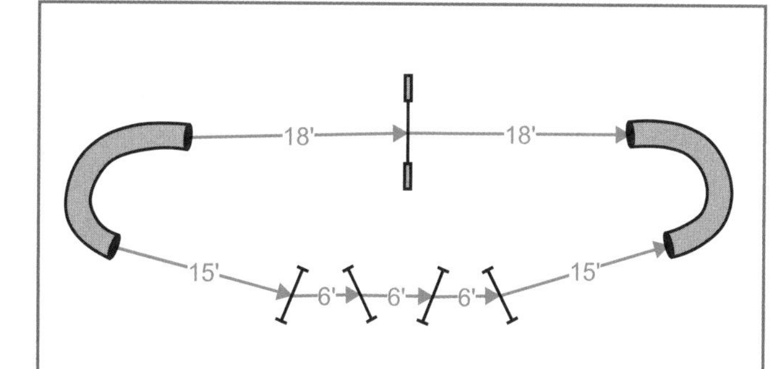

Jumps and Tunnels Grid - Oval Setup
Your dog's path to the tunnel opening should be relatively straight. The distances shown here are only examples. See "Jump Spacing and Height" to set up the grid for your dog.

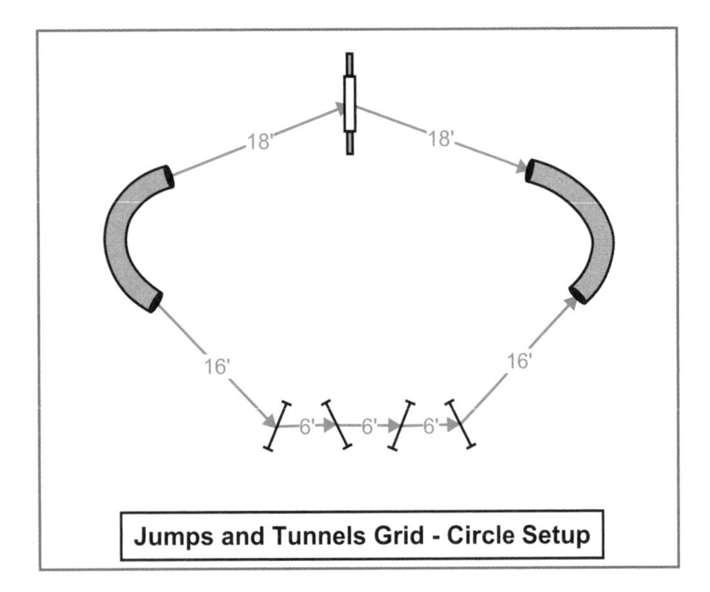

Jumps and Tunnels Grid - Circle Setup

Dogs will hit the tunnels with a great deal of speed so be certain the tunnels are anchored safely and securely.

To set up the grid, secure the first tunnel and then pace off the distance you will be using to the single jump and to the bounce grid. Build the bounce grid and set the single jump. Next pace off the distance to the second tunnel from the single jump and from the last jump of the bounce grid and secure the tunnel in place. It is a good idea to stand behind each tunnel at the center of the curve to determine if your dog's path to each tunnel entrance is relatively straight.

Jump Spacing and Height

Use the information below to determine the jump spacing and jump heights for the grid. Although I have used these distances with success at seminars, they are only guidelines and you may need to adjust them for your dog. Spacing between the jumps is measured from the center of one jump to the center of the next. Tunnel spacing is measured from the center of the jump to the tunnel opening.

Big Dogs

- *Single jump:* Set at your dog's competition jump height. The longer your dog's stride, the flatter his jumping arc will be. You do not want to encourage your dog to jump flat here, so start with 18' from the tunnel to the jump. When you are confident your dog can perform the exercise appropriately, you can open up your dog's stride by adding more space: 21'–23' from the jump to the tunnel.
- *Bounce/ladder grid:* Space the jumps 6' apart and set at 6"–8" in height. The height of these jumps never increases during the exercise. The first and last jump in the bounce grid should be 15'–16' from a tunnel opening.

Medium Dogs

- *Single jump:* Set at your dog's competition jump height. The longer your dog's stride, the flatter his jumping arc will be. You do not want to encourage your dog to jump flat here, so start with 15' from the tunnel to the jump. When you are confident your dog can perform the exercise appropriately, you can open up your dog's stride by adding more space: 18' from the jump to the tunnel.
- *Bounce/ladder grid:* Space the jumps 5' apart and set at 6" in height. The height of these jumps never increases during the exercise. The first and last jump in the bounce grid should be 18' from a tunnel opening.

Small and Tiny Dogs

- *Single jump:* Set at your dog's regulation jump height. The longer your dog's stride, the flatter his jumping arc will be. You do not want to encourage your dog to jump flat here, so start with 14' from the tunnel to the jump. When you are confident your dog can perform the exercise appropriately you can open up your dog's stride by adding more space: 16'–17' from the jump to the tunnel.
- *Bounce/ladder grid:* Space the jumps 4' apart and set at 4" in height. The height of these jumps never increases during the exercise. The first and last jump in the bounce grid should be 16' from a tunnel opening.

Target

The target moves for each stage of this grid as described in "Progressions."

Dog's Starting Position

Your dog can be in a sit, stand, or down to start.

When starting with the bounce grid, the distance between your dog and the first jump should be half the distance of the first space in the grid. For example, if jumps #1 and #2 are spaced 6' apart, then start your dog 3' from the first jump.

When starting from the single jump, set your dog up at a distance from jump #1 that is equal to one steady, short stride for him:

- Big dogs: 9'–11'
- Medium dogs: 7'–9'
- Small dogs: 5'–6'
- Tiny dogs: 4'–5'

Remember, the shorter the stride, the greater the balance and power. Find a good distance for your dog and become consistent with walking off that distance for your dog.

Handler's Position

Your position changes for each stage of this grid as described in "Progressions."

Progressions

A session consists of the following 10 repetitions:

1. Do the bounce grid going into the tunnel. Before you start, place the target 10' past the tunnel exit. Lead out halfway between the grid and the tunnel, release your dog, and begin to walk toward the tunnel. Do this exercise once and then do the bounce grid into the tunnel in the opposite direction.
2. Do the single jump going into the tunnel. Before you start, place the target 10' past the tunnel exit. Lead out halfway between the grid and the tunnel, release your dog, and begin to walk toward the tunnel. Do this exercise once and then do the single jump into the tunnel in the opposite direction.

Jumps and Tunnels Grid - Progressions, Stage 1
Do one repetition in each direction.

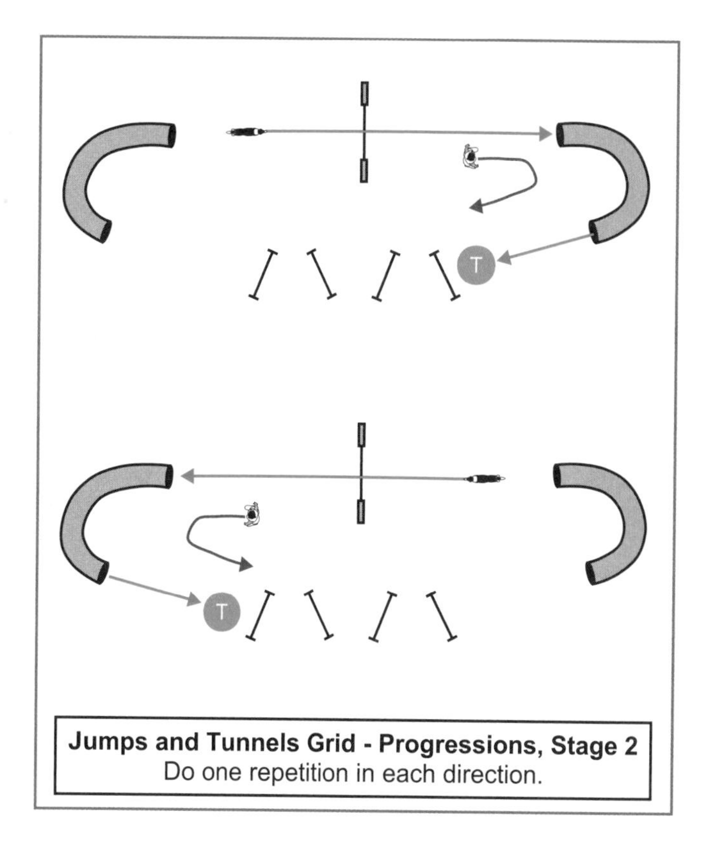

Jumps and Tunnels Grid - Progressions, Stage 2
Do one repetition in each direction.

"Lots of people talk to animals... Not very many listen though... that's the problem."
—Benjamin Hoff, The Tao of Pooh

3. Start your dog at the tunnel exit and do the bounce grid. Before you start, place the target 10' from the last jump of the bounce grid. Lead out and stand one step ahead of the target and one step laterally off the target. This allows your dog to get to the target without passing the plane of your body. Do this exercise once and then repeat in the opposite direction.
4. Start your dog at the tunnel exit and do the single jump. Before you start, place the target 10' from the single jump. Lead out and stand one step ahead of the target and one step laterally off the target. Do this exercise once and then repeat in the opposite direction.
5. Do the bounce grid, the first tunnel, the single jump, and the second tunnel. Lead out halfway between the grid and the tunnel, release your dog, and begin moving toward the tunnel. Rather than placing the target, carry it with you and drop it at your feet as you break off the exercise. Repeat in the opposite direction.

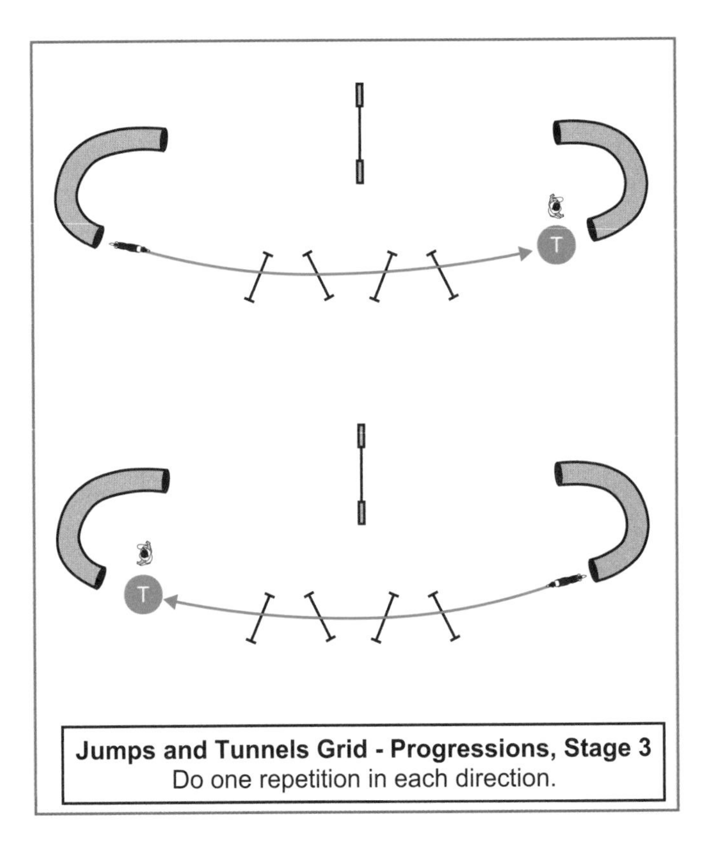

Jumps and Tunnels Grid - Progressions, Stage 3
Do one repetition in each direction.

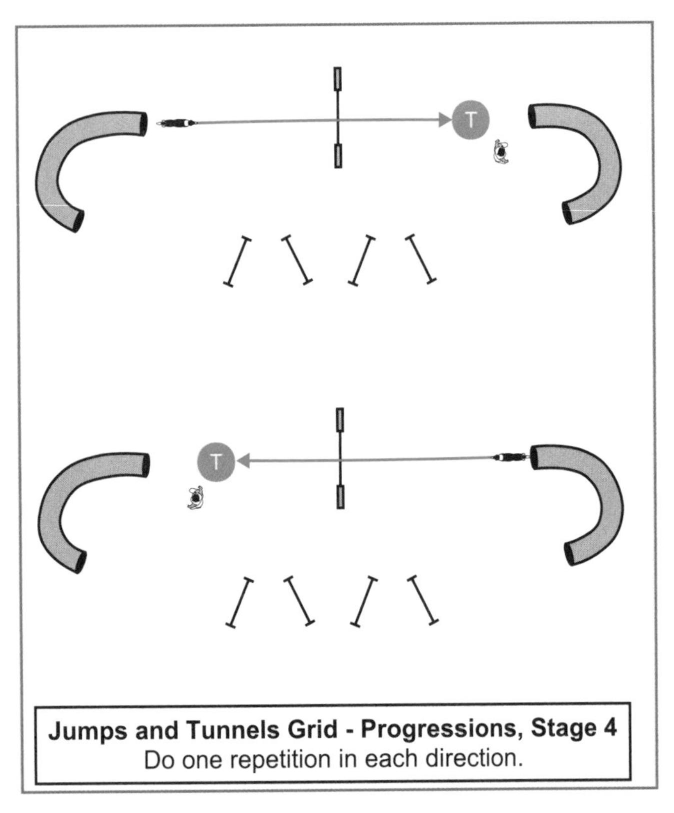

Jumps and Tunnels Grid - Progressions, Stage 4
Do one repetition in each direction.

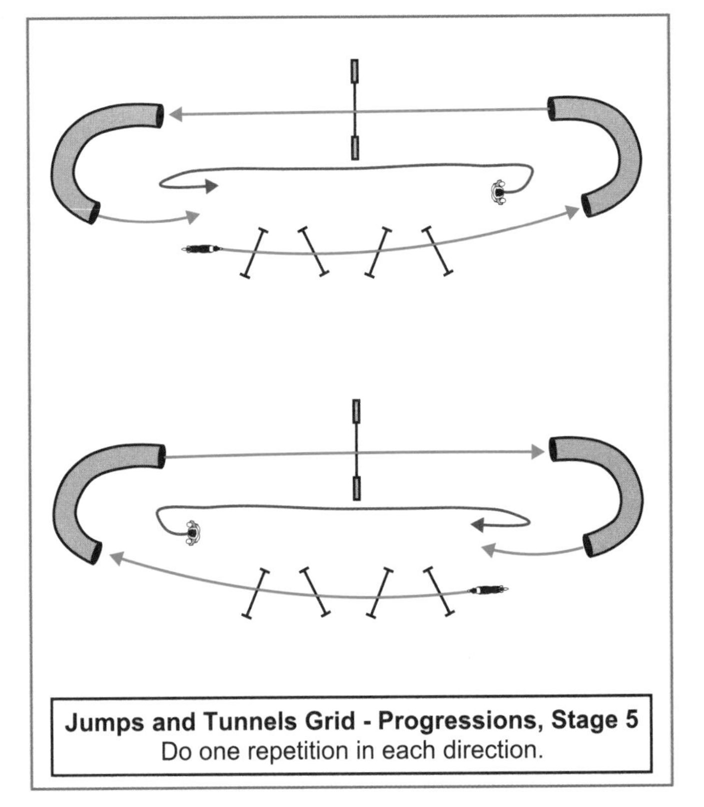

Jumps and Tunnels Grid - Progressions, Stage 5
Do one repetition in each direction.

Problem Solving

Problem: Your dog does not commit to the tunnel.

Solution: School the tunnel by itself until your dog is comfortable entering the tunnel and then try the sequence again.

Problem: Your dog knocks the bar of the single jump.

Solution: Use your target to focus your dog's attention. Place the target in front of the single jump and do one or two repetitions of tunnel to target. Then move the target to the landing side of the single jump and do the tunnel to the jump to the target. Then go back and try the entire sequence again.

You can also change the single jump to a hurdle that commands your dog's attention, such as a panel or wall jump. Alternatively, try a 3' bar with a stripe in the middle as described in the "Overview."

How Much to Practice?

Building the steps in "Progressions" prior to running the sequence is important until your dog is very comfortable with the exercise. Those steps provide good solid practice and progressive information to your dog.

Once your dog is successfully performing the sequence without flattening out or rushing through it, you can start a session with the full sequence. From time to time, however, you may need to break down the exercise again to ensure proper execution by your dog. When your dog reaches the point where breaking down the sequence is unnecessary, you will find that it is a fast, furious, and fun exercise for you and your dog.

With a trained dog, bend work is a skill that you need to practice monthly. It can be offered through the jumps and tunnels grid as well as other bending grids.

Proofing

Proofing this grid can be done in several ways. You can do a complete loop of all the obstacles so you are doing the bounce grid in both directions. You can also change out the single jump to another hurdle. Start with the more prominent jumps (such as the double or the panel) and then work your way to jumps with less of a presence. The goal would be to do the exercise with a low-profile nonwinged jump.

Adding Handler Motion

Handler motion is built into this grid through the progression. When you are doing the complete exercise, you can take a slight lead-out or you can run with your dog off the start line.

But I need to include a reminder here that adding handler motion should only enhance your dog's performance, never degrade his performance. If it is necessary for your dog, limit your motion as much as possible and gradually build up your speed.

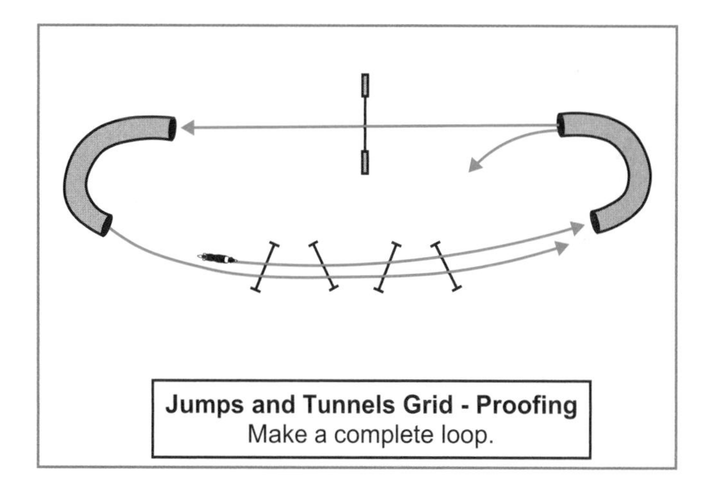

Jumps and Tunnels Grid - Proofing
Make a complete loop.

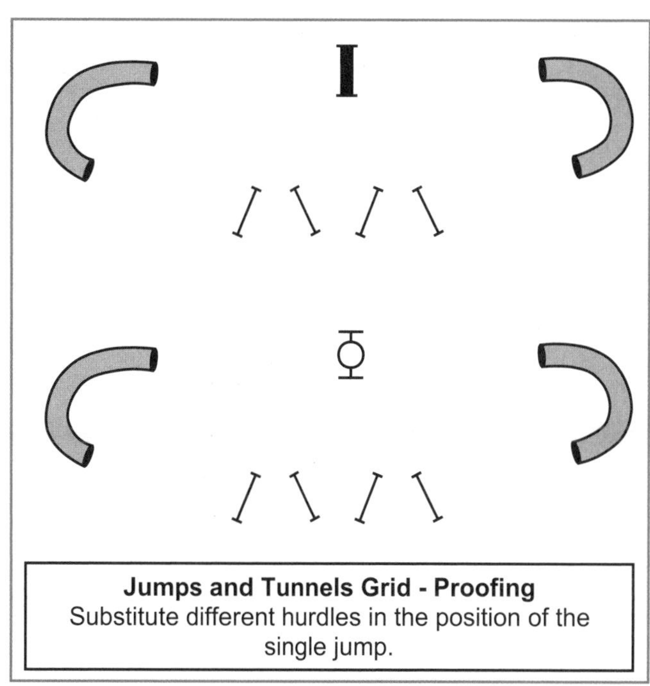

Jumps and Tunnels Grid - Proofing
Substitute different hurdles in the position of the single jump.

Adding Handling

There is no change of side in this exercise so crosses are not necessary. It is a fun speed circle.

Grid Variations

None.

© ERIC BOBKOWSKI

"Jump education has helped my dog Presto have a thoughtful, focused, and confident approach to jumping, even under the pressure of big events and driving to get around the course as quickly as possible."

—Terry Smorch, Multiple-time national champion and World Team member, agility judge

LADDER GRID #1 (FOUNDATION PLYOMETRIC EXERCISE)

Overview

The importance of the low, bounce/ladder grid cannot be overstated. This grid is an essential part of teaching our dogs speed, balance, and footwork done with precision and confidence. In foundation jumping training, the set point grid teaches our dogs to gather with power and elevate off the ground while this foundation plyometric grid teaches them to power through the air.

The jumps in this grid are set at a low height and spaced at a tight, "bounce" distance. The goal is for your dog to land centered in the distance between each jump and the next, and to leave the ground from the same spot where he landed. Your dog lands and leaves again simultaneously, requiring precision from all body parts. The more speed your dog carries, the more difficult this grid will be, because it becomes more difficult for your dog to keep his body under control.

Because of the tight spacing, a stride is not possible. Your dog remains in a continuous state of collection, which enables him to find his power source—his rear end.

When done with regularity, the low ladder grid is a wonderful way to build your dog's hind-end muscles and get more explosive power from him, which will serve him well when he is jumping at full height. The grid is also an excellent conditioning tool for dogs that need to build their fitness and dogs coming off an injury that need to build back up to performing at height.

Reference DVD

See Straight-Line Equal-Distance Grid on the *Foundation Jumping* DVD.

Setting Up the Grid

Height is not a part of this grid; the jumps are never raised. Some people build a set of PVC ladder grid pieces that are fixed at the height appropriate for their dog. Because the jumps are *not* adjustable, making them higher is not a possibility! If you are using regular jumps, nonwinged are best. You want to present this grid in as straightforward a manner as possible; you do not want the equipment to be busy or distracting.

I generally use five jumps for the foundation ladder grid, which is the *minimum* number necessary for working on speed, fluidity, and balance. Once your dog is comfortable with the skills required by the grid, you can add jumps if you have enough jumps and enough room. I have used as many as nine jumps. The more jumps, the more speed from your dog and the harder it is for him to perform the jumping function correctly. While it is fine to build the challenge for your dog, you can go too far. Keep in mind your dog's physical condition as you begin to work. This grid is strenuous enough with five jumps. If your dog is not in peak condition, do not add jumps.

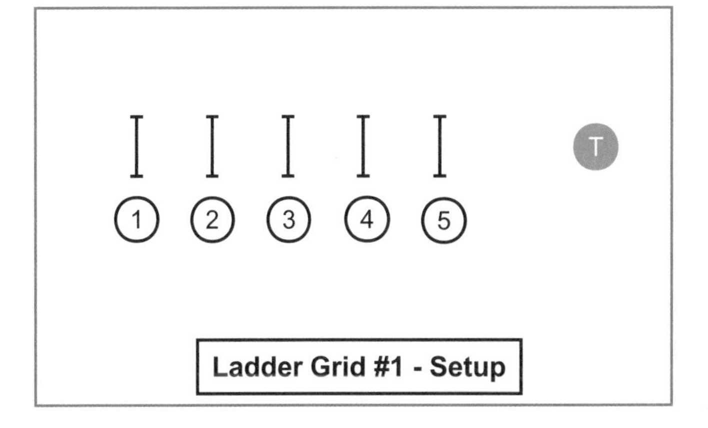

Ladder Grid #1 - Setup

Jump Spacing and Height

Use the information below to determine the jump spacing and jump heights for the grid. Although I have used these distances with success at seminars, they are only guidelines and you may need to adjust them for your dog. Spacing between the jumps is measured from the center of one jump to the center of the next.

Note: This is intended to be a bounce line, not a stride. The distances may need to be adjusted for some dogs to accomplish this.

Big Dogs

- Space the jumps 6' apart and set at 6"–8" in height. The height of these jumps never increases during the exercise.
- If you have a very large dog, you can increase the spacing to 7' with the jumps at 6"–8" in height.

Medium Dogs

- Space the jumps 5' apart and set at 6" in height. The height of these jumps never increases during the exercise.

- **Note:** The *Foundation Jumping* DVD allowed for the jumps to be set at 8" high for the medium dogs. However, after further observation of thousands of dogs, I feel that *any* unwanted shoulder action is counterproductive to what this grid is trying to teach. The lower jump height allows the dogs to better focus on speed, balance, and footwork.

Small Dogs

- Space the jumps 4' apart and set at 4" in height. The height of these jumps never increases during the exercise.

Tiny Dogs

- Space the jumps 3' apart and set at 4" in height. The height of these jumps never increases during the exercise.

Target

The target should be clearly visible to your dog from his starting position. Place it about 10' from the last jump *before* you take your dog to the start line. It needs to be far enough away from the last jump that it does not cause your dog to think about slowing down or stopping, which would negatively affect how he handles the last space of the grid (perhaps even to the point that he adds a stride in the last space.)

Dog's Starting Position

- Line up your dog so he is facing the center of the first jump.
- The distance between your dog and the jump should be half the distance of the first space in the grid. For example, if jumps #1 and #2 are 4' apart, then start your dog 2' from the first jump.
- Your dog can be in a sit, stand, or down.
- Your dog should be looking forward at the jump or target before you release him.

If you do not have a start-line stay, have a training partner restrain your dog.

Handler's Position

- Lead out and stand one step ahead of the target and one step laterally off the target. This allows your dog to get to the target without passing the plane of your body.
- Face the direction your dog is traveling, looking over your shoulder to watch him.
- Sometimes stand to the left of the target and sometimes stand to the right of the target, so that you are working your dog on both sides.

Note: This is not a grid that I would do as a send-away, at least at first, since dogs will carry their head a bit higher when traveling away from the handler if they are not confident they are correct. When your dog raises his head, his stride will always be shorter, causing extra strides.

Progressions

Do four repetitions of the grid, two on each side.

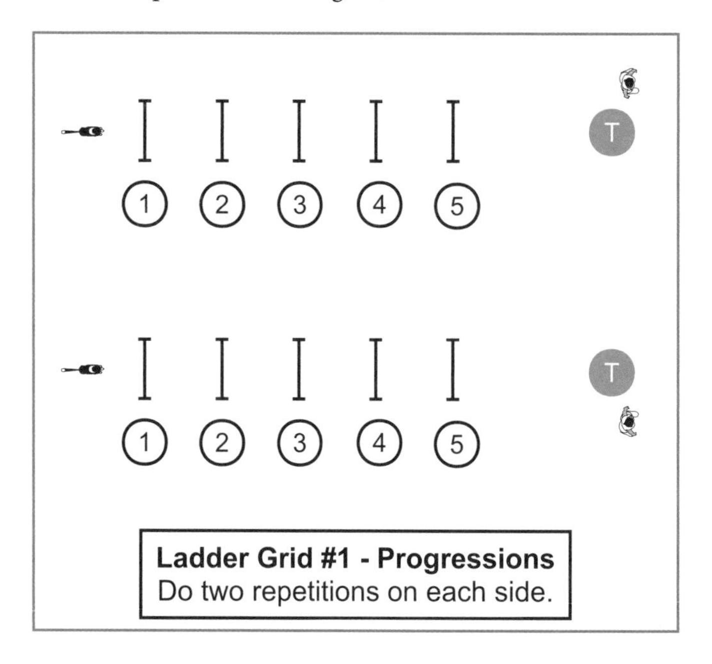

Ladder Grid #1 - Progressions
Do two repetitions on each side.

Problem Solving

Problem: Your dog runs from his start-line position directly to the target without entering the grid.

Solution: It can be overwhelming for your dog to look down the line and see so many bars so close together—remember, your dog has no clue about the desired outcome. Running around a grid is your dog's way of saying, "This is just too much and I don't understand what I am to do here." Break down the task into smaller parts and reward him for completing each part. By forward chaining the grid, you build the exercise from start to finish as shown in the diagram.

Problem: Your dog knocks the bar at jump #2.

Solution: This common problem happens when you set up your dog too close to jump #1. Your dog drives too deep to the base of jump #2 for a clean jumping effort. Setting up your dog at a distance from the first jump that is half the distance of the first space in the grid will solve the problem.

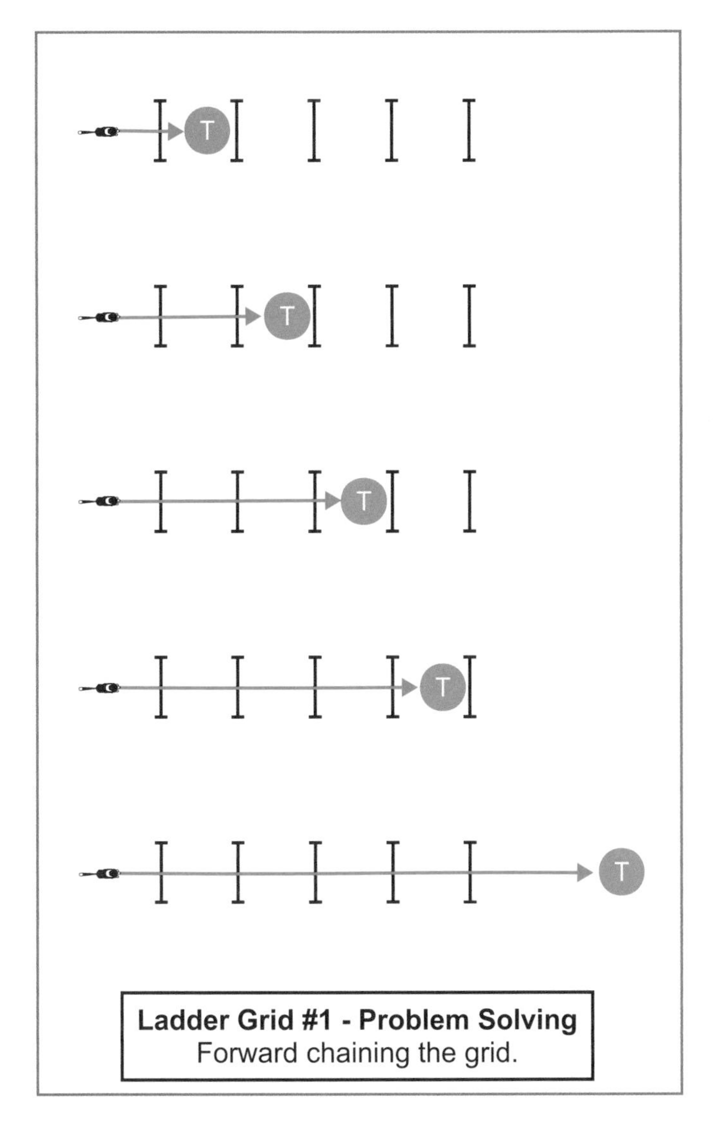

Ladder Grid #1 - Problem Solving
Forward chaining the grid.

Problem: Your dog jumps #4 and #5 as one spread jump rather than landing in the space between the two jumps.

Solution: This is a common problem that occurs when your dog begins to generate more speed than his body can coordinate. When this happens, place the target in front of jump #5. Repeat the grid two or three times with the target in this position to reinforce your dog for interacting with the space between jumps #4 and #5. Then move the target 10' after the last jump and try the grid again.

Problem: Your dog strides through the grid rather than bouncing.

Solution: Increase your dog's enthusiasm by using a higher value target. Or, instead of leading out all the way to the target, take a short lead-out, release your dog, and run to the target. If neither of these works to produce the fast, accurate bounce line we are looking for, then the distance may be too big for your dog. Shorten the spacing between the jumps until your dog will bounce the line.

How Much to Practice?

The low ladder (plyometric) grid gives a huge payoff for little effort on your part. It is one of the grids that can and should be done consistently. Doing it several times a week would not be too much at all. Elite tennis players, soccer players, football players, etc. do this type of plyometric exercise on a continuing basis to ensure that great footwork remains part of their athleticism.

With a trained dog, either this ladder grid or ladder grid #2 should be visited at least monthly as part of your jumping maintenance program. It is also an excellent grid to use to tune-up your dog's footwork and balance before a trial.

Proofing

You can begin proofing this grid once your dog is bouncing the line to his target with speed and ease of motion.

Set up your dog at a distance from jump #1 that allows him one steady, short stride:

- Big dogs: 9'–11'
- Medium dogs: 7'–9'
- Small dogs: 5'–6'
- Tiny dogs: 4'–5'

With success, gradually move your dog's starting distance farther back so he has more speed as he enters the grid. Do not proof your dog farther back than 12'–16'.

As you increase your dog's starting distance from the first jump, it is important to make sure he is not adding little pats of the ground as he tries to enter the grid. Your goal is for him to produce good, clean footwork. Your dog's movement should be a smooth, fluid stride or two strides, depending on how much space you have given him to enter the grid. Extra pats of the ground indicate that your dog is uncertain of how to step into the grid at speed. This should be a red flag to alert you that you are pushing the process by adding too much speed too quickly. Your dog must make a significant weight shift to enter this grid with speed. He has to be certain where he plans to step in to get the weight shift done correctly. Increase your dog's starting distance from jump #1 only as fast as is comfortable for him.

You can also proof this grid by gradually increasing your lateral distance from the target to a distance that reflects the normal working space between you and your dog.

Adding Handler Motion

The ultimate proofing is to add handler motion. During this process, remember that you are rewarding each effort whether it is a success or failure. Be sure not to push your dog past his current level of understanding. The goal is to carefully build success on success, so only go as far and as fast as determined by your dog's success. With some dogs, you will need to increase your motion even more slowly than described below.

Stage 1

Put your dog in his usual starting position and place the target 10' beyond jump #5. Begin next to your dog and walk down the line of jumps, releasing your dog as you pass jump #3. Continue walking forward. Take note of your dog's head position as he passes you. He should be looking forward and driving to the target. You do not want to see a head check as he drives past you.

Stage 2

Put your dog in his usual starting position and place the target 10' beyond jump #5. Begin next to your dog and walk down the line of jumps, releasing your dog as you pass jump #3. Continue moving forward, but change your speed to a jog. Again, take note of your dog's head position as he passes you. He should be looking forward and driving to the target. You do not want to see a head check as he drives past you.

Stage 3

Put your dog in his usual starting position and place the target 10' beyond jump #5. Lead out to jump #4, release your dog, and begin running toward the target.

Stage 4

Put your dog in his usual starting position and place the target 10' beyond jump #5. Release your dog and run off the line with him to the target.

Adding Handling

There is no change of sides in this exercise so crosses are not necessary.

Grid Variations

The foundation ladder grid can be done as a slice.

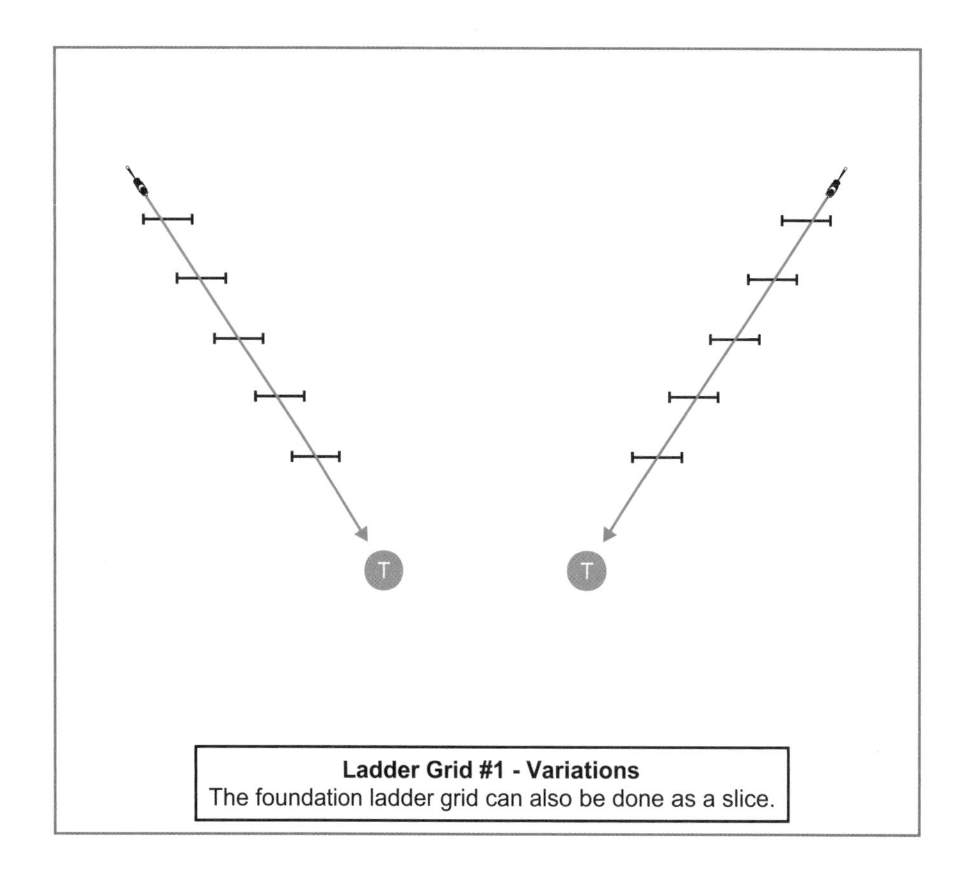

Ladder Grid #1 - Variations
The foundation ladder grid can also be done as a slice.

LADDER GRID #2 (ADVANCED PLYOMETRIC EXERCISE)

Overview

This grid is similar to the foundation ladder grid, but it is offered with larger spacing between jumps and slightly more jump height. This makes it a more advanced plyometric grid than ladder grid #1, requiring a great deal of core strength from your dog. Not all dogs are physically fit enough or have enough core strength to complete this grid without a good deal of practice over time.

If you have enough jumps and training spaces, I suggest you offer this grid and ladder grid #1 at the same time. Set them up side by side and alternate your dog between the two grids. This way you are building in scope so your dog recognizes the difference in task as you are leading out to the target.

Important: Do not introduce this grid until your dog can perform the ladder grid #1 smoothly and consistently.

Reference DVD

See Opened Up Bounce Grid on the *Tuning Up for Competition* DVD.

Setting Up the Grid

This grid required five winged jumps. I use winged jumps because they are more prominent and give the added space more definition to your dog as he looks down the line of jumps.

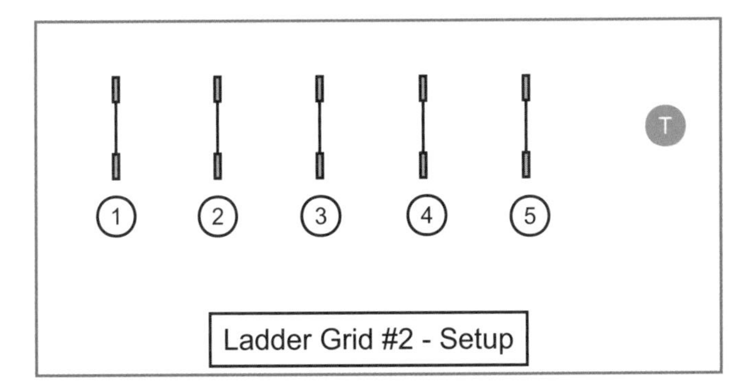

Jump Spacing and Height

Use the information below to determine the jump spacing and jump heights for the grid. Although I have used these distances with success at seminars, they are only guidelines and you may need to adjust them for your dog. Spacing between the jumps is measured from the center of one jump to the center of the next.

Note: This is intended to be a bounce line, not a stride. The distances may need to be adjusted for some dogs to accomplish this.

Big Dogs

- Space the jumps 10' apart and set at 16" in height. The height of these jumps never increases during the exercise.

Medium Dogs

- Space the jumps 9' apart and set at 16" in height. The height of these jumps never increases during the exercise.

Small Dogs

- Space the jumps 7' apart and set at 8" in height. The height of these jumps never increases during the exercise.

Tiny Dogs

- Space the jumps 6' apart and set at 6" in height. The height of these jumps never increases during the exercise.

Target

The target should be clearly visible to your dog from his starting position. Place it about 10' from the last jump *before* you take your dog to the start line. It needs to be far enough away from the last jump that it does not cause your dog to think about slowing down or stopping, which would negatively affect how he handles the last space of the grid (perhaps even to the point that he adds a stride in the last space.)

Dog's Starting Position

- Line up your dog so he is facing the center of the first jump.
- The distance between your dog and the jump should be half the distance of the first space in the grid. For example, if jumps #1 and #2 are 10' apart, then start your dog 5' from the first jump.
- Your dog can be in a sit, stand, or down.
- Your dog should be looking forward at the jump or target before you release him.

If you do not have a start-line stay, have a training partner restrain your dog.

Handler's Position

- Lead out and stand one step ahead of the target and one step laterally off the target. This allows your dog to get to the target without passing the plane of your body.
- Face the direction your dog is traveling, looking over your shoulder to watch him.
- Sometimes stand to the left of the target and sometimes stand to the right to work your dog on both sides.

Note: This is not a grid that I would do as a send-away, at least at first, since dogs will carry their head a bit higher when traveling away from the handler if they are not confident they are correct. When your dog raises his head, his stride will always be shorter, causing extra strides.

Progressions

Do four repetitions of the grid, two on each side.

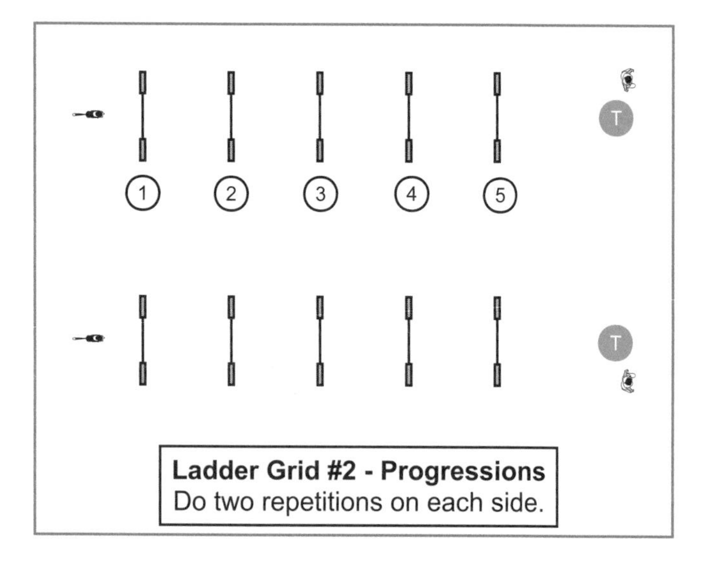

Problem Solving

Problem: Your dog runs from his start-line position directly to the target without entering the grid.

Solution: It can be overwhelming for your dog to look down the line and see so many bars so close together—remember, your dog has no clue about the desired outcome. Running around a grid is your dog's way of saying, "This is just too much and I don't understand what I am to do here." Break down the task into smaller parts and reward him for completing each part. By forward chaining the grid, you build the exercise from start to finish as shown in the diagram in the "Problem Solving" section of "Ladder Grid #1."

Problem: Your dog knocks the bar at jump #2.

Solution: This common problem happens when you set up your dog too close to jump #1. Your dog drives too deep to the base of jump #2 for a clean jumping effort. Setting up your dog at a distance from the first jump that is half the distance of the first space in the grid will solve the problem.

Problem: Your dog strides through the grid rather than bouncing.

Solution: Increase your dog's enthusiasm by using a higher value target. Or instead of leading out all the way to the target, take a short lead-out, release your dog, and run to the target. If neither of these works to produce the fast, accurate bounce line we are looking for, then the distance may be too big for your dog. Shorten the spacing between the jumps a bit.

If your dog still cannot do this grid without adding one or more strides in the provided spaces, you may need to do more work on ladder grid #1 and the set point exercise to build up your dog's strength before you work on this grid.

How Much to Practice?

This grid can be incorporated in your ongoing jump work, but you must be mindful of your dog's physical condition since this grid requires considerably more core strength than the foundation ladder grid. More practice is always good as long as it is not done in one long session. It's better to do just a few repetitions and visit the grid more often.

With a trained dog, either this ladder grid or ladder grid #1 should be visited at least monthly as part of your jumping maintenance program. It is also an excellent grid to use to tune-up your dog's footwork and balance before a trial.

Proofing

The best way to proof is to offer your dog both ladder grid #1 and #2 set up next to each other. Do a total of four repetitions alternating back and forth between the grids. Work on this set up in additional training sessions until your dog recognizes the difference in spacing and can accomplish both grids with equal ease.

You can also proof this grid by gradually increasing your lateral distance from the target to a distance that reflects the normal working space between you and your dog.

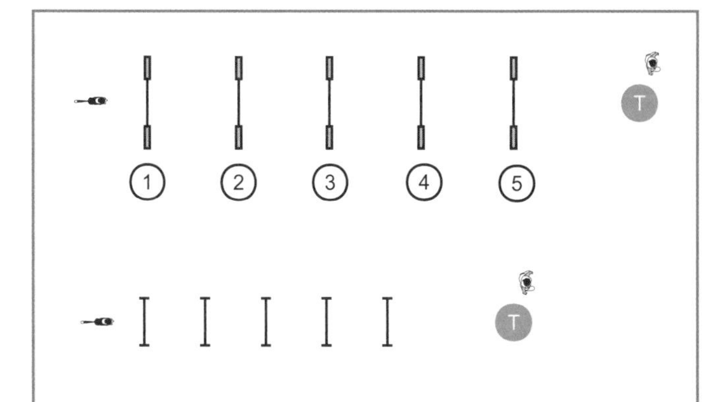

Adding Handler Motion

The ultimate proofing is to add handler motion. During this process, remember that you are rewarding each effort whether it is a success or failure. Be sure not to push your dog past his current level of understanding. The goal is to build carefully success on success, so only go as far and as fast as determined by your dog's success. With some dogs you will need to increase your motion even more slowly than described below.

Stage 1

Put your dog in his usual starting position and place the target 10' beyond jump #5. Begin next to your dog and walk down the line of jumps, releasing your dog as you pass jump #3. Continue walking forward. Take note of your dog's head position as he passes you. He should be looking forward and driving to the target. You do not want to see a head check as he drives past you.

Stage 2

Put your dog in his usual starting position and place the target 10' beyond jump #5. Begin next to your dog and walk down the line of jumps, releasing your dog as you pass jump #3. Continue moving forward but change your speed to a jog. Again, take note of your dog's head position as he passes you. He should be looking forward and driving to the target. You do not want to see a head check as he drives past you.

Stage 3

Put your dog in his usual starting position and place the target 10' beyond jump #5. Lead out to jump #4, release your dog, and begin running toward the target.

Dogs try so very hard to please the human; as such, I am a firm believer that a "try" should have value to the dog. After all, we are the only ones who know what success looks like; our dogs are unaware of the outcome we want. So to keep our dogs offering behaviors and to build value for the jumping effort itself, the try should always be rewarded.

Stage 4

Put your dog in his usual starting position and place the target 10' beyond jump #5. Release your dog and run off the line with him to the target.

Adding Handling

There is no change of side in this exercise so crosses are not necessary.

Grid Variations

None.

© CARRIE DEYOUNG

"Susan Salo's jumping program has given my dogs the opportunity to learn how to use their bodies with grace and power, as they confidently maneuver through the most complicated jumping sequences. It has resulted in educated dogs that know how to read distances, adjust striding, and put the appropriate amount of energy into each movement. I love watching my young dogs work their way through Susan's foundation program, as it builds value for jumping and allows the dog to develop proper form and striding without the messiness of handling. Then, as they develop their skills and conquer the most complicated of grids, it's thrilling to observe their athleticism. As I gradually introduce handling cues, taught first on the flat, my dogs tackle the job with confidence. And, regular revisiting of jump grids allows the dog to practice their skills in a thoughtful way. I can't imagine doing agility without this program!"

—Anne Stocum, Multiple-time AKC World Team member

LEAD CHANGE GRID

Overview

The lead change grid isolates your dog's ability to read his line and change leads appropriately. This lead change should happen as your dog leaves the ground for jump #6. Handling does come into play in this grid since there is a side change required for your dog to drive to jump #7 and his target. However, with this grid you do not have to move very far or very fast, so it is ideal for perfecting communication and connectedness between you and your dog, especially if your dog is very reactive to your motion.

This grid does not require as many jumps as some of the other grids and it does not take up much space, yet the skill set is isolated and can be worked on with great success. The footwork required of your dog is supported by the use of the plyometric arc grid, which then leads your dog to the two jumps set at competition height.

Important: Do not introduce this grid until you have completed the bend work foundation grid.

Reference DVD

None.

Setting Up the Grid

This grid requires five winged jumps and two nonwinged jumps. You can set up the grid to practice either a left-to-right lead change or a right-to-left lead change. You should work on each in a training session (you just need to move jumps #6 and #7) so your dog can work on providing a smooth, effortless change in each direction.

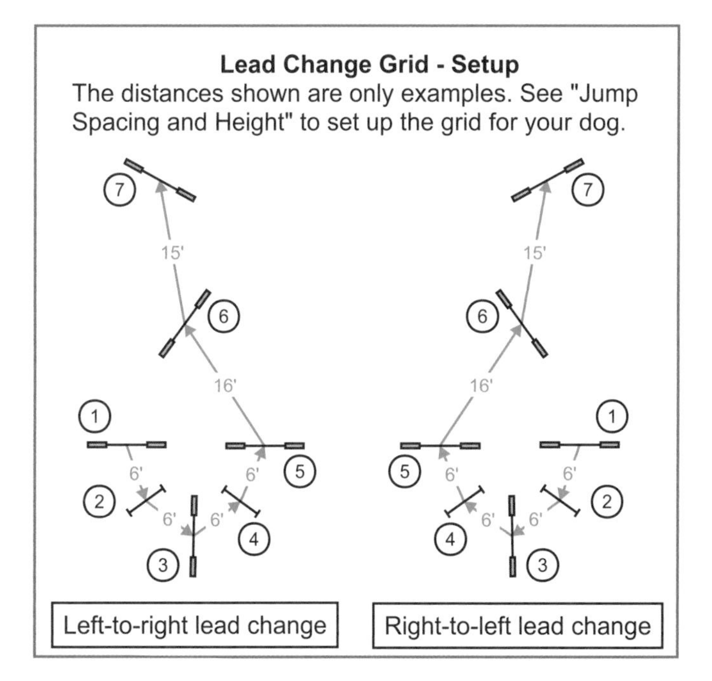

Begin by placing the winged jump that is the center of the plyometric arc, jump #3. Next place the two angled nonwinged jumps on either side of the center jump of the arc. Complete the arc with two winged jumps placed as shown. Pace off the appropriate distance from the exit jump of the arc to the first angled winged jump and then pace off the distance for the second angled winged jump.

Jump Spacing and Height

Use the information below to determine the jump spacing and jump heights for the grid. Although I have used these distances with success at seminars, they are only guidelines and you may need to adjust them for your dog. Spacing between the jumps is measured from the center of one jump to the center of the next.

Big Dogs

- *Arc:* Space jumps 6' apart and set at 6"–8" in height. The height of these jumps never increases during the exercise.
- *Jumps #6 and #7:* Place a winged jump (#6) at an angle 15'-18' from the exit of the arc. Place another winged jump at an angle 15'–18' from that one. Set the jumps at your dog's competition jump height.

Medium Dogs

- *Arc:* Space jumps 5' apart and set at 6" in height. The height of these jumps never increases during the exercise.
- *Jumps #6 and #7:* Place a winged jump (#6) at an angle 15' from the exit of the arc. Place another winged jump at an angle 15' from that one. Set the jumps at your dog's competition jump height.

Small Dogs

- *Arc:* Space jumps 4' apart and set at 4" in height. The height of these jumps never increases during the exercise.
- *Jumps #6 and #7:* Place a winged jump (#6) at an angle 14'–15' from the exit of the arc. Place another winged jump at an angle 14'–15' from that one. Set the jumps at your dog's competition jump height.

Tiny Dogs

- *Arc:* Space jumps 2'–3' apart and set at 4" in height. The height of these jumps never increases during the exercise.
- *Jumps #6 and #7:* Place a winged jump (#6) at an angle 12'–13' from the exit of the arc. Place another winged jump at an angle 12'–13' from that one. Set the jumps at your dog's competition jump height.

Target

The target moves for each stage of this grid as described in "Progressions."

Dog's Starting Position

The lead change grid begins with bend work. You want your dog to start with forward movement into the grid rather than starting from a stay.

- We do not want a sit or a stay for bend work; remember, your dog would prefer not to bend. You need to begin with forward motion into the grid. You will put your hand in your dog's collar, move forward with your dog, release him into the grid, and then rotate into the turn.
- Position your dog so he is centered on the first jump, facing straight ahead, and looking at the jump; do not place your dog on an angle to the first jump.
- Give yourself room to take several steps forward with your dog to guarantee he takes jump #2. Many handlers take only one step forward, say "Go," release their dog, and then abruptly stop motion. At that point their dog looks immediately for an exit to the grid to get back to the handler. This happens because motion overrides everything else, so leave yourself enough distance from the first jump of the grid to move forward and get your dog going.

Handler's Position

You need to move forward with your dog into the grid while *not* pushing your dog off the tight line. Think of this exercise as a wheel; you, the handler, are the hub of the wheel and the rotation of your hips and shoulders influences your dog's turn. Do not pass the plane of the center jump on the arc or you will push your dog off the tight line.

You will put your hand in your dog's collar, move forward with your dog, release him into the grid, and then rotate into the turn. Your shoulders and hips, not an extended hand or arm, should rotate to support your dog through each piece of the arc, . An arm supports distance and for this bend work there is no distance from your dog; you are right next to him. Try hard to keep your arm/hand "quiet" because it's essential for your dog to focus forward on the task while he "feels" you moving with him—if it has nothing to say, put it away.

It's important to turn while your dog is in the grid or you will push your dog off the tight line. Be careful not to race to intersect with the target or you will be pushing your dog off the tight line that we want him to find and drive. If you're using a toy, your dog should drive to the target, get it, and then come to you for play.

Progressions

This grid is built up progressively during a training session.

Stage 1

First you will practice a left-to-right lead change. Place the target on the tight line after jump #5. Make sure you give your dog enough room to land from jump #5 while still keeping him driving on a bend through the last jump.

Do a total of three repetitions, alternating direction each time.

Stage 2

Place the target 10' past jump #6 on your dog's line. Do two repetitions.

When your dog is committed to completing the arc, it is important to show motion toward jump #6 and the target.

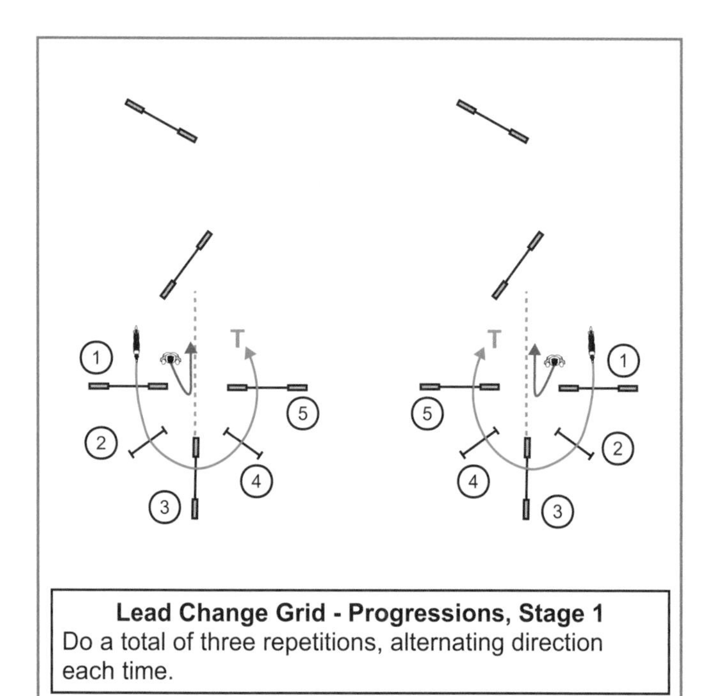

Lead Change Grid - Progressions, Stage 1
Do a total of three repetitions, alternating direction each time.

Dogs will see the target and continue to drive to it with or without their handlers. At this point, handlers often perceive they are finished and do not follow through with motion to the target. When you slow down and stop, your dog should follow suit. Failing to support the target with appropriate forward motion will desensitize your dog to your deceleration, something you will regret later.

Stage 3

Place the target 10' past jump #7 on your dog's line. Do three or four repetitions.

A front or rear cross is required to get to jump #7. Be certain to walk both options before running your dog through the exercise. If you are doing a front cross, you will need to cross the plane of the center jump of the arc. If you are doing a rear cross, you will not cross this plane.

Stage 4

Flip jumps #6 and #7 horizontally (a mirror image as shown in the setup diagram) so you can repeat stage 3, this time practicing a right-to-left lead change.

Problem Solving

This grid really should not present problems, as that is not its intent.

If your dog fails to recognize or drive to the jump out of the arc (jump #6), you can target in front of jump #6 and retry the exercise once. But if your dog is still struggling, select a grid with even less motion so you can create the understanding your dog needs to allow him to drive to the next logical obstacle to find his target.

How Much to Practice?

You build this grid starting at stage 1 *every* time you offer it to your dog. Once you have built up to stage 3 in a training session, three or four repetitions working a left-to-right lead change and three or four repetitions working a right-to-left lead change are sufficient for that session.

This is a great "go-to" grid to set up for your dog before a trial for tuning up his footwork and lead changes. It can also be used as part of your monthly maintenance program.

Proofing

This grid is proofing a lead change. There is no other proofing required.

Adding Handler Motion

Handler motion is built into this grid. If handler motion is problematic for your dog, this is a good grid to practice because you do not have to travel very far. Your motion can be slow and not significantly stimulating for your dog.

Adding Handling

Once you are doing the full grid, you will need to use a front or rear cross to change sides. Try both options to determine which is the smoothest and fastest for your dog. The eventual goal is to have your dog's jumping form constant regardless of which cross you use.

Grid Variations

None.

Lead Change Grid - Progressions, Stage 2
Do two repetitions.

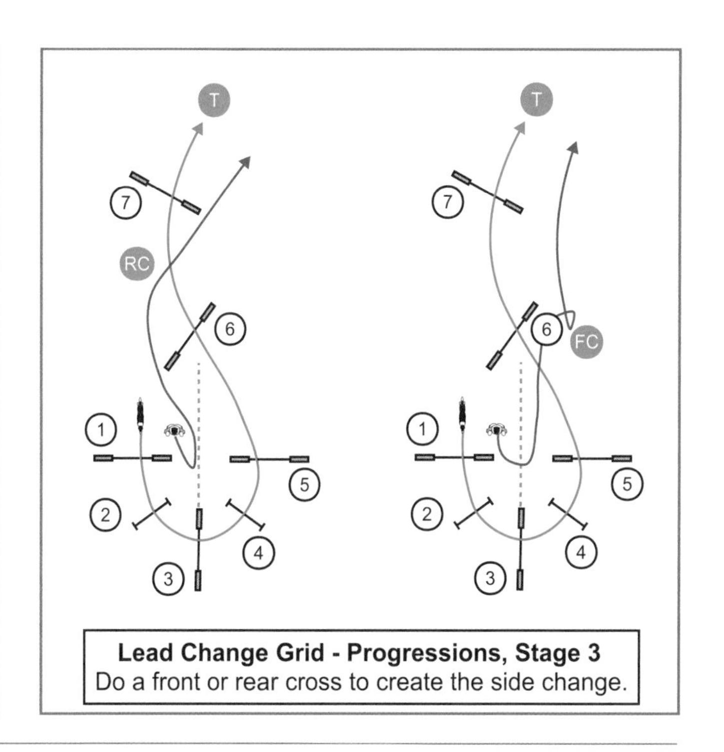

Lead Change Grid - Progressions, Stage 3
Do a front or rear cross to create the side change.

© JUKKA PATYNEN

"I have been following Susan's jumping program for the past 10 years. It is the first work I go to with my pups and my students' dogs to teach forward focus to the dogs and lateral independence from the handlers. Without forward focus, it is pretty difficult to do our job as handlers. Our dogs spend far more time on the ground between the obstacles than they do performing them. My puppies and adult dogs love jump grids. The predictability of the exercises builds confidence, independence, and speed. The progression to more advanced grids just naturally flows. Once my pup has forward focus, the handling is so much easier to add to the mix. Height is just one piece of the jumping equation. Susan's program educates our dogs on all aspects of jumping. Thank you so much Susan for all that you've taught me!"

—Nicki Gurr, Canadian national champion and multiple-time Canadian World Team member, owner and instructor Animotion Agility

OVAL TO FIGURE-8 GRID

Overview

When I set up this grid for people who have done the circle to figure-8 grid many times, they do not recognize the grid as a variation; they perceive it as a totally different grid, and in many ways it is. Once the shape is changed from a circle to an oval, the lines across the top and bottom of the grid become softer, offering your dog the option to maintain his lead of choice until he reaches the jump at the farthest edge of each oval. This turn is sharp and your dog must change leads. The handling line also changes considerably.

With the circle to figure-8 grid, most handlers can get into the "hub" position and support the dog's line with little motion. But when the shape changes to an oval, the handling line changes and you have to move farther to support the jump at the far end of the oval and then get into position for the change of side. The jumps in the oval basically become slices for your dog until the sharp-turning jump at the far end, so your dog is working on a skill set that's a little bit different from other circle grids.

This grid is several notches up in difficulty from the circle grid, but as with the circle grid, the training stages are built up systematically to prevent your dog from failing.

Important: Do not introduce this grid until your dog can perform the circle to figure-8 grid smoothly and consistently.

Reference DVD

None.

Setting Up the Grid

This grid requires 12 jumps (more if you use the shortest recommended distances between jumps). I like to use a combination of winged and nonwinged jumps.

Set the center jump in the middle of your work area. I often use an ascending double for the center jump. If you don't have a double, depending on the specific construction of your jumps, you may be able to make one by placing two single jumps close together. Place a facilitator jump on one side of the center jump to create a set point.

Next set four jumps, two off each side of the center jump, to form an "X" as shown in the diagram. Use a mix of 18'–21' between jumps, measured from the center of one jump to the center of the next jump. The spacing does *not* have to be the same on each of the circles.

Note: The fact there is more spacing between jumps in this grid than in the circle to figure-8 grid makes this a more advanced grid because many young dogs are eager to open up and flatten out their stride, making the biomechanics of jumping difficult. In a sense, they self-destruct given too much distance between jumps when they don't have sufficient knowledge to be successful.

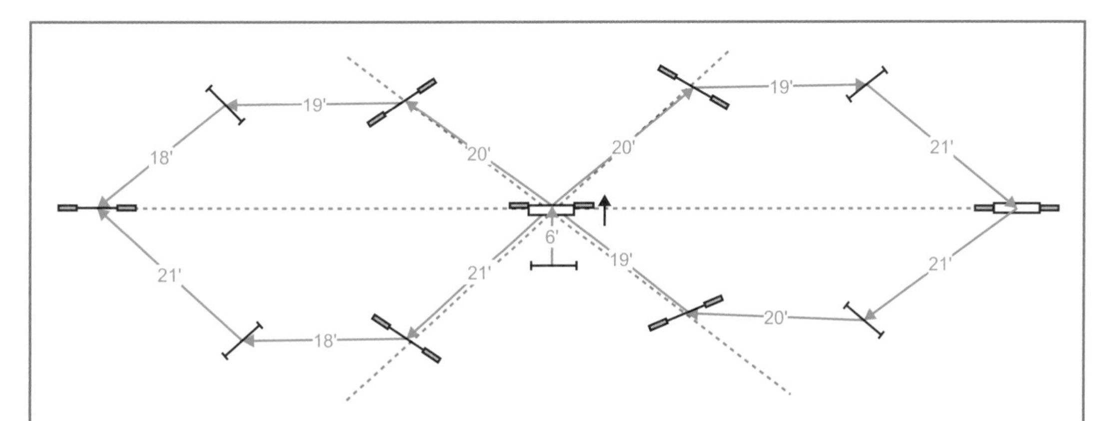

Oval to Figure-8 Grid - Setup
First place the center jump in the middle of your work area with a set point facilitator on one side. Then place four jumps, two on each side to form an X (red dashed lines). Finally place the remaining jumps to create two ovals. There should be a straight horizontal line through the middle of the grid as shown by the third red dashed line. You can use a mix of 18'-21' spacing between jumps, and you can use a double as the turning jump at the far edge of the oval. The spacing for each oval can be different.

Place the remaining jumps to complete the oval, interspersing winged jumps and nonwinged jumps, and again using a mix of spacing between 18'–21'. The goal is to create an oval on each side of the set point. The turns on the oval are sharper than they are on the circle to figure-eight grid.

I prefer to use a double as the turning jump at one end of the oval to test a dog's skill set for initiating a turn for a double. But if your dog is struggling with the grid, change the double jump to a single winged jump.

Go to each end of the "X" and look through the jumps to make sure your dog has a clear path on each slice. Do not worry about the facilitator jump being on the slice path because it will be removed for the slice exercise. Also, check that there is a clear path across the top of the exercise. Do not worry if it's not a perfect straight line, as long as it's a reasonable line for your dog to perform. I encourage dogs to find these lines because they do appear on courses.

Note: While the grid looks perfect in the diagram, it never looks the same for me when I set it up! I have built this grid numerous times and it always seems to be slightly different each time. In reality this is a good thing, as long as your "X" is in place and you have two ovals for your dog to work.

Jump Spacing and Height

Use the information below to determine the jump spacing and jump heights for the grid. Although I have used these distances with success at seminars, they are only guidelines and you may need to adjust them for your dog. Spacing between the jumps is measured from the center of one jump to the center of the next.

Big Dogs

- *Set point:* Space the facilitator jump 6' from the center jump. Set the center jump at your dog's competition jump height and set the facilitator jump at a maximum of 6" in height.
- *Ovals:* Space the jumps 18'–21' apart. All jumps on the ovals should be at your dog's competition jump height or close to that height.

Medium Dogs

- *Set point:* Space the facilitator jump 5' from the center jump. Set the center jump at your dog's competition jump height and set the facilitator jump at a maximum of 4"–6" in height.
- *Ovals:* Space the jumps 18'–21' apart. All jumps on the ovals should be at your dog's competition jump height or close to that height.

Small Dogs

- *Set point:* Space the facilitator jump 4' from the center jump. Set the center jump at your dog's competition jump height and set the facilitator jump at a maximum of 4" in height.
- *Ovals:* Space the jumps 18'–21' apart. All jumps on the ovals should be at your dog's competition jump height or close to that height.

Tiny Dogs

- *Set point:* Space the facilitator jump 2'–3' from the center jump. Set the center jump at your dog's competition jump height and set the facilitator jump at a maximum of 4" in height.
- *Ovals:* Space the jumps 18'–21' apart. All jumps on the ovals should be at your dog's competition jump height or close to that height.

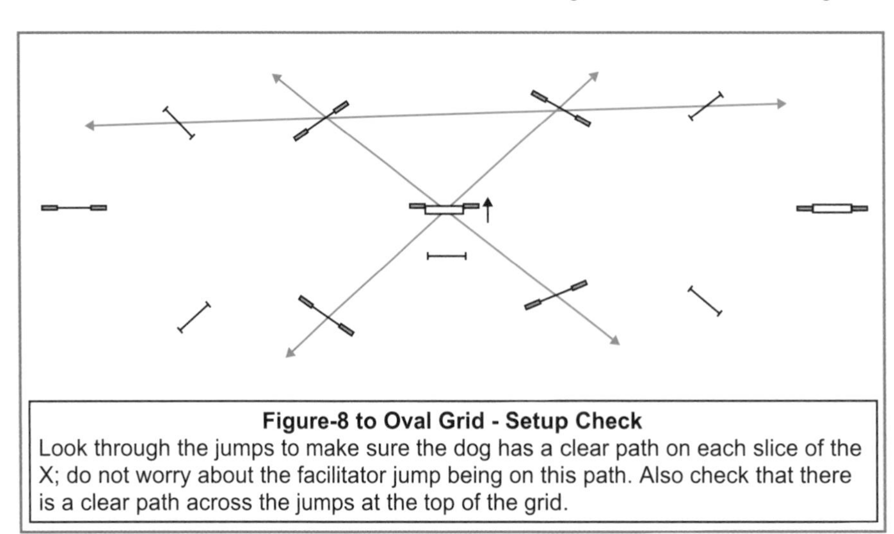

Figure-8 to Oval Grid - Setup Check
Look through the jumps to make sure the dog has a clear path on each slice of the X; do not worry about the facilitator jump being on this path. Also check that there is a clear path across the jumps at the top of the grid.

Target

The target moves for each stage of this grid as described in "Progressions."

Dog's Starting Position

For stages 1–4:

- Line up your dog so that he is facing the center of the facilitator jump.
- The distance between your dog and the facilitator jump should be half the distance of the space in the set point grid. For example, if the facilitator jump and the center jump are spaced 6' apart, start your dog 3' from the first jump.
- Your dog can be in a sit, stand, or down.
- Your dog should be looking forward at the jump or target before you release him.

If you do not have a start-line stay, have a training partner restrain your dog.

Once the initial stages of the grid have been performed and the oval becomes the figure-8 in stage 5, the facilitator jump is removed from the grid. At this point, your dog needs to start at a distance from jump #1 that is equal to one steady, short stride for him:

- Big dogs: 9'–11'
- Medium dogs: 7'–9'
- Small dogs: 5'–6'
- Tiny dogs: 4'–5'

Remember, the shorter the stride, the greater the balance and power. So find a good distance for your dog and then become consistent with walking off that distance for your dog.

Handler's Position

Your position changes for each stage of this grid as described in "Progressions."

This picture is worth a thousand words. The dog has turned himself inside out in attempt to save the bar. Clearly this effort did not work for the dog, but it needs to be shown and stated just how hard the dog tried. The dog failed to read a tight distance and drove too deep to his take off spot.

Progressions

This grid is built up progressively *each time* you do it. Even when your dog is performing the complete figure-8 with ease in both directions, you will always start the training session by building the grid up from stage 1 up to stage 7. Consider stages 1 through 3 to be a warm-up for stages 4 and 5, and think of stages 6 and 7 as a cool down from the pressure of handler movement.

Stage 1

Place the target 10' past the center jump in the set point exercise on an arc that leads your dog toward jump #2. The target should be visible to your dog Lead out and stand one step ahead of the target and one step laterally off the target. This allows your dog to get to the target without passing the plane of your body.

Do the exercise several times and then move the target to jump #2 on the opposite oval and repeat.

If your dog is successful and comfortable with the exercise, move on to stage 2.

Stage 2

Your dog will be performing the set point to a jump. Place the target 10' past jump #2 where it's visible to your dog when he's taking jump #1. Lead out and stand one step ahead of the target and one step laterally off the target.

Do the exercise several times and then move the target so it's 10' past jump #2 on the opposite oval and repeat.

If your dog is successful and comfortable with the exercise, move on to stage 3.

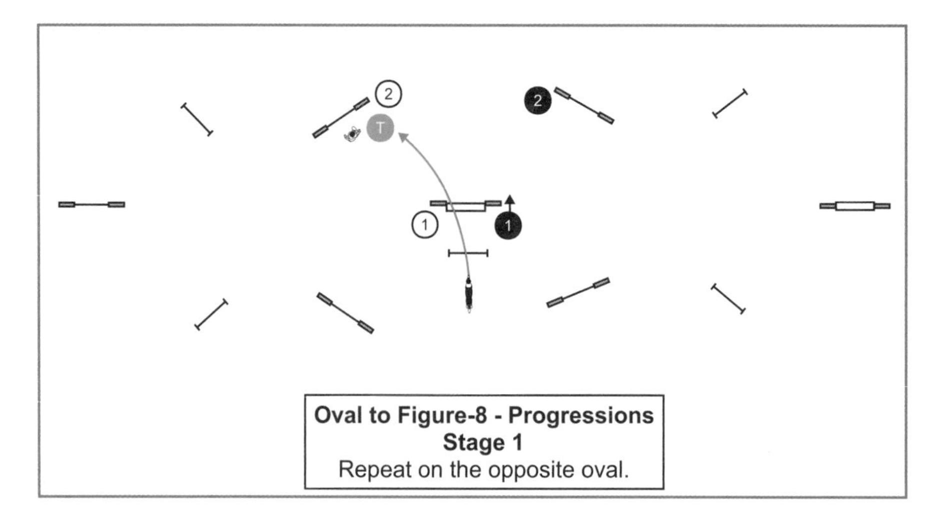

Oval to Figure-8 - Progressions
Stage 1
Repeat on the opposite oval.

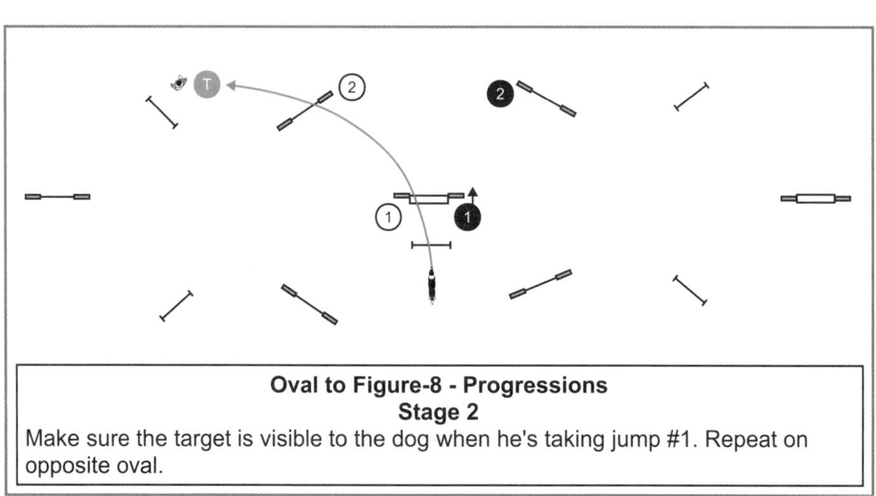

Oval to Figure-8 - Progressions
Stage 2
Make sure the target is visible to the dog when he's taking jump #1. Repeat on opposite oval.

Stage 3

Your dog is performing the set point to two jumps on the arc. Place the target 10' past jump #3 where it is visible to your dog when he's taking jump #2. Lead out and stand one step ahead of the target and one step laterally off the target.

Do the exercise several times and then move the target so that it's 10' past jump #3 on the opposite oval and repeat.

If your dog is successful and comfortable with the exercise, move on to stage 4.

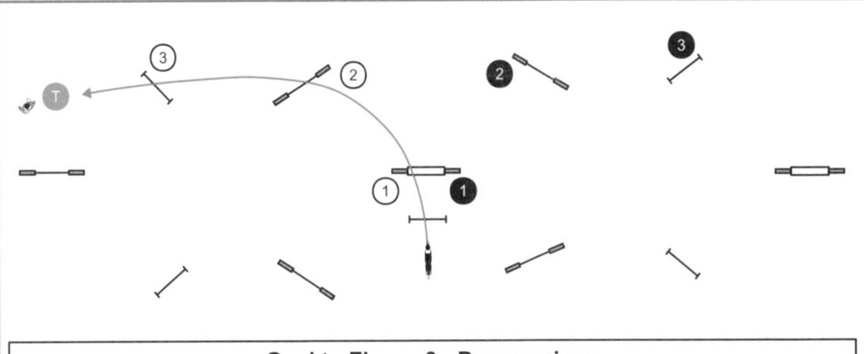

Oval to Figure-8 - Progressions
Stage 3
Place target so that it's visible to the dog as he's taking jump #2. Repeat on opposite oval.

Stage 4

Drop the target directly behind your dog at the start line. Your dog will now drive from the set point and continue around the circle of jumps back to his target.

At this stage you will be increasing your lateral distance from your dog and you will need to introduce some minimal motion. Preferably you can lead out to the center "hub" position of the circle and move slowly in a small circle, supporting your dog by turning your shoulders and hips as your dog performs the jumps. If it's necessary for you to be closer to the jumps to support your dog while he does the oval, then work on gradually adding more lateral distance until you can handle from the center of the oval.

Do two or three repetitions and then repeat the exercise on the opposite oval.

Do not progress to the next stage until your dog can complete the oval smoothly and with consistent success *in both directions.*

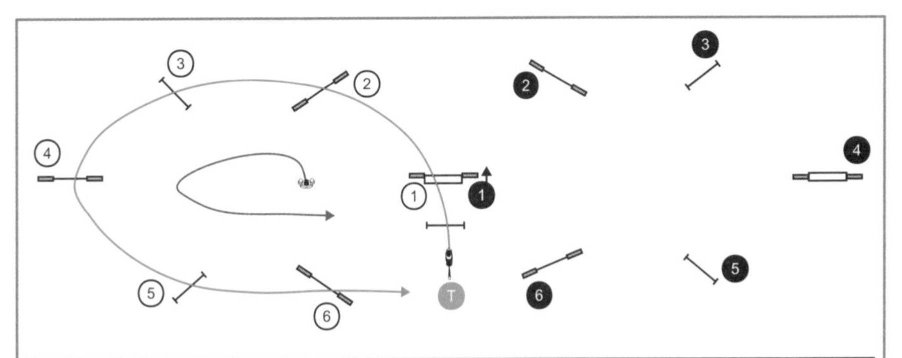

Oval to Figure-8 - Progressions
Stage 4
Build up lateral distance until you can handle from the center of the oval. Repeat the exercise on the opposite oval.

Few people realize that part of their dog's jumping problem begins before the dog is ever released from the start line. In the first photo you can see that the dog's head is down. This puts the dog's weight onto the forehand, and the elbows are just beginning to abduct. The second photo shows the same dog sitting with an erect spine and good balance: an appropriate time to release the dog to jump.

Stage 5

Remove the facilitator jump.

In this stage you are going to do a complete figure-8, which means you will need to use a front or rear cross at #7 to change sides. Be certain to walk both options prior to running your dog through the exercise. You will have to travel much farther here to support the jumps in the oval than you did in the circle to figure-8 grid.

To start the exercise, set up your dog in front of jump #1 at a steady, short one-stride distance. Rather than placing the target, carry it with you and drop it at your feet as you break off the exercise after jump #12.

Do two or three repetitions and then repeat the exercise starting with your dog on your left and traveling into the oval to start.

Once you build up to stage 5, you always want to do stages 6 and 7 before ending the training session.

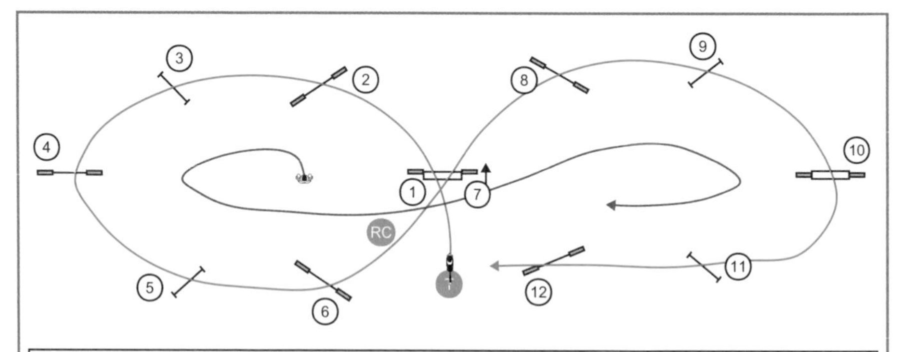

Oval to Figure-8 - Progressions
Stage 5
Facilitator jump has been removed. Do a front or rear cross at jump #7. Repeat the exercise in the opposite direction, starting with the other oval.

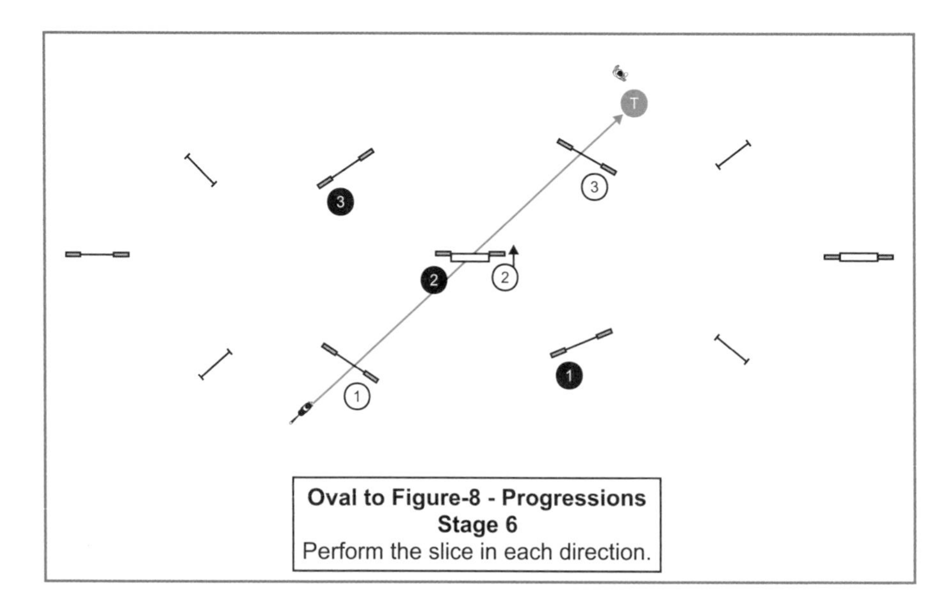

Oval to Figure-8 - Progressions
Stage 6
Perform the slice in each direction.

Stage 6

After the handling stage it is important to back off the handling and offer your dog the chance to perform the slices through the center of the grid (the "X") and the line across the top of the grid quietly and without the pressure of handler motion. I believe that dogs need the chance to settle and think again when motion, followed by more motion or faster motion, is offered. Offering motion signals "game on" and can easily push many young dogs over the top with arousal. Some give and take of that pressure becomes increasingly important for the young, motion-reactive dogs as a reminder that they must still execute their job with thought and care—even once it becomes "game on." In addition, your dog has worked through many repetitions of circle work with this drill; the straight lines allow your dog to lengthen his spine and relax his muscles prior to ending a session of bend work.

Also, the use of the target at the end of the training session provides balance. Once we are handling and the target is no longer on the ground, we become the dominant information to our dogs. By bringing the target back into the picture, you help encourage your dog to be looking ahead and task oriented again.

Place the target 10' past jump #3. Lead out and stand one step ahead of the target and one step laterally off the target.

Do the exercise once and then move the target so it's 10' past jump #3 on the opposite circle and repeat.

Stage 7

Place the target 10' past jump #4. Lead out and stand one step ahead of the target and one step laterally off the target.

Do the exercise once and then move the target and repeat, going in the opposite direction.

Problem Solving

Problem: Your dog either drops a bar or pulls off the turning jump at the top of the oval.

Solution: If the bar is dropped, place a target after that jump on the line to the next jump once or twice and then try the complete sequence again. If your dog pulls off the jump, correct your handling on the next repetition by supporting that jump a little longer. You need to wait for affirmation that your dog has read the turning jump *and* has eyes locked onto the next jump in sequence before moving away.

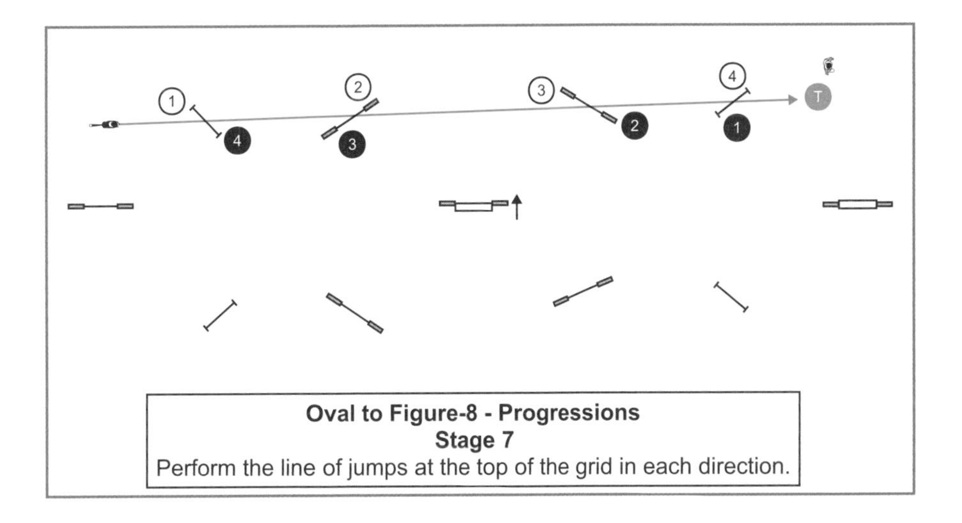

Oval to Figure-8 - Progressions
Stage 7
Perform the line of jumps at the top of the grid in each direction.

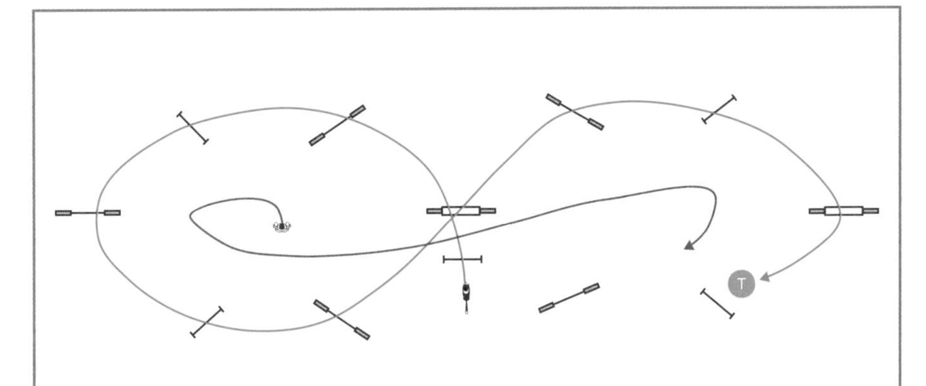

Oval to Figure-8
Problem Solving
If the dog is pulling off the turn jump of the oval, place a target on the landing side of the jump, leading toward the next jump of the oval.

This dog experienced and talented jumping dog is actually running through the air here because he was not able to set himself up at all; he is pushing off the ground from one hind leg. Poor motion from the handler caused this situation. I see this all too often at trials when motion from handlers is either inappropriate or poorly timed, so the dog must try to organize faster than he actually can.

Problem: Your dog begins dropping bars once handling motion increases.

Solution: Reduce your motion until your dog settles into his work. Handler motion is a huge stimulant to your dog and should not be rushed into before your dog has the skills to deal with it. Go back to the step where your dog was consistent; for example, instead of running you can jog or instead of jogging you can walk. Work that step a bit longer and then try gradually increasing your speed.

Problem: Your dog aborts the third jump on the center slice.

Solution: Place the target in front of jump #3 and do jumps #1 and #2 to the target once and then retry the entire slice. If your dog still refuses the jump, repeat the targeting exercise and lower the height of jump #3. Slice jumps are an acquired skill for many dogs. Even though we perceive the slice as a straight line, most dogs do not and many struggle with it. Meet your dog where he "thinks he can" and build from there. Remember, it is only your dog's perception of the difficulty that counts here, since your dog is the one performing the task.

Problem: Your dog cannot find the straight line across the top of the grid.

Solution: This is a common problem depending on how hard that line is for your dog to find. Often when this grid is set up, your dog does not see the obvious line until he has committed to the prior jump. If your dog needs help, I would offer assistance through the use of the target, as opposed to handling. Build the line by offering the target prior to jump #3, then move it in front of jump #4, and then finally move the target 10' after jump #4. It is much easier to handle a dog that is always looking ahead for the next logical obstacle that is supported by your motion, as opposed to a dog that requires you be at each jump. If the latter is your dog, you are likely slowing him down. Handling a dog that is schooled, skilled, and has sharp mental acuity is a supporting role, not a dominant role. Take the time to train your dog to look ahead for obstacles and then enjoy the ride!

How Much to Practice?

You should build this grid starting at stage 1 *every* time you offer it to your dog, though you can reduce the number of repetitions in stages 1–3 so you aren't doing as many set points. As I said before, the grid setup always comes out a bit different and the use of different jumps can be of influence. Take the time to target your dog's path in stages 1 through 3 before you start the stages that require handler movement. Think of it this way: stages 1 through 3 are a warm-up for stages 4 and 5, and stages 6 and 7 are a cool down from the pressure of handler movement.

If you see or sense your dog is struggling with any part of the exercise, break off the session and finish with something your dog finds easier and can be successful with. Always try to finish on a positive note.

With a trained dog, bend work is a skill that you need to practice monthly. It can be offered through the oval to figure-8 grid as well as other bending grids.

Proofing

You are systematically proofing your dog as you gradually add difficulty to this grid and introduce handler motion.

You can also work on increasing your lateral distance from your dog. Your handling for the turning jump at the far end of the oval is critical and may take some time to perfect. Just remember that your dog is correct and should be rewarded if you pull him off the turning jump by moving too suddenly or by not adequately supporting it. You need to learn what it looks like when your dog has locked onto the turning jump and plans to take it. As soon as you recognize that point of commitment, you can leave and support the jump from a distance.

Adding Handler Motion

Handler motion is built into this grid when you get to stages 4 and 5, but only go as far and as fast as determined by your dog's success. With some dogs you will need to start the exercise with you at a walk and then slowly increase handler motion over time.

Remember that an extended hand/arm is intended to support distance. If you are in the hub position of the circle/oval or laterally off your dog's path, then the hand/arm is suitable. But if you are running alongside your dog as he jumps, the hand can distract your dog from focusing forward on the task.

Adding Handling

Once you are doing the full figure-8, you will need to use a front or rear cross at the center jump to change sides. Try both so you can determine which option is the smoothest and fastest for your dog. The eventual goal is to have your dog's jumping form remain constant regardless of which cross you use.

Grid Variations

Circle to figure-8 grid

PROGRESSIVE GRID

Overview

The progressive grid offers a different type of distance question to your dog. It is the canine version of the acceleration ladder used by human sprinters. An acceleration ladder teaches sprinters to open up their stride with each step, as each space in the ladder is wider than the one before it. The progressive ladder teaches your dog to open up his stride and bounce between the jumps, even though each distance is greater than the previous one.

Your dog needs to look ahead and drive to the appropriate midpoint between two jumps to be ready for the next jump, while adjusting his stride between each pair of jumps. Because each distance is greater than the last, each stride must be more powerful than the one before it. You would like to see your dog landing relatively centered, which makes each effort equal for him. If your dog lands shallow, then the distance to the next jump becomes a big reach; your dog will land shallow again and he will have an even greater distance to the next jump. Eventually he will run out of room to compensate and will likely have to add a stride. Your dog must learn to look far enough ahead down the line of jumps to avoid this problem.

For most dogs this is a straight-forward extension grid that allows them to stretch out and relax. Dogs enjoy doing the progressive grid, particularly after they have worked on a difficult exercise. After doing bend work, for example, the progressive grid offers a release of pressure, provided that your dog understands plyometric grids.

Important: Do not introduce this grid until your dog can perform the ladder grid #1 smoothly and consistently.

Reference DVD

See Progressive Grid on the *Foundation Jumping* DVD.

Setting Up the Grid

This grid requires five nonwinged jumps placed in a straight line. The jumps are spaced at gradually increasing distances and are set at a low height. Height is not a part of this grid; the jumps are *never* raised.

I do not add extra jumps to this grid. This grid is not intended as a means to see how big a distance your dog can cover.

Important: This grid is *not* bidirectional; it is only used to teach extension. Sor never let dogs go backward through the grid (compression).

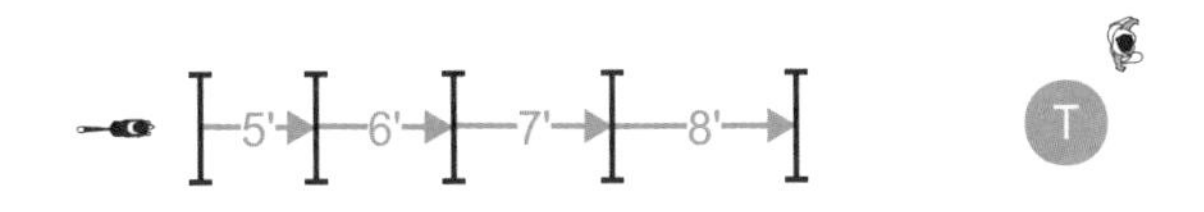

Progressive Grid - Setup
Each space in the grid is larger than the one before it. Use the spacing information that is appropriate for your dog's size.

Jump Spacing and Height

Use the information below to determine the jump spacing and jump heights for the grid. Although I have used these distances with success at seminars, they are only guidelines and you may need to adjust them for your dog. Spacing between the jumps is measured from the center of one jump to the center of the next.

Big Dogs

- First space is 6', second space is 7', third space is 8', and last space is 9'. Set the jumps at 6"–8" in height. The height of these jumps never increases during the exercise.

Medium Dogs

- First space is 5', second space is 6', third space is 7', and last space is 8'. Set the jumps at 6" in height. The height of these jumps never increases during the exercise.

Small Dogs

- First space is 4', second space is 5', third space is 6', and last space is 7'. Set the jumps at 4" in height. The height of these jumps never increases during the exercise.

Tiny Dogs

- First space is 2', second space is 3', third space is 4', and last space is 5'. Set the jumps at 4" in height. The height of these jumps never increases during the exercise.

Target

The target should be clearly visible to your dog from his starting position. Place it about 10' from the last jump *before* you take your dog to the start line. It needs to be far enough away from the last jump that it does not cause your dog to think about slowing down or stopping while in the grid, which would cause him to shorten his stride.

Dog's Starting Position

- Line up your dog so he is facing the center of the first jump.
- The distance between your dog and the jump should be half the distance of the first space in the grid. For example, if jumps #1 and #2 are 4' apart, then start your dog 2' from the first jump.
- Your dog can be in a sit, stand, or down.
- Your dog should be looking forward at the jump or target before you release him.

If you do not have a start-line stay, have a training partner restrain your dog.

Handler's Position

- Lead out and stand one step ahead of the target and one step laterally off the target. This allows your dog to get to the target without passing the plane of your body.
- Face the direction your dog is traveling, looking over your shoulder to watch him.
- Sometimes stand to the left of the target and sometimes stand to the right to work your dog on both sides.

Note: This is not a grid that I would ever do as a send-away unless you have a very high drive dog.

Progressions

Do three repetitions of the grid, alternating which side you work your dog on.

Problem Solving

Problem: Your dog enters the grid, bounces between jumps #1 and #2, and then begins to add strides in the remaining spaces.

Solution: Allow your dog two or three repetitions of the grid to figure out what he should offer in each space. Generally dogs will correct themselves.

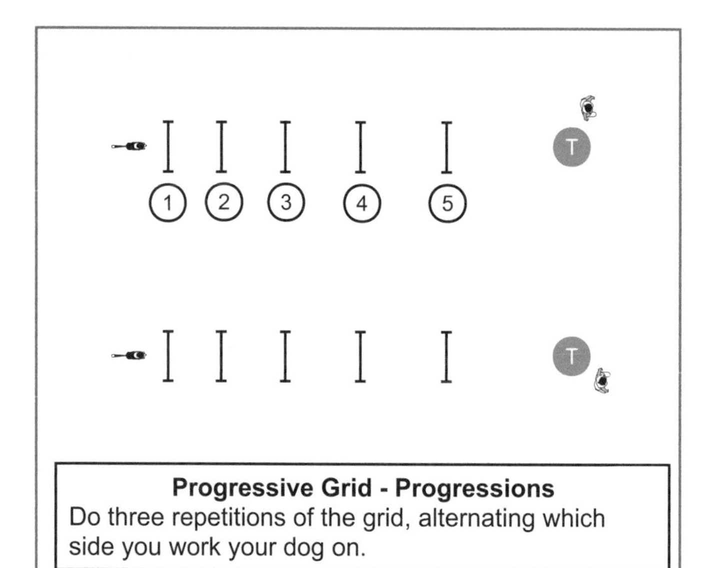

Progressive Grid - Progressions
Do three repetitions of the grid, alternating which side you work your dog on.

Problem: Your dog bounces through the beginning of the grid but cannot complete the grid without adding a stride in the last space.

Solution: Make sure your target is at least 10' from the last jump. If target placement is not the problem, remember that energy creates energy. Increase your dog's enthusiasm by using a higher value target. Or, instead of leading out all the way to the target, take a short lead-out, release your dog, and run to the target.

Problem: You dog consistently adds a stride in the last space within the grid.

Solution: Shorten the distance in *each* space by 6"–12". Although it is logical to think you only need to shorten the last space, the line of jumps encourages your dog to incrementally increase his stride length all the way through the grid, not simply the last space.

How Much to Practice?

If your dog understands this grid, it is a great one to offer after a difficult training session or a session that required a lot of thought from your dog. This grid provides a fun release of pressure for dogs that are comfortable performing the skills required.

If your dog is struggling to assess the task ahead of him, more practice would serve your dog well. Remember, more repetitions in a session do not get the end result you seek. Visiting the grid a bit more often is more useful for a dog that is slow to assess the task and respond appropriately. We want to work on the grid regularly until your dog can survey the task ahead of him, quickly assess what he needs to do, and accomplish that task with ease.

Proofing

You can proof this grid by gradually increasing your lateral distance from the target to a distance that reflects the normal working space between you and your dog.

Adding Handler Motion

This is a great grid to which to add motion, particularly for dogs that struggle with powering up their stride. Some dogs will do much better on this grid when you run with them.

Because the grid requires your dog to power up his stride and come forward, it is not appropriate for you to walk. When you add motion to the progressive grid, you need to run with intent to beat your dog to the target or lead out far enough that you can beat your dog to the target.

Adding Handling

There is no change of side in this exercise so crosses are not necessary.

Grid Variations

None.

I cannot think of any handlers who do not spend practice time working on their dogs' contact performances. Even though their dogs perform contact behaviors with great precision, they still require regular practice to maintain that level of excellence. The same is true of weave pole entries. Much training time is devoted to that skill set throughout the dog's career. Should the dog's jumping skills get any less attention? I think not, considering that every course the dog will ever set a paw on will be mostly made up of jumps! Yet jumping skills remain the least taught and least understood aspect of the agility dog's training. Is it really such a hard concept that we need to allow the dog practice time for jumping skills? Not simply as jumping relates to the handler, meaning while running sequences, but actually setting aside training time for work on the mechanical skills of jumping. Doing so will help the dog's physical skills as well as help maintain his confidence as it relates to jumping.

© PIX 'N PAGES

"Never underestimate the fragility of a dog's brain. No matter how difficult a training session may be, never blame the dog. Their behavior, both good and bad, is just a reflection of their current level of understanding. While it might not appear evident at first, blaming the dog for mistakes will chip away at the fabric of your relationship. Take care to break down behaviors into understandable pieces as in the gridwork, lavish the desired responses with reinforcement, and you will develop a confident, fast dog."

—Mary Lou Hanlon, Multiple-time national finalist, instructor Agility University, inventor of Hit It Board, Touch It, Squiggle It, and Move It!

S GRID

Overview

The S grid is an excellent one to do after completing the foundation bend work. The difficulty in this grid is the supple lead changes your dog must produce to drive with speed through the grid, without adding strides. For your dog to accomplish this, he must be working and looking for the next logical obstacle rather than looking at you. If you have not yet done enough work with your dog focusing on and driving to the target, this grid might be too advanced.

This is another plyometric grid where adding height is *not* appropriate. Even the most advanced dogs have problems with this from time to time, which demonstrates the need for handlers to practice the S grid a bit more often since smooth lead changes are crucial to agility.

Your dog enters the grid on one lead and exits the grid on the other lead. If you see your dog make adjustments in his footwork before the second bend, it indicates that your dog does not understand how to make the lead change while stepping over the facilitator jump. This causes your dog to add a stride before the bend to gather himself to change leads. It is important to build the grid and your dog's understanding to "follow the work" before attempting the entire grid at once.

This grid requires handling because there is a side change. I have found that handlers have more trouble with it than the dogs because of the tight spacing.

Important: Do not introduce this grid until you have completed the bend work foundation grid, because your dog is meant to be producing a given lead here.

Reference DVD

See Exercise #3 on the *Advanced Jumping* DVD.

Setting Up the Grid

The S grid uses two winged jumps and seven nonwinged jumps set up in an S pattern. On the *Advanced Jumping* DVD, this grid is shown with one fewer jump, but adding a jump to the center of the grid allows you a bit more handling room. It also increases the challenge for your dog because there is more speed into the turn and lead change.

As the diagram shows, there are two nonwinged jumps on the curve to the first winged jump, followed by three nonwinged jumps across the relatively straight section, and then another winged jump followed by two nonwinged jumps on the second curve.

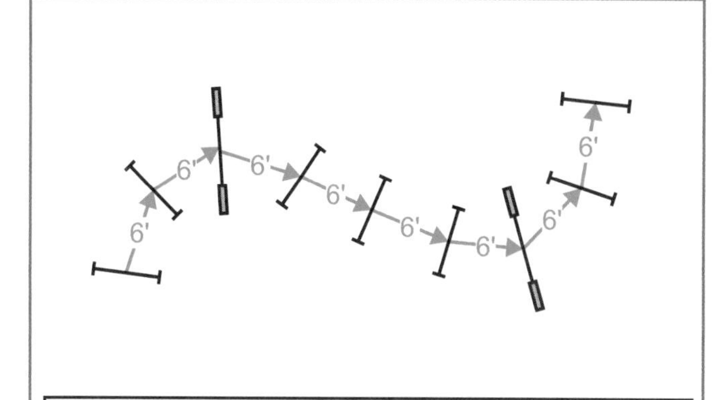

S Grid - Setup
S grid setup with spacing for big dogs. Use the spacing recommended for your dog.

Jump Spacing and Height

Use the information below to determine the jump spacing and jump heights for the grid. Although I have used these distances with success at seminars, they are only guidelines and you may need to adjust them for your dog. Spacing between the jumps is measured from the center of one jump to the center of the next.

Big Dogs

- Space the jumps 6' apart and set at a maximum of 6"–8" in height. The height of these jumps never increases during the exercise.

Medium Dogs

- Space the jumps 5' apart and set at a maximum of 6" in height. The height of these jumps never increases during the exercise.

Small Dogs

- Space the jumps 4' apart and set at a maximum of 4" in height. The height of these jumps never increases during the exercise.

Tiny Dogs

- Space the jumps 2'–4' apart and set at a maximum of 4" in height. The height of these jumps never increases during the exercise.

Target

The target moves for each stage of this grid as described in "Progressions."

Dog's Starting Position

We do not want a sit or a stay for bend work; remember, your dog would prefer not to bend. You need to begin with forward motion into the grid. The arcs in this grid are set up to be a plyometric exercise for your dog; they are *not* spaced at a one-stride distance as in the circle grid. Set up your dog in front of the first jump, giving yourself just enough room to take several steps forward with your dog to guarantee he takes jump #2.

Position your dog so he is centered on the first jump, facing straight ahead, and looking at the jump. Do *not* place your dog on an angle to the first jump.

Handler's Position

Your position changes for each stage of this grid as described in "Progressions."

Progressions

This grid is built up progressively, starting at stage 1 *each time* you do it.

Stage 1

You are going to do only the first arc of the grid. Place the target in front of jump #5. Begin with your dog, stepping forward and rotating your shoulders through the first arc. Do two or three repetitions.

If your dog is successful and comfortable with the exercise, move on to stage 2.

Stage 2

You are now going to do the exit arc of the grid. Place the target on the tight line at the end of the bend, giving your dog room to get to it without landing on it. Begin with your dog, stepping forward and rotating your shoulders through the arc. Do two or three repetitions.

If your dog is successful and comfortable with the exercise, move on to stage 3.

Stage 3

Once your dog is comfortable with both bends, you can try the whole grid. Rather than placing the target, carry it with you and drop it at your feet on the tight line as your dog finishes the grid. This is one of the few grids where leaving the target on the ground can be problematic. Your dog will see the target as he comes out of the first arc, which may cause him to cut across your feet to

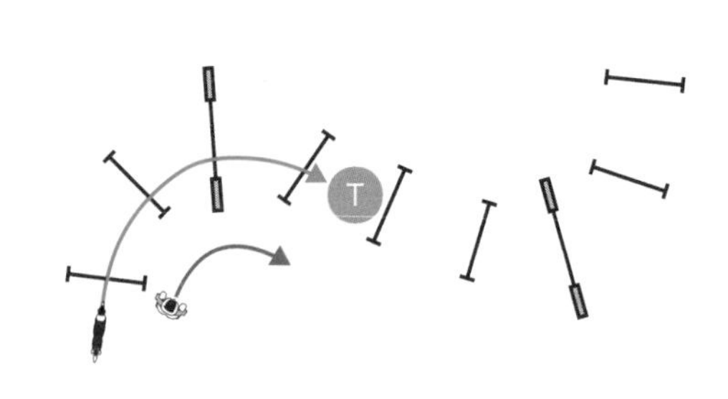

S Grid - Progressions
Stage 1
Do the arc at the beginning of the grid two to three times.

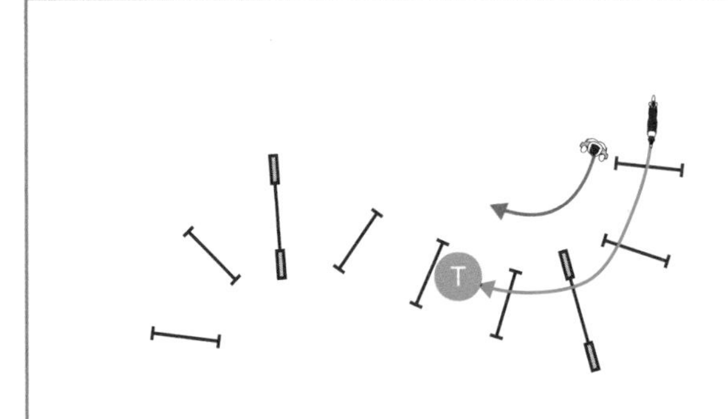

S Grid - Progressions
Stage 2
Do the arc at the exit of the grid two to three times.

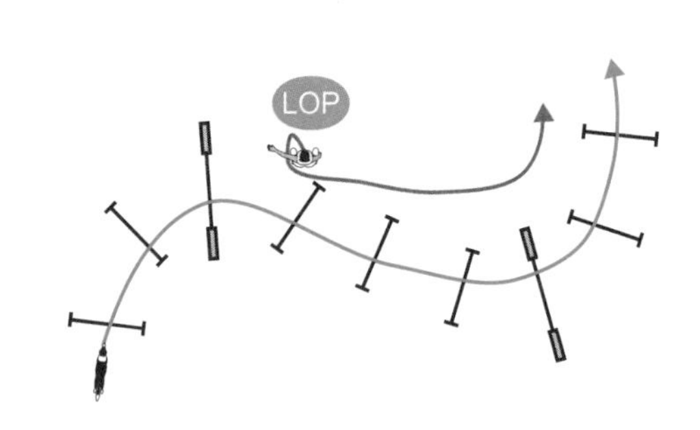

S Grid - Progressions
Stage 3
Handle the lead change in whatever manner works best for you. You could use a lead-out pivot or rear cross among other options.

get to it. The goal is not to build frustration for either you or your dog while doing the work, so carry the target with you until you get to the proofing stage for this grid.

You will need to do a lead-out pivot, a recall to heel, a rear cross, or some handling maneuver to deal with the change of side required. Be certain to walk your handling plan before running your dog through the exercise.

When handling each arc, the wing jump in the center of the arc is a reminder that you should be turning your shoulders to support the bend. You should not be moving past that jump wing in a straight line that would drive your dog off the tight line.

Do four or five repetitions.

Problem Solving

Problem: Your dog cuts across your feet without entering the arc and goes straight for the target in stages 1 or 2.

Solution: Start again, slipping your finger into your dog's collar to help him into the grid, releasing the collar as your dog commits to the first jump. You will feel your dog want to go forward as he understands where to go.

Problem: While attempting to do the entire grid, your dog fails to look for the next obstacle and gets stuck looking you.

Solution: The dog getting stuck at the handler's side is something that happens frequently with this grid because handlers do not anticipate just how fast their dog will be moving through the grid. Handlers get caught watching their dog rather than offering information via motion so the dog "stalls out" once he reaches the handler. Once you release your dog, get moving!

Problem: Your dog gets stuck looking up at your hand.

Solution: Remember the hand supports distance and there is no distance in this grid. Keep your hand quiet and move. Jim Basic of Power Paws Agility has a wonderful saying, "No arm, no harm." Very true! Your dog just needs motion information here. If you are too busy worrying about pointing, it can keep you from moving appropriately.

Problem: Your dog will not drive past you so you can do a rear cross.

Solution: This grid can help to keep your dog moving while you change sides, providing that your dog understands to continue to follow the work (jumps). If this understanding is not in place, then you need to work on your rear crosses away from jump grids.

How Much to Practice?

With a trained dog, bend work is a skill that you need to practice monthly. This can be offered through the S grid as well as other bending grids. This is an excellent drill for practicing footwork and lead changes so your dog's efforts can be fluid and smooth on course.

Proofing

When your dog is comfortably and accurately performing the S grid, try putting the target at the end of the grid on the tight line. See if your dog understands to continue the work that takes him to his reward (the target). If you are successful, congratulations! Your dog has an excellent understanding of the task.

Another way to proof this grid is to open up the jump spacing through the center of the grid, not on the curve, to encourage more speed into the lead change, which increases the difficulty. I only use an additional 6" of space.

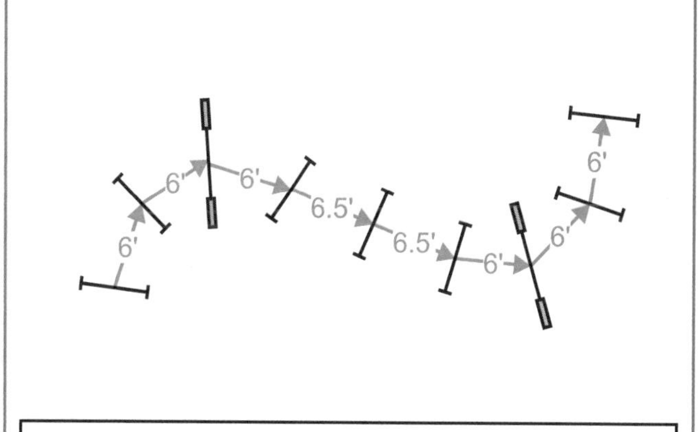

S Grid - Proofing
You can open up the spacing in just the center of the grid to add more speed into the lead change.

Adding Handler Motion

Handler motion is built into this grid.

Adding Handling

Once you are doing the full grid, try all the handling options available to you and determine which gets the smoothest, fastest result from your dog. Then work on the handling maneuvers that are weak until your dog's grid performance comes together smoothly, no matter what handling you choose.

Grid Variations

None.

"I think of grids as a giant puzzle for my young girl. They have her learning not only the mechanics of jumping, but they have helped her build confidence. It has been amazing to see how she mentally and physically works through the challenges that the grids present her, and to see her understanding progress over time. It's reflected clearly in her approach and in the speed at which she progresses through them. As a team we value our ability to work on our distance skills within the grids."

—Lisa Schwellinger, Agility trainer and part owner Think Pawsitive Dog Training in New Berlin, WI

SERPENTINE GRID

Overview

Serpentine lines can be difficult for dogs to find and execute tightly without proper education. Some handlers feel the need to soften serpentine lines by making big loops to ensure their dog jumps cleanly, but we really want our dogs to drive these lines in a tight, flat manner. This is a skill set that requires time and practice in both your handling and your jumping training.

The grids from the *Proofing Jump Work with Motion* DVD were designed not only to enhance your dog's jumping performance but to isolate small pieces of information given from handler to dog and vice versa. Developing connectedness requires time to develop understanding between you and your dog. Information give and take between you and your dog needs to be perfected, and helping you build that connectedness is one of the goals of this drill.

Note: You need to have trained your dog to understand the cues you use to perform serpentines before attempting this grid.

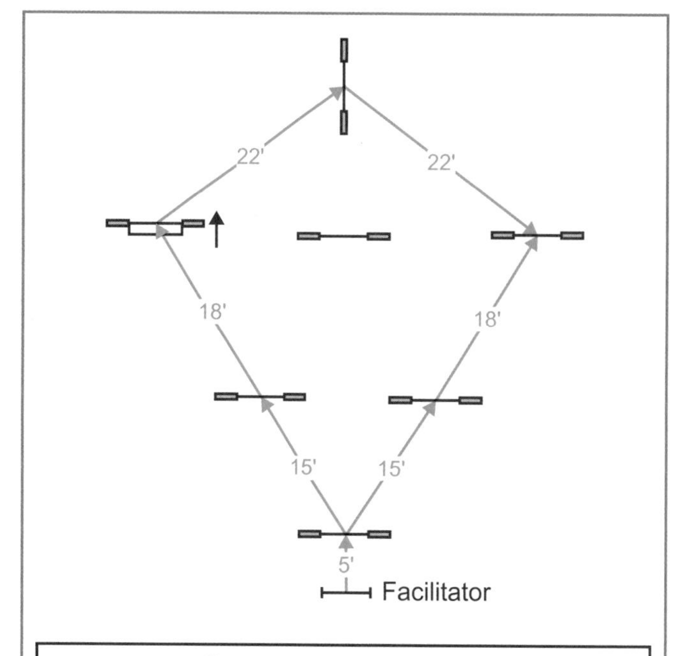

Serpentine Grid - Setup
The distance from the facilitator jump to the first jump changes depending on the size of the dog. See "Jump Spacing and Height."

Reference DVD

See Exercise 2 on the *Proofing Jump Work with Motion* DVD.

Setting Up the Grid

Six winged jumps, an ascending double spread jump, and one facilitator jump are required for this grid.

Start by setting up the inverted triangle in the center of your work area, then add the line of three jumps across the back of grid, and finally add the jump that is by itself at the top of the grid.

Note: I have changed this grid slightly from the one used on the *Proofing Jump Work with Motion* DVD. I deleted the second serpentine line and added the jump at the top of the arc. It has been my experience that people rarely trained with the more widely spaced second serpentine line because more practice was needed on the tighter serpentine line. The addition of the jump at the top allows your dog to open up and flow after the pressure of working the serpentine.

Once motion is added to the exercise, the facilitator jump is removed.

Jump Spacing and Height

Use the information below to determine the jump spacing and jump heights for the grid. Although I have used these distances with success at seminars, they are only guidelines and you may need to adjust them for your dog. Spacing between the jumps is measured from the center of one jump to the center of the next.

Jump Spacing

The spacing between the jumps is measured from the center of one jump to the center of the next.

Follow the guidelines for the "Set Point Exercise" to set up the set point at the tip of the inverted triangle.

Next measure 15' on the slice from the set point jump to the winged jumps that form the base of the triangle.

Measure 18' on the slice from these two jumps to the two jumps on the ends of the row of three jumps. Center a winged jump between those jumps in the same row.

Center the jump at the top of the grid as shown. Generally this distance will be about 22' on each side. But it can vary, depending on how the rest of the grid sets up.

Jump Height

With the exception of the facilitator jump, which is never higher than 4"–6" depending on your dog's size (see "Set Point Exercise" for specific heights), all jumps for this grid are set at your dog's competition jump height.

Target

The target moves for each stage of this grid as described in "Progressions."

Dog's Starting Position

For stages 1 and 2:

- Line up your dog so he is facing the center of the facilitator jump on the slice. Your dog should not be placed in a position that would cause him to twist or bend to get on the straight line. He should be able to look through the jumps and see the slice he is to drive.
- The distance between your dog and the facilitator jump should be half the distance of the space in the set point grid. For example, if the facilitator jump and the center jump are spaced 4' apart, start your dog 2' from the facilitator jump.
- Your dog can be in a sit, stand, or down.
- Your dog should be looking forward at the jump or target before you release him.

Once the initial stages of the grid have been performed and the facilitator jump is removed from the grid, your dog needs to start at a distance from jump #1 that is equal to one steady, short stride for him:

- Big dogs: 9'–11'
- Medium dogs: 7'–9'
- Small dogs: 5'–6'
- Tiny dogs: 4'–5'

Handler's Position

Your position changes for each stage of this grid as described in "Progressions."

Progressions

This grid is built up progressively *each time* you do it.

Stage 1

Place the target 10' past the jump in the set point exercise. The target should be visible to your dog. Lead out and stand one step ahead of the target and one step laterally off the target. This allows your dog to get to the target without passing the plane of your body.

Do one repetition of the set point on your right and one on your left.

If your dog is successful and comfortable with the exercise, move on to stage 2.

Stage 2

Place the target 10' after jump #2 on the slice. The target should be clearly visible to your dog from his starting position. Lead out and stand one step ahead of the target and one step laterally off the target. This allows your dog to get to the target without passing the plane of your body.

Do one repetition of the slice from white #1–#2 and one repetition of the slice from black #1–#2.

If your dog is successful and comfortable with the exercise, move on to stage 3.

Stage 3

Remove the facilitator jump.

Place the target 10' after jump #3 on the slice. The target should be clearly visible to your dog from his starting position. Lead out and stand one step ahead of the target and one step laterally off the target. This allows your dog to get to the target without passing the plane of your body.

Do one repetition of the slice from white #1–#3 and one repetition of the slice from black #1–#3.

If your dog is successful and comfortable with the exercise, move on to stage 4.

Stage 4

Place the target 10' after jump #3. Lead out as far as you need to in order to cue the turn in a "quiet" manner with minimal motion. Do one repetition from white #1–#3 and one repetition from black #1–#3.

If your dog is reading your cues for the turn well, move on to stage 5.

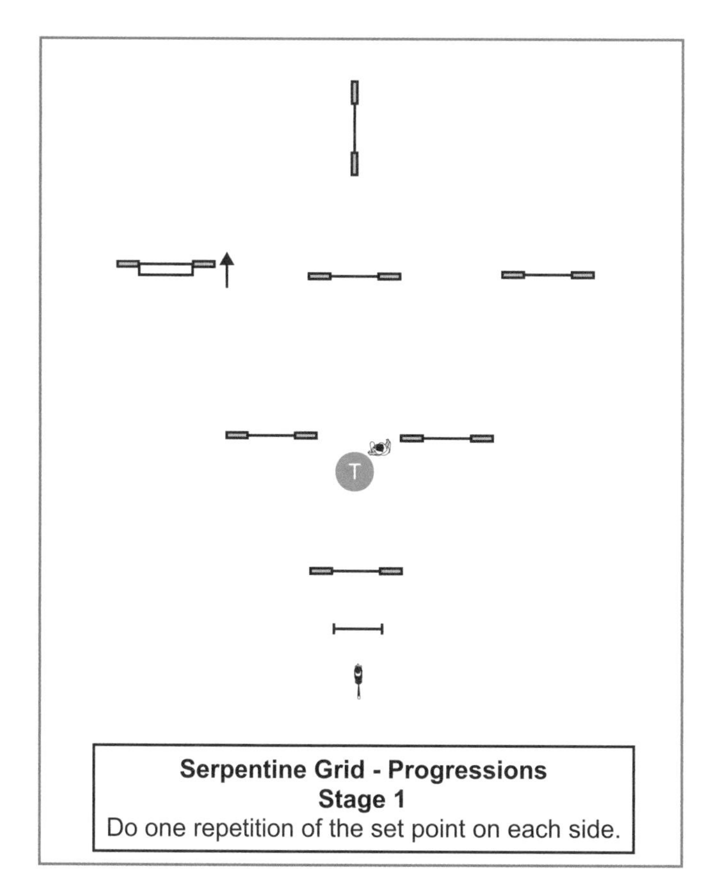

Serpentine Grid - Progressions
Stage 1
Do one repetition of the set point on each side.

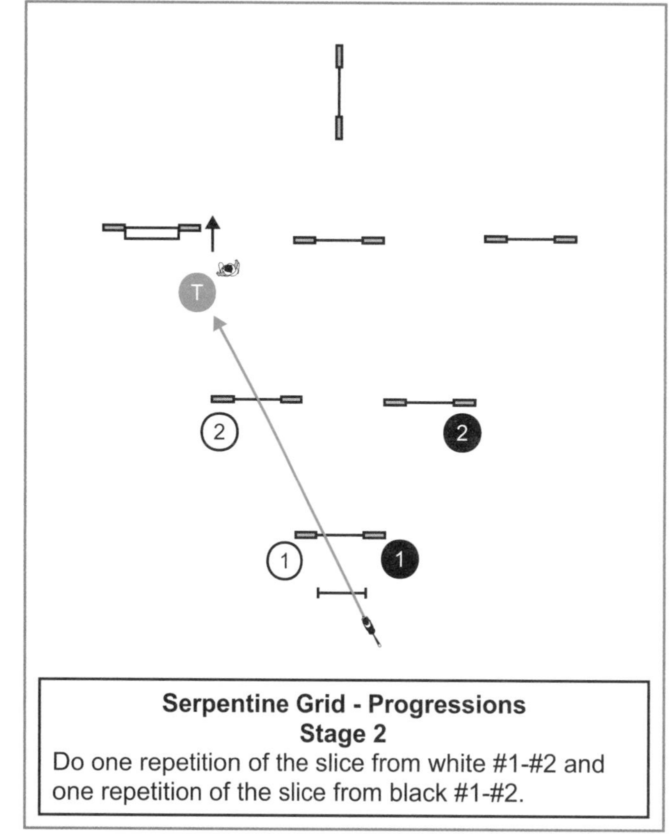

Serpentine Grid - Progressions
Stage 2
Do one repetition of the slice from white #1-#2 and one repetition of the slice from black #1-#2.

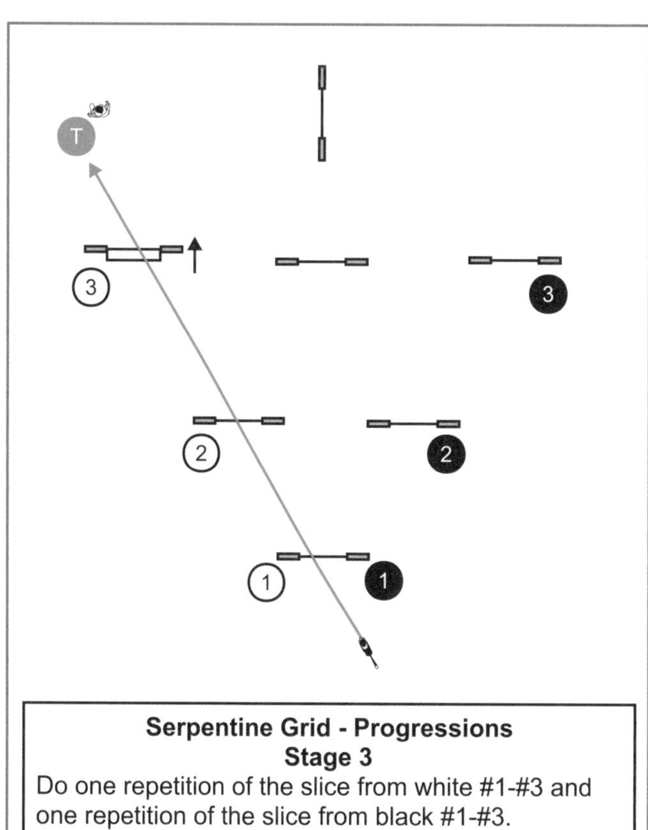

Serpentine Grid - Progressions
Stage 3
Do one repetition of the slice from white #1-#3 and one repetition of the slice from black #1-#3.

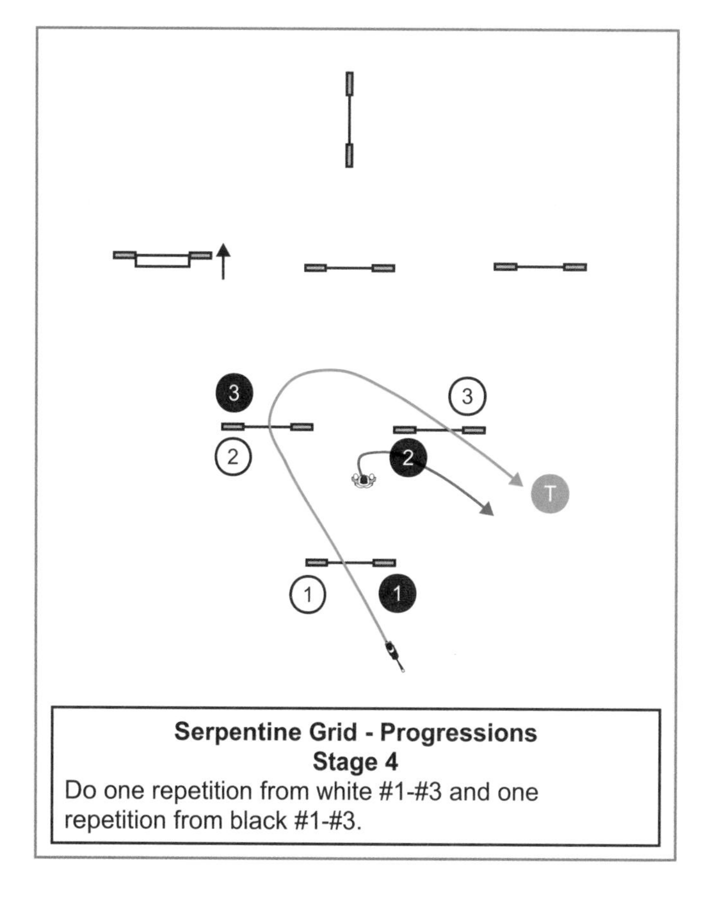

Serpentine Grid - Progressions
Stage 4
Do one repetition from white #1-#3 and one repetition from black #1-#3.

Stage 5

Do #1–#5 and perform the serpentine. Rather than placing the target, carry it with you and drop it at your feet as you break off the exercise. Do the exercise two or three times in each direction.

Stage 6

This progression ends the session by allowing the dog to flow while you simply support the dog as he works. Rather than placing the target, carry it with you and drop it at your feet as you break off the exercise. Do the exercise two or three times in each direction.

Problem Solving

Problems with this grid usually come in the form of timing. One reason I love this grid is that it is systematic in approach, meaning that if the full serpentine line presents trouble, simply go back to the triangle to fix your timing and then try the full serpentine line again.

You will likely find that communication with your dog is easier on one side than the other. This does not mean you should drill your dog on the weaker side. Rather, it means that you should go back a step or two on the weaker side. For example, while you may be doing the full serpentine when working your dog on the right, if you left side is weak, you may need to focus on the slice and the turn after the first jump.

How Much to Practice?

The serpentine grid can be included as part of your dog's jumping maintenance program and as part of a tune-up plan for a big competition.

Proofing

You are proofing this grid as you work through the stages of building it. It's a good idea to pay close attention to the turn you get in stage 4 and see how close you can come to that performance when your dog has more speed and you are showing more motion in stage 5. Perfection at anything comes in small pieces and that feeling is what keeps most of us wanting more. Mother Goose sums it up, "Good, better, best. Never rest, til good be better and better best." Just not all in one training session!

Adding Handler Motion

Handler motion is built into this grid as you work through the progressions.

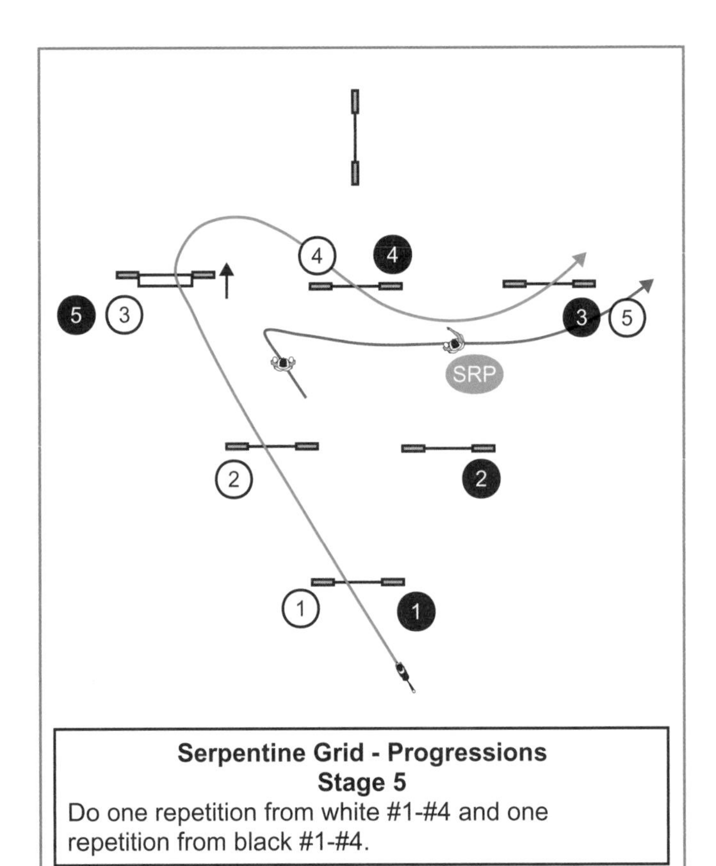

Serpentine Grid - Progressions
Stage 5
Do one repetition from white #1-#4 and one repetition from black #1-#4.

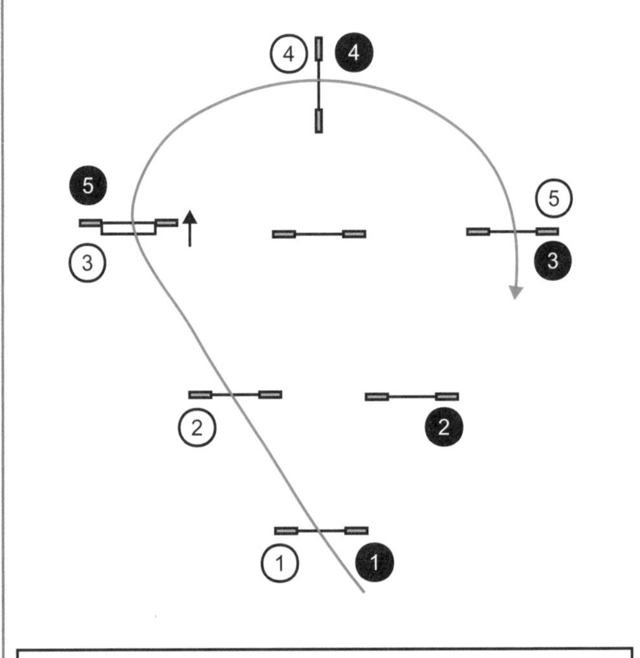

Serpentine Grid - Progressions
Stage 6
Do two to three repetitions in both directions, rotating in the direction of the double when you follow the black numbers.

Adding Handling

This grid relies on you having trained cues for handling serpentines. But remember that the focus in gridwork is always on your dog, not the sequence. Reward the behaviors you wish for your dog to repeat. If you only focus on running the "entire" serpentine sequence, you may well miss the opportunity to reward something your dog has offered that is worthy of note. If you want your dog to understand that a particular turn is better than another, then you need to mark it and reward. You are not handling a sequence, you are handling your dog. Mark good behaviors and reward your dog with praise, and play and/or treats. Dogs do not hear our appreciation nearly enough. If you want a dog that is willing to perform heroics in the ring to save the day for you, make sure he knows that you really appreciate the effort he is putting forth.

Grid Variations

You can offer the version of the serpentine grid from the *Proofing Jump Work with Motion DVD.*

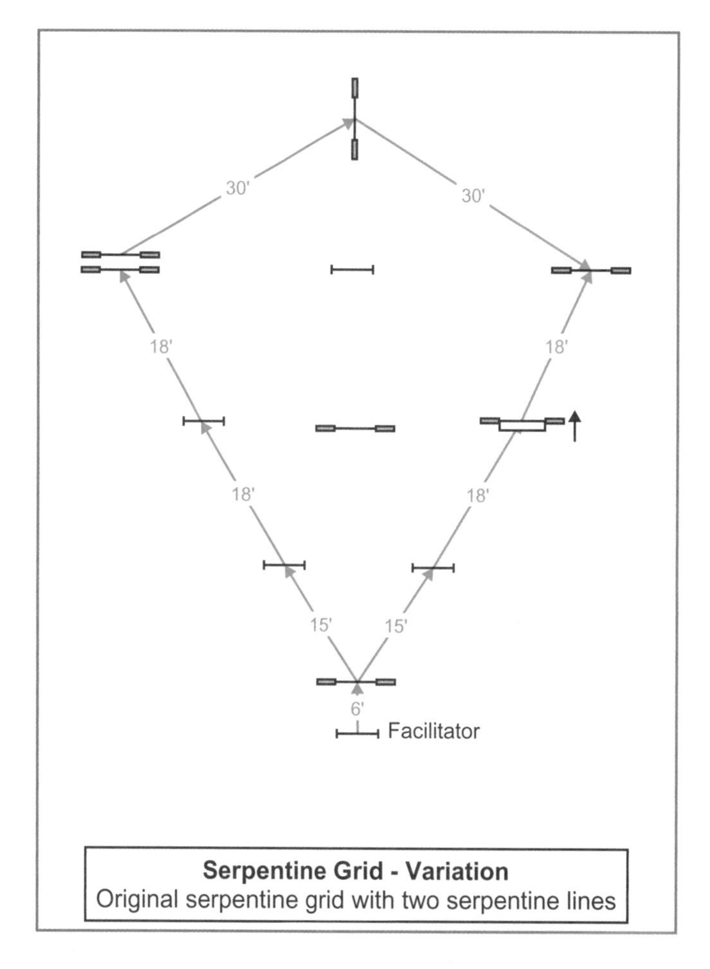

Serpentine Grid - Variation
Original serpentine grid with two serpentine lines

Here is a great example of a well-executed set point. The dog has just lifted off the ground. The rear legs are tight together, the front legs are up under the chin, the head is down, and the shoulders have moved forward slightly.

"Although nobody expects a child to solve algebra problems without having learned arithmetic, some riders persist in trying to win hunter or jumper competitions with horses that cannot negotiate a simple, single fence without revealing a weak or nonexistent elementary foundation for jumping. This is both sad and unnecessary, for giving the animal good fundamental skills for it to realize its full potential isn't all that complicated or time-consuming. As in teaching any other skill, it depends on using a method that is rational and progressive." —William Steinkraus, Olympic Gold Medal Equestrian

SET POINT EXERCISE

Overview

The set point is the only exercise where the mechanical aspect of how your dog gathers (or organizes) himself to come off the ground can be effectively addressed. By eliminating the elements that get dogs into trouble with their jumping—speed, distance, and pressure or handler motion—the set point becomes a supportive tool for your dog to learn the skill of successful, clean jumping.

The set point teaches your dog how to power off the ground and make elevation by setting him up to be correct. The proper takeoff spot is clearly presented to your dog—he does not have to seek it out—and there is no forward speed into the grid. Your dog is prepared for the jumping effort since his feet are right under him. The set point exercise gives your dog the opportunity to feel the correct form for jumping and repeat it many times.

Your dog steps into the space presented, rocks his weight back onto his hips (loading the spring), and fires off the ground. Ultimately you are looking for your dog's back feet to be placed tightly together, his back to be relaxed and slightly rounded, and his head to bob slightly downward and forward as he lifts off the ground. Your dog will likely offer several different efforts at the set point jump until he finds the one that feels comfortable to him. This ease of motion is intuitively correct to your dog and, being so clever, he will duplicate that jumping effort over and over again, thus learning the correct feel of the effort. Once he is consistently using the same form, you will know your dog understands the task.

Note: If your dog's head is too high as he comes off the ground, then correct shoulder motion will be impeded, often causing a bar to fall.

The set point is a powerful and explosive jumping effort by your dog, which is why it is taught from a stationary position without forward speed. Your dog's stride becomes longer once he begins to meet jumps at real speed, making the arc of the stride lower to the ground. Your dog's center of gravity is directly behind his shoulder blades. When your dog takes a long stride, much of his length is behind his center of gravity, all of which must come up under his center to create the correct angle of elevation, which is approximately 45° relative to the height of the jump. While the set point exercise offers a perfect takeoff space for this jump, the perfect takeoff space will vary once your dog has learned to meet jumps from a forward stride. But it's foolish to assume that a dog will know where that spot is without being trained! Once again, as a rider, I would never assume a young horse actually "knows" where to takeoff for his jump without many months of showing the horse where that spot is.

Reference DVD

See Set Point Exercise on the *Foundation Jumping* DVD and Set Point Warm-up on the *Advanced Jumping* DVD.

In the photo on the left, the dog displays excellent form with lots of power. Note that his head is down and his shoulders have come up nicely and tightly while still advancing forward.

In the photo on the right, the dog is lifting off at set point. His hind feet are planted close together for maximum power, his head is down, and his shoulders have come up beautifully. This will be a well-executed jump.

This dog has chosen an excellent set point for the spread jump, yet his head position is a bit too high, which will limit the reach of his shoulders through the air. This head position often results from the dog watching the handler or the handler's hand.

Setting Up the Grid

The set point requires little equipment and minimal space. All you need is a facilitator jump and a jump of some kind.

Facilitator Jump

You need facilitator jump for the set point exercise. The facilitator jump can be a PVC jump bump, a jump with a fixed base, or a nonwinged jump set at a low height (see "Jump Spacing and Height"). The facilitator jump never offers height; it is simply a marker of the space that is available for your dog and places him at the takeoff place required for the set point jump. We never raise the height of the facilitator jump because it would cause too much shoulder action when we want our dog to concentrate on using his hindquarters.

Alternatively, you can also use the V-bounce apparatus for set point work instead of a facilitator jump, which will guarantee your dog does not load into the space on his shoulders. Plans for building and using a V-bounce apparatus are included in "Appendix 4."

The Jump

The set point jump can be a single jump or a double or oxer (horse terminology). For the sake of training and educating dogs, I prefer an ascending double where the back bar is one jump height higher than the front bar. When using an ascending double, it is important to make sure either both bars match or the more dominant-looking bar is the highest. I also prefer using two separate jumps to make the double rather than using a fixed double. A fixed double does not allow you the flexibility to alter the width of the spread for your dog, if necessary.

Set Point Exercise - Setup
The set point exercise set up with a double made up of two jumps (left) and with a single verticle jump (right). The distances shown here are only examples. See "Jump Spacing and Height" to set up the grid for your dog.

It is a myth that dogs require more forward speed to perform a double cleanly; the reality is that your dog simply needs to generate more power off the ground. The ascending double gives your dog clear information to get his shoulders up and out of the way quickly whereas a single vertical jump does not. The double also encourages a nice stretch of the neck and back as the dog leaves the ground, creating good form for your dog.

The set point jump should be changed out often to school your dog through different types of hurdles in this picture: ascending double, parallel double, triple, extended spread, tire, wall jump, viaduct, and panel. I do not use the broad jump or long jump in this exercise; I isolate and school this obstacle separately. The broad jump is just an extended stride with little to no elevation, so using it for the set point exercise would be counter-intuitive for your dog's understanding of the task.

The V-bounce apparatus makes it very clear to the dog where he is to organize himself to get off the ground.

Jump Spacing and Height

The space between the facilitator jump or the V-bounce apparatus and the set point jump is determined by your dog's length of back. It is important to offer your dog enough space to comfortably step into the grid, but not so much room as to allow him to be lazy or sloppy with the performance.

Use the information below to determine the jump spacing and jump heights for the grid. Although I have used these distances with success at seminars, they are only guidelines and you may need to adjust them for your dog. Spacing between the jumps is measured from the center of one jump to the center of the next.

The set point jump can be offered at your dog's competition jump height. However, when working the exercise you should change the jump height frequently (as often as each pass). Moving the bar up and down challenges your dog to pay better attention than he would if the jump were always presented in a static way.

The set point exercise is also a permissible place to "over school" your dog, meaning you can set the bar 2" higher than his competition height so he builds up a bit more core strength.

Large Body Type

Place the set point jump 5'–6' from the facilitator jump. The facilitator jump is set at a maximum of 4"–6" in height, and the set point jump is set between 8" and your dog's competition height.

Note: I have worked with many very large breeds such as Bernese Mountain Dogs, Mastiffs, and Irish Wolfhounds. While it may seem suitable to give them 7' or more to the set point jump, it actually does not serve their jumping education. These dogs must learn to organize themselves more quickly, which will not happen if the space is too large.

Border Collie/Aussie Body Type

Place the set point jump 4'–5' from the facilitator jump. The facilitator jump is set at a maximum of 4"–6" in height, and the set point jump is set between 8" and your dog's competition height.

Sheltie Body Type

Place the set point jump 3'–4' from the facilitator jump. The facilitator jump is set at a maximum of 4"–6" in height and the set point jump is set between 8" and your dog's competition height.

JRT Body Type

Place the set point jump 2'–3' from the facilitator jump. The facilitator jump is set at a maximum of 4" in height and the set point jump is set between 8" and your dog's competition height.

Very Small Body Type

Place the set point jump 1.5'–2' from the facilitator jump. The facilitator jump is set at a maximum of 4" in height and the set point jump is set between 8" and your dog's competition height.

Target

The target should be clearly visible to your dog from his starting position. It needs to be placed at the point where your dog will complete his stride *after* landing, not at his landing point. This is at least 6' away from the jump for small dogs and 9'–10' from the jump for larger dogs. Placing the target too far away from the last jump will encourage your dog to jump flat, which is not desirable. We want him to have just enough space between the jump and the target that he can land and get all four feet on the ground before he reaches the target, encouraging balance to be maintained through the jumping effort.

Dog's Starting Position

- Line up your dog so he is facing the center of the facilitator jump.
- The distance between your dog and the facilitator jump should be half the distance of the space in the grid. For example, if the distance is 4', start your dog 2' from the facilitator jump or the point of the V-bounce apparatus.
- Your dog can be in a sit, stand, or down.
- Your dog should be looking forward at the jump or target before you release him.

If you do not have a start-line stay, have a training partner restrain your dog.

If you are starting your dog from a sit position, make sure your dog's weight is on his haunches. If your dog starts an exercise in a crouching or "vulture" position, then his weight is on his front and the angle of his shoulders is closed. This is not desirable and can cause knocked bars. See "General Guidelines for Gridwork" for photos that show the correct position. An easy way to get a dog to sit upright (which puts his weight on his haunches and opens up the angle of his shoulders) is to ask for a high hand touch after he sits.

Handler's Position

- Lead out and stand one step ahead of the target and one step laterally off the target. This allows your dog to get to the target without passing the plane of your body.
- Face the direction your dog is traveling, looking over your shoulder to watch him.
- Sometimes stand to the left of the target and sometimes stand to the right to work your dog on both sides.

Note: This is not a grid that I would do as a send-away, at least at first, since dogs will carry their head a bit higher when traveling away from the handler if they are not confident they are correct. When your dog raises his head, his stride will always be shorter, causing extra strides.

Progressions

Do three to five repetitions of the grid, alternating which side you work on.

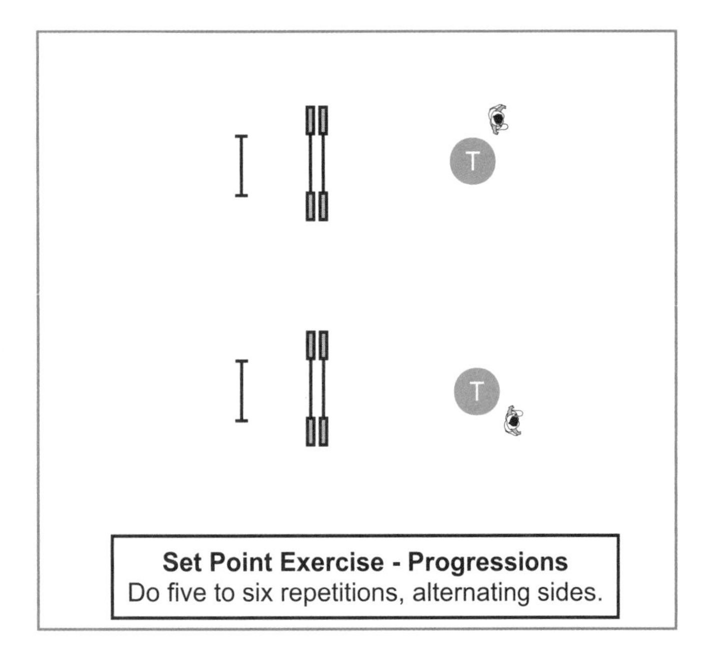

Set Point Exercise - Progressions
Do five to six repetitions, alternating sides.

Problem Solving

Problem: Your dog attempts to take the facilitator jump or V-bounce apparatus and the set point jump as one obstacle.

Solution: Lower the height of the set point jump. Place the target in front of the set point jump and do one or two repetitions. Move the target back to its original position, raise the bar back up, and try again.

Problem: Your dog goes around the facilitator jump or V-bounce apparatus.

Solution: Place the target in front of the set point jump and do one or two repetitions. If using the V-bounce apparatus, open up the point of the V 4"–6" to create a clearer path for your dog to enter.

Problem: Your dog fails to organize his body well in preparation for liftoff.

Solution: Change the set point jump to an ascending double.

Problem: Your dog is having trouble transferring his weight to his hips.

Solution: If you're not getting good weight transfer and your dog is getting "stuck over his shoulders" (unable to get his shoulders out of the way in time), replace the facilitator jump with the V-bounce apparatus. Using a diagonal bar under the bar of a single jump or the front bar of a double can also help a dog that is having difficulty with weight transfer.

Problem: Your dog's head stays too high.

Solution: Change the set point jump to a parallel double (bars set at the same height, not ascending) and make it a bit wider than usual. Lower the height of the jump, as the challenge is the width not the height. This should encourage your dog's head to come down and his back to round a bit. For dogs with very erect body types, you may need to offer the set point in this manner frequently.

Problem: Your dog fails to look at the target or set point jump and just stares at you.

Solution: This is a learned behavior. Take your dog away from all equipment. Work on getting your dog to focus forward on the target, then release him and play. Repeat this until your dog is keenly focusing on the target, then try the set point exercise again.

Problem: When you are doing the set point variation on a bend or slice (see "Variations"), your dog lands on the step-out bar.

Solution: Now we are shaping the arc of flight, which your dog often cannot fully control in the beginning stages of training. Lower the jump height and place target in front of the step-out bar to encourage your dog to use the space offered. Repeat several times. Add jump height back to the exercise and see if your dog understands to land within the given space.

How Much to Practice?

The set point is the only jump grid that can be practiced frequently within a session without harm. If your dog steps in and jumps out with little or no effort and with apparent ease of motion, then three to five repetitions are enough for that training session. If, however, each repetition seems a bit different than the last, your dog is still processing how to make the jumping effort work for him. Do a few more repetitions for that session. Your end goal is for the first repetition of any session to look spectacular and subsequent repetitions to look just the same as that first one.

The set point can be used as a warm-up before an agility training session and it can be incorporated into the training session: if your dog makes a jumping error, break off the sequence and do a couple of set points before going back and trying the sequence again.

The set point is also a vital part of your dog's jumping maintenance program.

Proofing

Since the set point is the only grid that helps your dog "clean up" the mechanical process of jumping, I do not believe in doing any type of proofing that could ruin this one tool handlers have to keep their dogs' jumping clean and successful. I strongly suggest that you keep the set point simple and clear, and allow your dog to be quiet in his mindset.

The only proofing you should do for this grid is to replace the set point jump with all the different hurdles you will see on courses (except for the broad jump or long jump, as previously noted).

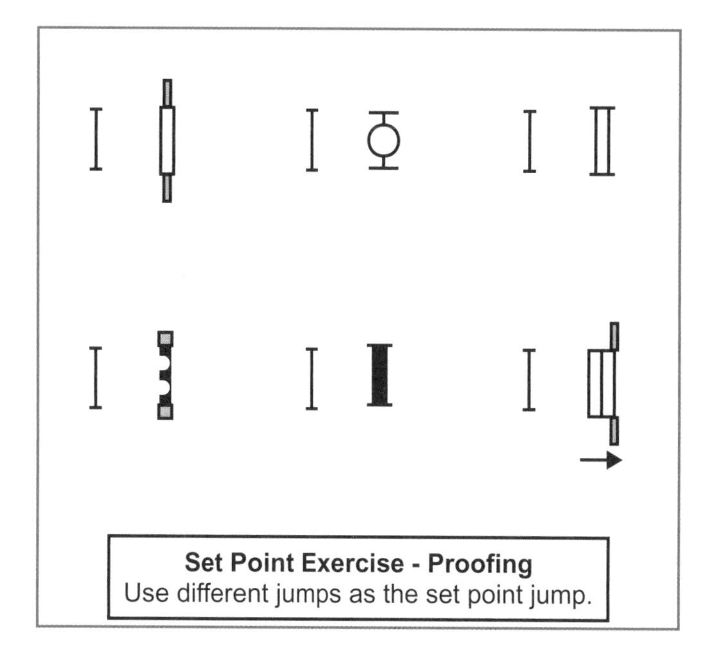

Note: I do not use the V-bounce apparatus when using a tire as the set point jump because as I feel the visual picture becomes too complicated and overpowers your dog's thought process. Use just the facilitator jump before the tire.

Adding Handler Motion

For the set point exercise, I would not add too much motion because the spacing is so tight. The most motion I would offer is a walk toward the target as my dog does the exercise.

Adding Handling

There is no change of side in this exercise so crosses are not necessary.

The jump bar here is very dominant. It has a larger diameter than a normal bar and the striping is very bold, giving the dog a lot to look at, which results in a nice jumping effort. If all your jump bars look the same, dogs can become a bit lazy in their effort from time to time. When schooling for a big event, use equipment that brings out the best performance in your dog.

Grid Variations

The set point exercise does not always have to be schooled straight on. It can be offered on a slice or on a bend. In these more advanced versions of the exercise, you place a facilitator jump after the set point jump (step-out facilitator) as well as in front of the set point jump (step-in facilitator.). By including the step-out, you are shaping your dog's arc.

Note: When you are doing the set point exercise on a slice or bend, do *not* use the V-bounce apparatus.

Bend Variation

- Use the spacing and height guidelines provided earlier for the straight-line set point exercise.
- Place the target on the tight line of the circle at the end of the bend, giving your dog room to get to it without landing on it.
- Position your dog so he is centered on the first jump, facing straight ahead, and looking at the jump; do not place your dog on an angle to the first jump. Give yourself room to take several steps forward with your dog to guarantee he takes the second jump.
- Put your hand in your dog's collar, move forward with your dog, release him into the grid, and then rotate into the turn. Your shoulders and hips, not an extended hand or arm, should rotate to support your dog through the grid.
- Be sure to work in each direction to practice a left-lead bend as well as a right-lead bend. Place your target on the tight line.

Slice Variation

In the slice variation of the set point exercise, the standard of one jump is positioned at the center of the previous jump, and a step-out facilitator is used. The slice can be made more severe as your dog's understanding progresses.

- The target should be clearly visible to your dog from his starting position. Place it about 10' from the last jump before you take your dog to the start line.
- The distance between your dog and the step-in facilitator jump should be half the distance of the first space in the grid.
- Lead out and stand one step ahead of the target and one step laterally off the target.
- Work a left-to-right slice as well as a right-to-left slice.

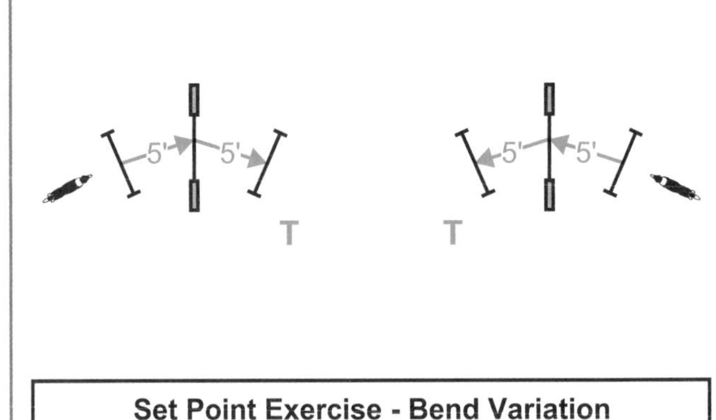

Set Point Exercise - Bend Variation
Be sure to work in each direction so you are practicing a left-lead bend as well as a right-lead bend.

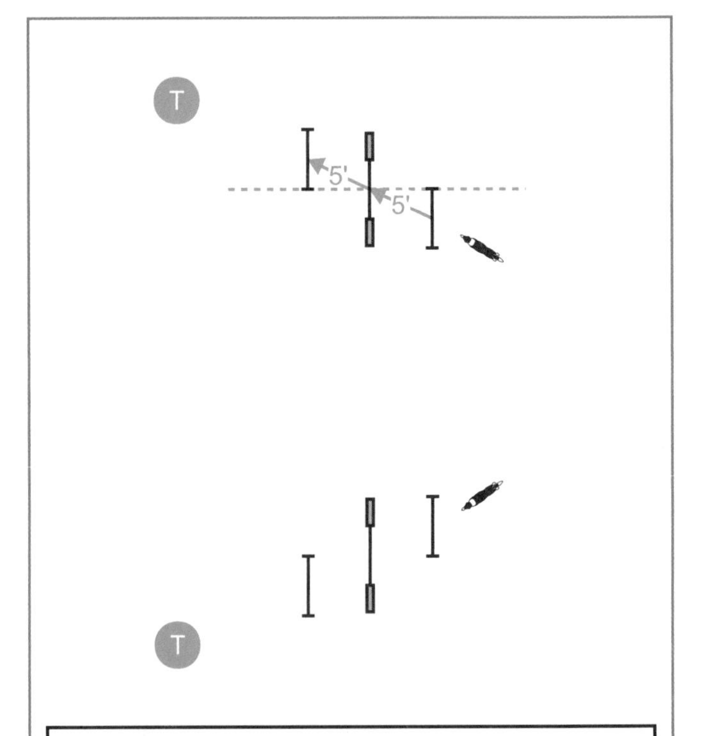

Set Point Exercise - Slice Variation
Initially, the end of each facilitator should line up with the center of the set point jump. Gradually increase the degree of the slice for more advanced work. Be sure to work both a right-to-left slice and a left-to-right-slice.

The dog stepping into the offered space of a set point on a slice (top) and the dog in flight after completing the step in (bottom).

© BARRY ROSEN PHOTOGRAPHY

"Justy is almost 11 years old and still jumping happily and enjoying agility. As a youngster, he was unable to judge his takeoff point and had no idea what to do with his body. Working with Susan's methods, he learned to adjust his stride and improve his jumping accuracy. Thanks to her we are still going strong. Justy has his MX and MXJ and we are slowly working toward a MACH."

—Laurie Rossi Sherck, Running Norfolks in agility for 15 years

STRAIGHT-LINE STRIDE GRID

Overview

For many years, this grid was a staple of the work I did after foundation training. But I stopped using it for a long time because it became increasingly clear that young dogs, in particular, struggle once they have to negotiate a line of jumps at height. The reason for the struggle is that they cannot produce the necessary weight shift for several jumps in a row. Often you will see young dogs sequence two jumps nicely but as you add jumps to the line they will begin to run around the jumps, go under them, or otherwise abort the effort. This is simply a result of the dogs attempting to inform their handler that they are over faced by the challenge. That is the first reason I chose to put this grid away for a time. The second reason is that our dogs will never have to perform a line of jumps in competition that are all spaced at an equal distance. In addition, we want the dog to understand that he can adjust the length of his stride. Therefore, schooling with any regularity on a straight line of jumps spaced at an equal one-stride distance is counterproductive.

While I still use a line of competition-height jumps for this grid, the spacing between the jumps is never equal.

Reference DVD

See Steady One-stride Grid on the *Advanced Jumping* DVD.

Setting Up the Grid

You need four jumps for this grid. Initially you will set up only three jumps, but then you will add a fourth jump. The fourth jump allows your dog to jump into the grid, produce two more good strides, and jump out.

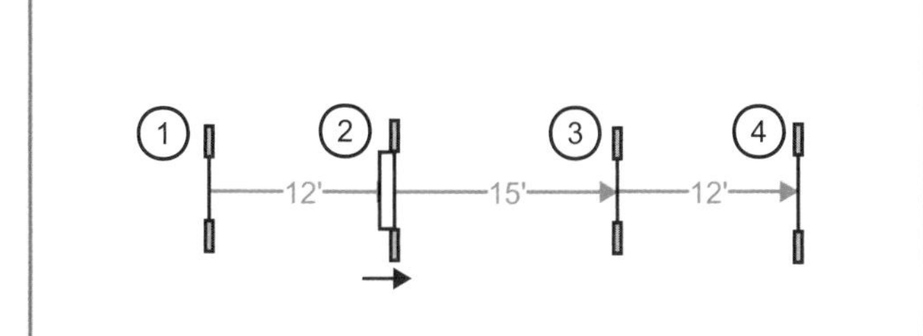

Straight-Line Stride Grid - Setup
Initially only set up jumps #1-#3. Jump #4 can be added during the training session. These jumps are spaced for a small dog.

Initially, use three winged jumps and an ascending double or use four winged jumps. When you start proofing, you will mix up the types of jumps you offer (excluding the broad jump or long jump).

I usually offer the dog's shortest stride distance between jumps #1 and #2 and then add a few feet for the space between jumps #2 and #3. When adding jump #4 to the line, I use the dog's shortest stride distance again. Your dog will jump into the space between jumps #1 and #2 without forward speed and then build length of stride between jumps #2 and #3. He will likely appreciate the shorter distance between jumps #3 and #4 to rebalance himself.

Jump Spacing and Height

Use the information below to determine the jump spacing and jump heights for the grid. Although I have used these distances with success at seminars, they are only guidelines and you may need to adjust them for your dog. Spacing between the jumps is measured from the center of one jump to the center of the next.

Big Dogs

- *Jumps #1 and #2:* Space 15' apart.
- *Jumps #2 and #3:* Space 18' apart.
- *When you add jump #4:* Place the fourth jump 15' from jump #3.
- Set the jumps at your dog's competition height.

Medium Dogs

- *Jumps #1 and #2:* Space 14' apart.
- *Jumps #2 and #3:* Space 17' apart.
- *When you add jump #4:* Place the fourth jump 14' from jump #3.
- Set the jumps at your dog's competition height.

Small Dogs

- *Jumps #1 and #2:* Space 12' apart.
- *Jumps #2 and #3:* Space 15' apart.
- *When you add jump #4:* Place the fourth jump 12' from jump #3.
- Set the jumps at your dog's competition height.

Tiny Dogs

- *Jumps #1 and #2:* Space 10' apart.
- *Jumps #2 and #3:* Space 12' apart.
- *When you add jump #4:* Place the fourth jump 10' from jump #3.
- Set the jumps at your dog's competition height.

Target

The target should be clearly visible to your dog from his starting position. Place it about 10' from the last jump *before* you take your dog to the start line.

Dog's Starting Position

Your dog can be in a sit, stand, or down. The distance between your dog and the first jump should equal one steady, short stride for your dog:

- Big dogs: 9'–11'
- Medium dogs: 7'–9'
- Small dogs: 5'–6'
- Tiny dogs: 4'–5'

This will allow your dog to begin with the most power and greatest balance. Starting your dog farther from the jump may cause even a well-educated jumping dog to want to flatten out or become frenetic.

Handler's Position

- Lead out and stand one step ahead of the target and one step laterally off the target. This allows your dog to get to the target without passing the plane of your body.
- Face the direction your dog is traveling, looking over your shoulder to watch him.
- Sometimes stand to the left of the target and sometimes stand to the right to work your dog on both sides.

Note: This is not a grid that I would do as a send-away, at least at first, since dogs will carry their head a bit higher when traveling away from the handler if they are not confident they are correct. When your dog raises his head, his stride will always be shorter, causing extra strides.

Progressions

Do two repetitions of three jumps, one on your left and one on your right. Add a fourth jump and then do two more repetitions.

Problem Solving

Problem: Your dog jumps #1 and exits the grid to go to the target.

Solution: Your dog may not be prepared to offer the second weight shift for jump #2. Lower the bar on jump #2 by one jump height and try the sequence again. If the dog comes out of the grid again, place the target in front of jump #2 and repeat. If your dog is successful, move the target back to the end of the line and repeat. If he is successful again, raise the height of jump #2.

If your dog comes off the line a third time, go back to set point work for several repetitions and then try this line one more time. If your dog meets the challenge, break off the exercise, reward him, and go on to an easier grid to end the session.

Problem: Your dog drives too deep to his takeoff place for jump #4, failing to recompress his stride.

Solution: Place the target in front of jump #4, to encourage your dog to recompress his stride, and do one repetition. Move the target back to the landing side of #4 and try the line again. Dogs love to flatten out their stride and jumping arc, but this can lead to many dropped bars; they need to learn to read the line and collect where required.

Another solution is to place a diagonal bar with one end resting in the jump cup above the current jump height and the other end resting on the ground approximately 8" from in front of the base of the jump. This bar reorients your dog to a takeoff place slightly farther back from the base of the jump. It is very effective but must be faded as soon as possible to encourage your dog to assess the problem without a visual aid.

How Much to Practice?

This grid can be included in your dog's maintenance training as one you visit every two or three months. I also use it as part of a tune-up for a big competition.

Proofing

- When the dog is comfortable with the exercise, play with the spacing between the jumps. Allow for more room or less room depending on what a particular dog needs at a particular point in time. For example, if the spacing for the line is currently 15', 18', 15', you could try offering 15', 15', 18' for the first proofing repetition. Then change the spacing to 15', 18', 20' for the next repetition. For the final repetition, go back to the original spacing of 15', 18', 15'. A big part of this jumping methodology is to produce both athleticism and a quick mental response from dogs, so changing things up within a session is a good idea unless your dog is struggling with the exercise.
- Proofing this grid also means rotating in the different hurdles you will see on courses (except for the broad jump or long jump).
- You can also gradually increase your lateral distance from the target to a distance that reflects the normal working space between you and your dog.

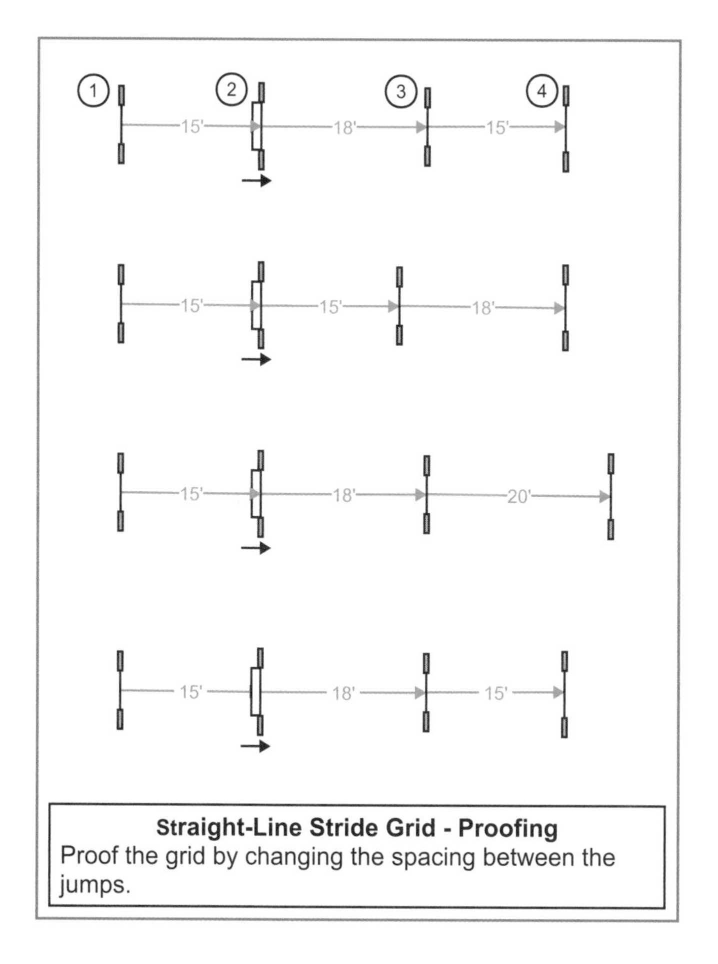

Straight-Line Stride Grid - Proofing
Proof the grid by changing the spacing between the jumps.

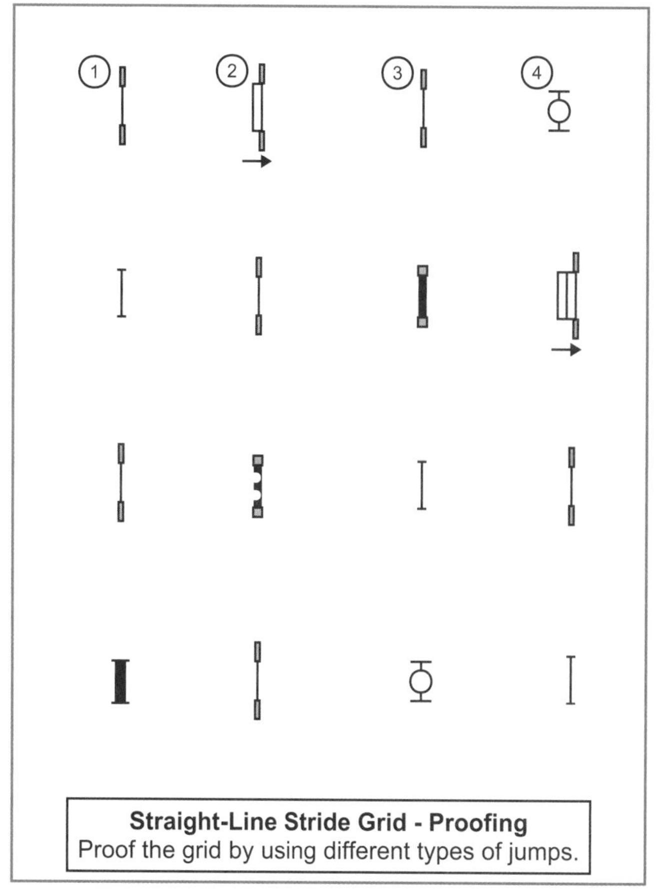

Straight-Line Stride Grid - Proofing
Proof the grid by using different types of jumps.

Adding Handler Motion

Adding handler motion is appropriate for this grid, providing that you are aware of the spacing and do not offer acceleration motion into a space that does not warrant it. For example, if the last space in the grid is the tight 15' distance, then you do not want to power forward and open up your stride because it cues your dog to open up his stride into a tight space that requires some deceleration from your dog. If you are uncertain about how to help your dog, it is always best to lead out to the target, be still, and allow your dog to figure out what he needs to do to accomplish the task.

Most handlers rush into running with their dogs before the dog understands the mechanical effort needed to do the task with precision. There is much work needed to get your dog to the point where he's ready for you to be in motion. Adding handler motion should only begin after you have completed the proofing work above, and your dog is producing a reliable one stride between the jumps at varying distances.

As always, remember to work your dog on both your left and right side.

1. Lead out halfway through the grid, release your dog, and move forward at a walk. Your dog should complete the grid correctly and continue driving forward toward the target. As you walk, your dog will pass you so it's a good idea to have a trained "Go On" cue that you can give as your dog catches up with you.
2. Lead out halfway through the grid, release your dog, and move forward at a jog.
3. Lead out halfway through the grid, release your dog, and move forward at a run.
4. Run with your dog from the start.

These steps should be done incrementally so your dog's performance does not change. If your dog starts to have difficulty with your motion, then you are increasing your speed too quickly. Your dog needs the opportunity to become comfortable with your motion while still focusing on his job.

Adding Handling

There is no change of sides in this exercise so crosses are not necessary.

Grid Variations

None.

X GRID

Overview

The X grid can pose a relatively simple distance question to your dog or an extremely complicated question involving distance, collection, extension, and problem solving. The grid addresses the all-important set point as well as variable distances in striding to a jump. The initial stages require your dog to go from collection to extension. But when presented in its most difficult form, where your dog will perform the grid from end to end in either direction, he will be jumping into the grid in extension, gathering for collection, and then opening up again to extension. We are building a true test of his athleticism.

Dogs often will not have the answer for this grid until they do it a few times. The X grid offers a slice, which will strongly influence one lead over the other from your dog. Many dogs that have not done enough bend work will struggle a bit with this concept. As you work through the grid in a progressive manner, your job is to build success on success rather than failure on failure. This means you will not always accomplish all the stages of this grid in one session, but remember that latent learning is powerful. While your dog may struggle with this grid initially, the next time you present it he may be assessing what needs to take place and how best to accomplish it as soon as you place him at the start line.

Important:

- Do not introduce this grid until you have completed the bend work foundation grid.
- Because stage 3 of this grid involves jumping into compression, this stage should not be done with puppies.

Reference DVD

See Exercise #4 on the *Advanced Jumping* DVD.

Setting Up the Grid

This grid requires nine jumps: one winged jump for the center, four nonwinged jumps that function as facilitator jumps, and four jumps of various styles for the corners: winged, nonwinged, double, extended spread, triple, panel, tire, wall, or viaduct. Any type of jump is fine with the exception of the broad jump or long jump.

First build the small X in the center of the grid. Place a winged jump in the center of your work area. This jump

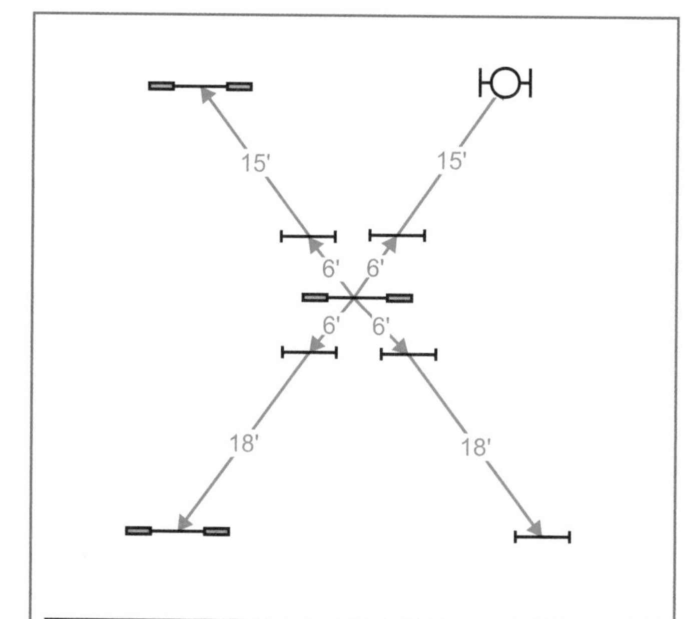

X Grid - Setup
Set up for the X grid with the four facilitator jumps spaced for big dogs. See "Jump Spacing and Height" to set up the grid for your dog.

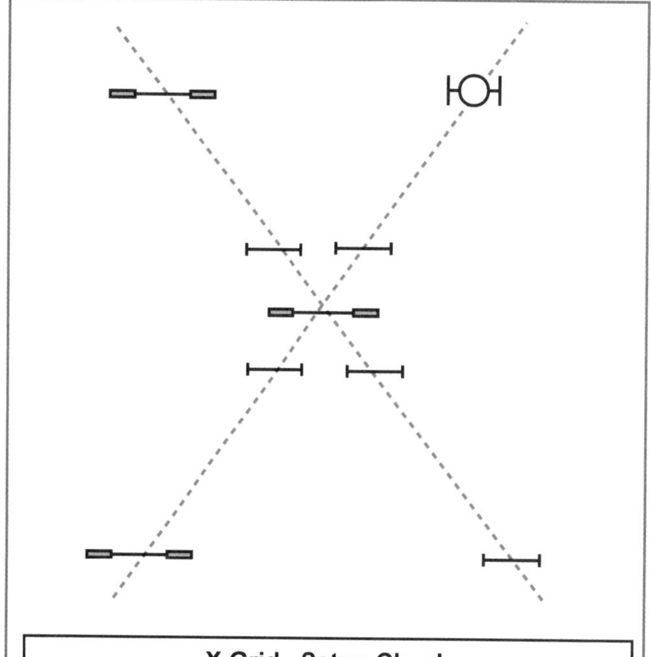

X Grid - Setup Check
Stand behind the corner jumps to make sure you have a straight slice that is centered from corner to corner.

will be set at your dog's competition height. Then place the four nonwinged facilitator jumps on a slice to form the step-in and step-out set points for the main jump. These facilitator jumps serve only to shape your dog's jumping arc and inform him where to take off and land; therefore, they have no height.

Once the small X is in place, walk off 15' from two of the facilitator jumps to place the jumps in each corner at one end of the X (measure from the center of one jump to the center of the next). Pace off 18' from the opposite two facilitator jumps to place the corner jumps at the other end of the grid. By setting up the spacing in this manner, you are asking your dog to assess the difference in distances and offer an adjustable stride. The corner jumps are set at your dog's competition height.

Stand behind a corner jump at each end of the "X" and look through the jumps to make sure that the slice is a straight line centered from corner to corner.

Jump Spacing and Height

Use the information below to determine the jump spacing and jump heights for the grid. Although I have used these distances with success at seminars, they are only guidelines and you may need to adjust them for your dog. Spacing between the jumps is measured from the center of one jump to the center of the next.

Important: When you have your dog doing the entire line of four jumps, it may be advisable to open up the spacing between the center jump and the facilitator jumps by 6"–12" to allow for the speed and length of stride your dog will be driving with. It is still by all accounts maximum collection, but it needs to be offered in a fair manner to avoid unnecessary stress on your dog's body.

Big Dogs

- *Facilitator jumps and center jump:* Space the four facilitator jumps 6' from the center winged jump. Set the center jump at your dog's competition jump height and set the facilitator jumps at a maximum of 6" in height.
- *Corner jumps:* Space the two corner jumps on one side of the grid 15' from the facilitator jumps on that side. Space the two corner jumps on the opposite side of the grid 18' from the facilitator jumps. Set all of the corner jumps at your dog's competition jump height.

Medium Dogs

- *Facilitator jumps and center jump:* Space the four facilitator jumps 5' from the center winged jump. Set the center jump at your dog's competition jump height and set the facilitator jumps at a maximum of 6" in height.
- *Corner jumps:* Space the two corner jumps on one side of the grid 15' from the facilitator jumps on that side. Space the two corner jumps on the opposite side of the grid 18' from the facilitator jumps. Set all of the corner jumps at your dog's competition jump height.

Small Dogs

- *Facilitator jumps and center jump:* Space the four facilitator jumps 4' from the center winged jump. Set the center jump at your dog's competition jump height and set the facilitator jumps at a maximum of 4" in height.
- *Corner jumps:* Space the two corner jumps on one side of the grid 15' from the facilitator jumps on that side. Space the two corner jumps on the opposite side of the grid 18' from the facilitator jumps. Set all of the corner jumps at your dog's competition jump height.

Tiny Dogs

- *Facilitator jumps and center jump:* Space the four facilitator jumps 2'–3' from the center winged jump. Set the center jump at your dog's competition jump height and set the facilitator jumps at a maximum of 4" in height.
- *Corner jumps:* Space the two corner jumps on one side of the grid 15' from the facilitator jumps on that side. Space the two corner jumps on the opposite side of the grid 18' from the facilitator jumps. Set all of the corner jumps at your dog's competition jump height.

Target

The target should be clearly visible to your dog from his starting position. Place the target about 10' from the last jump *before* you take your dog to the start line.

Dog's Starting Position

For stages 1 and 2:

- Line up your dog so he is facing the center of the facilitator jump on the slice. Your dog should not be placed in a position that causes him to twist or bend to get on the straight line. He should be able to look through the jumps and see the slice he is to drive.
- The distance between your dog and the facilitator jump should be half the distance of the space in the set point grid. For example, if the facilitator jump and the center jump are spaced 6' apart, start your dog 3' from the facilitator jump.
- Your dog can be in a sit, stand, or down.
- Your dog should be looking forward at the jump or target before you release him.

For stage 3, when you are starting at one of the corner jumps, your dog needs to start at a distance from jump #1 that is equal to one steady, short stride for him:

- Big dogs: 9'–11'
- Medium dogs: 7'–9'
- Small dogs: 5'–6'
- Tiny dogs: 4'–5'

Remember, the shorter the stride, the greater the balance and power. Find a good distance for your dog and become consistent with walking off that distance for your dog.

Handler's Position

- Lead out and stand one step ahead of the target and one step laterally off the target. This allows your dog to get to the target without passing the plane of your body.
- Face the direction your dog is traveling, looking over your shoulder to watch him.

Progressions

Until your dog is very comfortable with the X grid, it should be built up progressively *each time* you do it. When your dog is performing each complete slice with ease in both directions, you can start the training session with stage 3.

Stage 1

Initially you will work just the center portion of the grid, which is basically a set point on a slice. You are shaping your dog's jumping arc. Do four repetitions, alternating direction and the side on which you are working your dog.

Before progressing to stage 2, be certain your dog can perform this without stepping on the bar of the step-out facilitator jump.

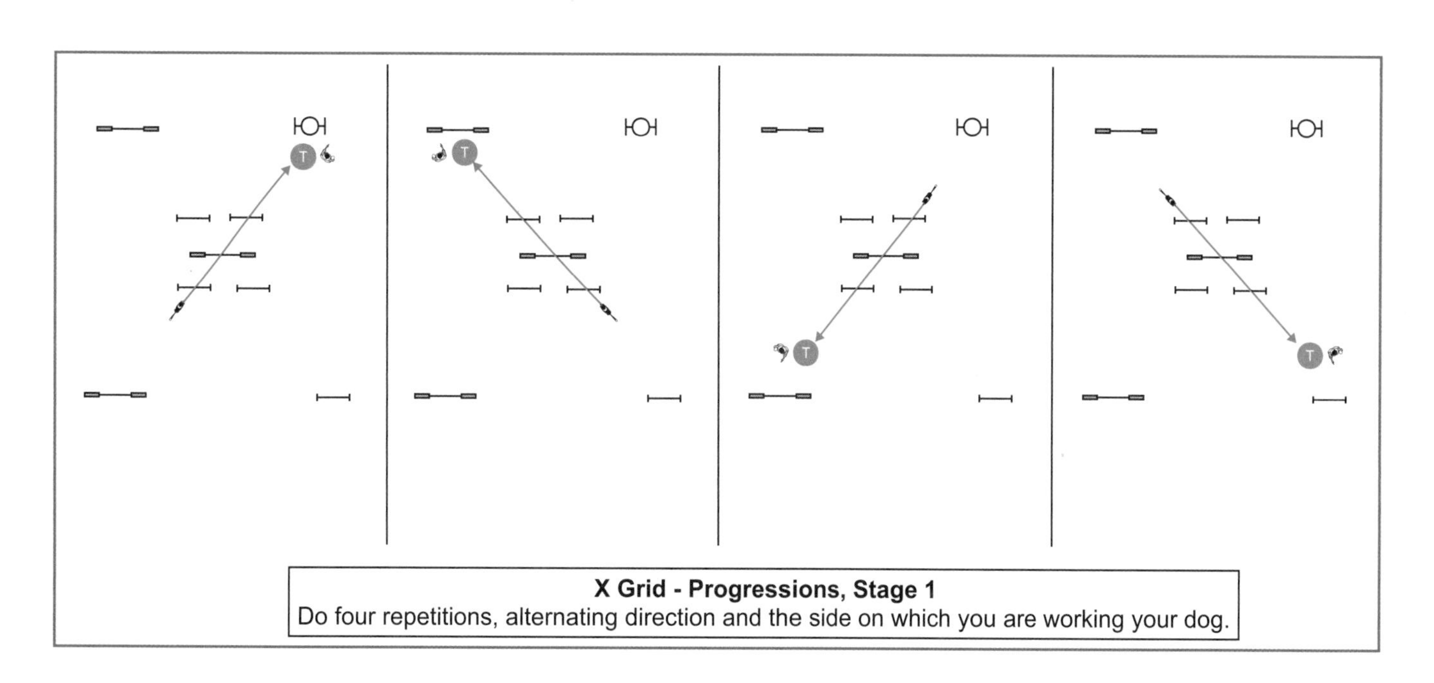

X Grid - Progressions, Stage 1
Do four repetitions, alternating direction and the side on which you are working your dog.

Stage 2

Now you are going to ask a distance question. Your dog will jump from the center of the grid to each of the outside jumps. Each line is designed to be one stride for your dog even though the distances are different. Do one repetition to each corner jump.

It is likely that you will need to practice stages 1 and 2 for several training sessions before you try to move on to stage 3. If you are not planning to move on to stage 3 in a training session, you can do another repetition of each of these slice lines.

Stage 3

If all is going well, you can attempt to jump the entire slice line from end to end. Your dog will be jumping from extension into tight collection and then going back to extension. This is a difficult exercise; do not overdo it.

Do one repetition starting from each corner jump.

Considering the difficulty of this slice, be certain to reward with something of high value to your dog. Remember to reward the "try" regardless of whether it is successful. The whole point of practice is that there will be failures. Accept it and reward your dog. Tomorrow is another day. Olympic diver Greg Louganis once reminded me that he needed to achieve over 100 *flawless* repetitions to perfect each dive he performed. Just imagine how many repetitions he did that were not perfect to achieve his end goal of Olympic gold.

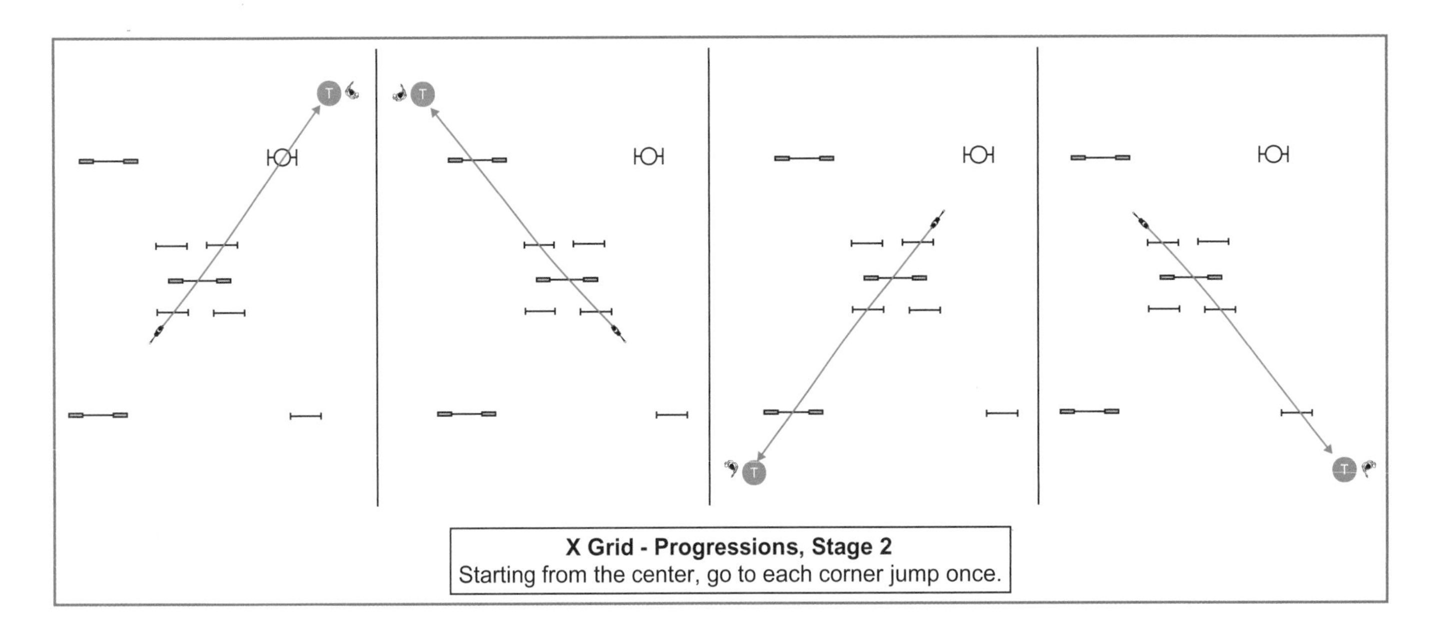

X Grid - Progressions, Stage 2
Starting from the center, go to each corner jump once.

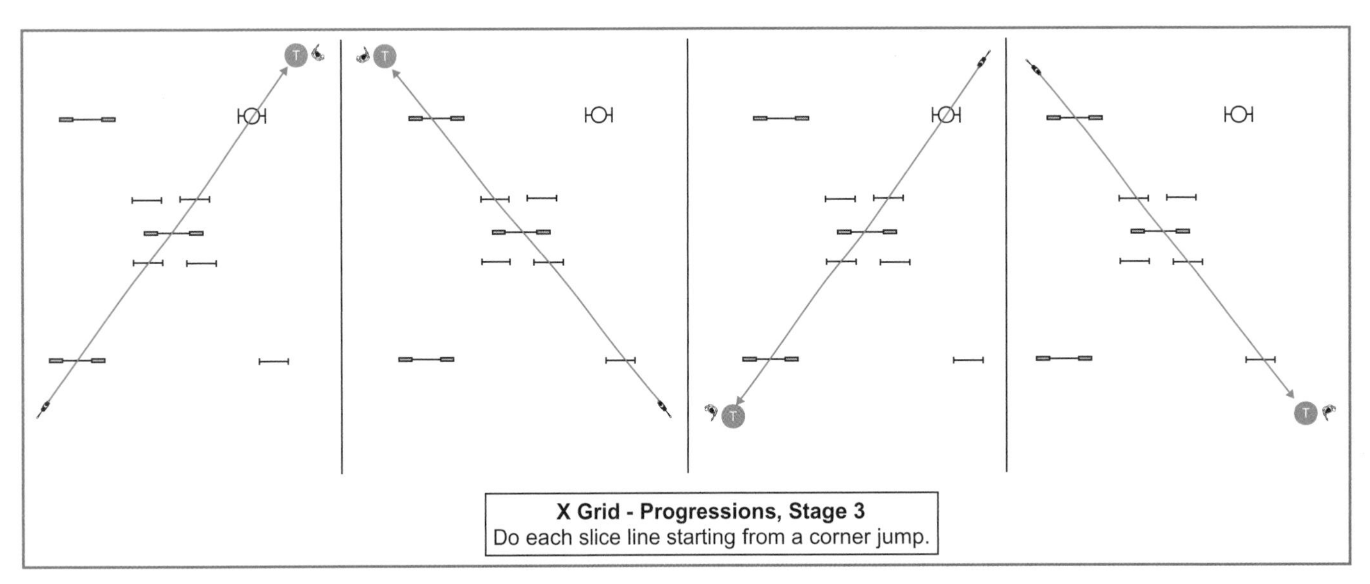

X Grid - Progressions, Stage 3
Do each slice line starting from a corner jump.

Problem Solving

Problem: Your dog will not enter the small "X" on one slice or the other.

Solution: Because slice jumps strongly influence one lead over the other, many dogs will have difficulty with one slice or the other because the slice encourages his weaker lead. Lower the bar on the center jump by one jump height and place the target directly in front of the jump to encourage your dog to step into the space. Once your dog will enter the space, move the target back to its position after the step-out facilitator jump.

If the lead is particularly weak, you may need to lower the jump height more to help your dog sort it out. Work at his speed and do not be in too big a rush to get to the next stage of training.

Problem: While working on the small "X", your dog steps on the step-out bar.

Solution: Lower the bar on the center jump by one jump height. Place the target in front of the step-out jump to encourage your dog to land in the offered space. Once your dog realizes he *can* land there, he will respect the space and use it. Move the height of the center jump back to your dog's competition height.

If your dog continues to step on the bar after you raise the center jump again, open up the space between the center jump and the facilitator jumps by 6".

Problem: Your dog takes the center jump and the step-out facilitator bar as one obstacle, failing to use the space offered between the center jump and the step-out facilitator jump.

Solution: This can happen if your dog is not accustomed to having his jumping arc shaped. Lower the bar on the center jump by one jump height. Place the target in front of the step-out facilitator jump to encourage your dog to land in the space offered. Do two or three repetitions. Move the height of the center jump back to your dog's competition height.

Problem: Your dog does not recognize the path to the outside jump after he completes the set point slice in the middle.

Solution: Place the target half way to the corner jump to correct your dog's path and do one repetition. Move the target so it is right in front of the corner jump and do one repetition. Move the target back to its original position on the landing side of the corner jump and try the entire slice again.

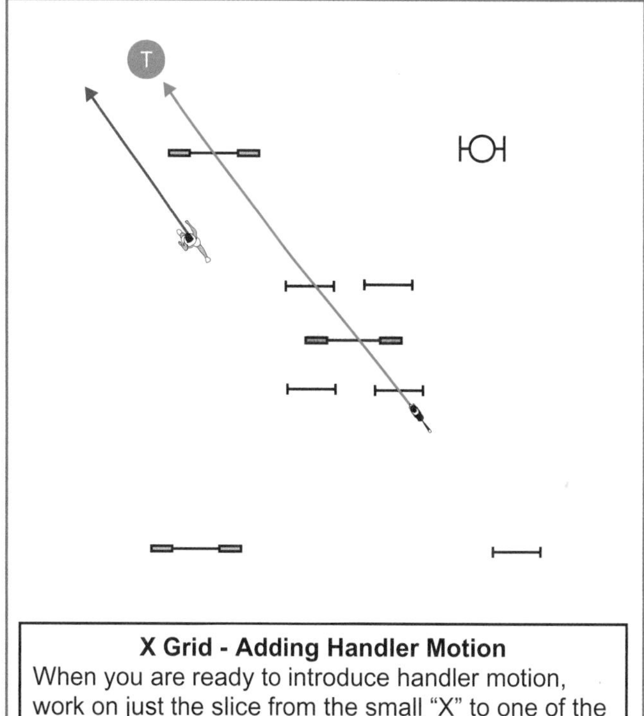

X Grid - Adding Handler Motion
When you are ready to introduce handler motion, work on just the slice from the small "X" to one of the corner obstacles.

Problem: When going from end to end, your dog fails to get the weight shift necessary to enter the small "X" and he performs the set point slice in a frightening manner.

Solution: Immediately go back to stage 2, working the small "X" to the outside jumps.

Speed without thought of execution is a fruitless effort for the agility dog and he should not be encouraged to have this mindset. He needs to address the collection required. The next time you work on stage 3, instead of doing the entire slice line, work from one of the corner jumps back into the small "X" to the target, which should be placed after the step-out facilitator. This way he does not get the opportunity to open up and accelerate, which allows him to focus on the collection aspect of the grid.

If this does not fix the problem, you are moving too fast with the exercise.

How Much to Practice?

This grid can be included in your dog's maintenance training as one you visit every two or three months. It is a particularly good grid for tuning up your dog prior to competition or for a dog that has become careless with collection.

Proofing

- You can gradually increase your lateral distance from the target to a distance that reflects the normal working space between you and your dog.
- Proofing this grid also means working it with all the different hurdles you will see on courses inserted into the corner jump spots (except for the broad jump or long jump, as previously noted).

Adding Handler Motion

The initial training of this grid is done with you motionless and neutral, allowing your dog to focus on making the crucial weight shift necessary to perform the small "X" cleanly. Do not be in a rush to add motion to the exercise. Remember, adding handler motion should only enhance your dog's performance, never degrade it. If the motion is adversely affecting your dog's performance, limit your motion as much as possible and gradually build up your speed.

When you are ready to introduce handler motion, work on just the slice from the small "X" to one of the corner obstacles.

1. Lead out halfway between the step-out facilitator jump and the corner jump your dog is going to take. Release your dog and move forward at a walk. Your dog should complete the grid correctly and continue driving forward toward the target. As you walk, your dog will pass you so it's a good idea to have a trained "Go On" cue that you can give as your dog catches up with you.
2. Lead out halfway again, release your dog, and move forward at a jog.
3. Lead out halfway again, release your dog, and move forward at a run.
4. Run with your dog from the start or take a short lead-out.

When you think your dog is ready, follow the same steps for adding motion while working the entire slice line, from corner jump to corner jump. It is important to remember that when you are doing the entire line, you need to provide deceleration information for your dog as he enters the small "X."

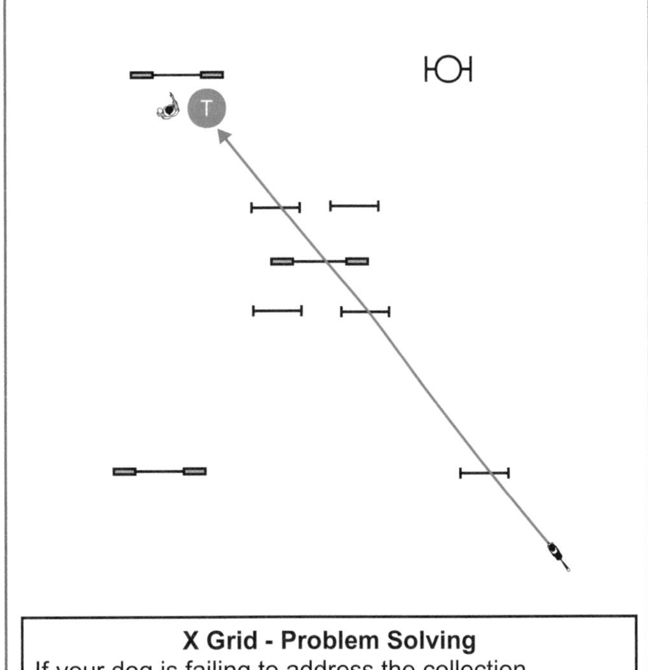

X Grid - Problem Solving
If your dog is failing to address the collection required, take away his opportunity to move back into extension.

Adding Handling

There is no change of side in this exercise so crosses are not necessary.

Grid Variations

See X Bend Grid.

X BEND GRID

Overview

The X grid offered on a bend is a very difficult exercise. Your dog needs to have successfully worked through the original X grid before you offer this version, because the biomechanics of bending off the ground and through jumps is significantly more difficult for your dog to produce.

As with other jumping grids, there are layers of understanding and athleticism that need to be built carefully so you do not challenge your dog to a higher degree than appropriate at that point of your dog's understanding.

Reference DVD

None.

Setting Up the Grid

This grid requires ten jumps: six winged jumps and four nonwinged jumps that function as facilitator jumps.

First build the small X in the center of the grid. Place a winged jump in the center of your work area. This jump will be set at your dog's competition height. Then place the four nonwinged facilitator jumps at an angle off the center jump. These form the step-in and step-out set points for the main jump. They serve only to shape your dog's jumping arc and inform him where to take off and land; therefore, they have no height.

Once the small X in the middle is in place, position the four winged jumps at the corners of the grid. The two jumps on the left side are placed at a different distance from the facilitator jumps than the two jumps on the right side of the grid. By setting up the spacing in this manner, you are asking your dog to assess the difference in distances and offer an adjustable stride. The corner jumps are set at your dog's competition height.

The final winged jump is centered between the two jumps on the right side of the grid to make an arc.

Important:

- Do not introduce this grid until you have completed the bend work foundation grid.
- Because stage 3 of this grid involves jumping into compression, this stage should not be done with puppies.

Jump Spacing and Height

Use the information below to determine the jump spacing and jump heights for the grid. Although I have used these distances with success at seminars, they are only guidelines and you may need to adjust them for your dog. Spacing between the jumps is measured from the center of one jump to the center of the next.

Big Dogs

- *Facilitator jumps and center jump:* Space the four facilitator jumps 6' from the center winged jump. Set the center jump at your dog's competition jump height and set the facilitator jumps at a maximum of 6" in height.

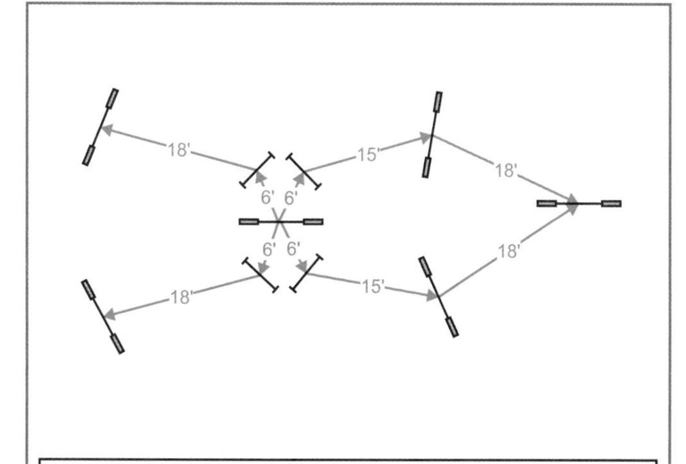

X Bend Grid - Setup
Set up for the X bend grid with jumps spaced for big dogs.

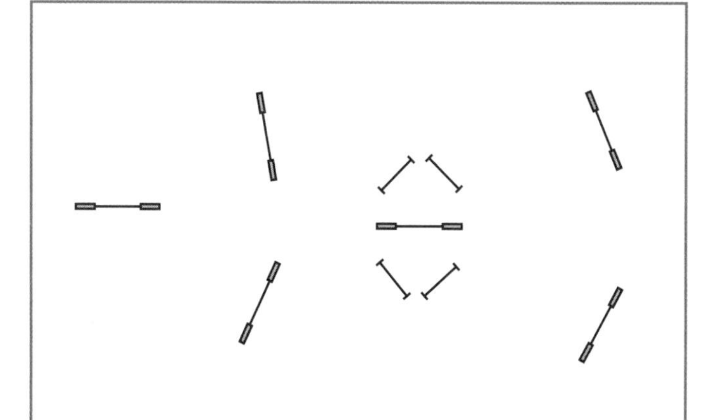

X Bend Grid - Mirror Image Setup
Although the text refers to the single jump being set up on the right side of the grid, the mirror image of this grid should also be practiced.

- *Corner jumps:* Choosing a measurement between 15'–18', space the two corner jumps on one side of the grid at the same distance from the facilitator jumps on that side. Choosing a different measurement between 15'–18', space the two corner jumps on the opposite side of the grid at the same distance from the facilitator jumps. Set all of the corner jumps at your dog's competition jump height.
- *Arc jump:* Position this jump 18' from the winged jumps on one side of the grid. It should be set at your dog's competition jump height.

Medium Dogs

- *Facilitator jumps and center jump:* Space the four facilitator jumps 5' from the center winged jump. Set the center jump at your dog's competition jump height and set the facilitator jumps at a maximum of 6" in height.
- *Corner jumps:* Choosing a measurement between 15'–18', space the two corner jumps on one side of the grid at the same distance from the facilitator jumps on that side. Choosing a different measurement between 15'–18', space the two corner jumps on the opposite side of the grid at the same distance from the facilitator jumps. Set all of the corner jumps at your dog's competition jump height.
- *Arc jump:* Position this jump 18' from the winged jumps on one side of the grid. It should be set at your dog's competition jump height.

Small Dogs

- *Facilitator jumps and center jump:* Space the four facilitator jumps 4' from the center winged jump. Set the center jump at your dog's competition jump height and set the facilitator jumps at a maximum of 4" in height.
- *Corner jumps:* Choosing a measurement between 13'–15', space the two corner jumps on one side of the grid at the same distance from the facilitator jumps on that side. Choosing a different measurement between 13'–15', space the two corner jumps on the opposite side of the grid at the same distance from the facilitator jumps. Set all of the corner jumps at your dog's competition jump height.
- *Arc jump:* Position this jump 18' from the winged jumps on one side of the grid. It should be set at your dog's competition jump height.

Tiny Dogs

- *Facilitator jumps and center jump:* Space the four facilitator jumps 2'–3' from the center winged jump. Set the center jump at your dog's competition jump height and set the facilitator jumps at a maximum of 4" in height.
- *Corner jumps:* Choosing a measurement between 12'–14', space the two corner jumps on one side of the grid at the same distance from the facilitator jumps on that side. Choosing a different measurement between 12'–14', space the two corner jumps on the opposite side of the grid at the same distance from the facilitator jumps. Set all of the corner jumps at your dog's competition jump height.
- *Arc jump:* Position this jump 18' from the winged jumps on one side of the grid. It should be set at your dog's competition jump height.

Target

Place the target on the tight line of the bend, giving your dog room to get to it without landing on it.

Dog's Starting Position

- We do not want a sit or a stay for bend work; remember, your dog would prefer not to bend. You need to begin with forward motion into the grid. You will put your hand in your dog's collar, move forward with your dog, release him into the grid, and then rotate into the turn.
- Position your dog so he is centered on the first jump, facing straight ahead, and looking at the jump; do not place your dog on an angle to the first jump.
- Give yourself room to take several steps forward with your dog to guarantee he takes jump #2. Many handlers take only one step forward, say "Go," release their dog, and then abruptly stop motion. At that point their dog looks immediately for an exit from the grid to get back to the handler. This happens because motion overrides everything else, so leave yourself enough distance from the first jump of the grid to move forward and get your dog going.

Handler's Position

You need to move forward with your dog into the grid while *not* pushing your dog off the tight line. Rotate your hips and shoulders to support the turn.

Take a lead-out as necessary to ensure that you can move at a slow pace while supporting your dog rather than having to run. You want your dog to be able to focus on this very difficult jumping task before you increase your motion.

Progressions

Until your dog is very comfortable with the X bend grid, it should be built up progressively *each time* you do it. When your dog is performing the full grid with ease, you can start a training session with stage 3.

Stage 1

Initially, you will work just the center portion of the grid. You are shaping your dog's jumping arc. It is important not to create too much momentum from your dog into the grid. The more speed he carries, the more difficult it will be for him to perform the bend, which makes it easier for him to take the off-course facilitator jump.

Do one repetition starting at each facilitator jump in the center.

If your dog has any difficulty with this exercise, do not try to move on to stage 2. Instead, do an additional four repetitions at this stage. Do not move on to stage 2 until your dog is comfortable and demonstrates ease of motion, and until he understands his task is to bend.

Stage 2

Now you are going to ask a distance question. Your dog will jump from the center of the grid to each of the corner jumps. Each line is designed to be one stride for your dog even though the distances are different.

Place the target on the tight line on the landing side of the corner jump, giving your dog enough room to get to it without landing on it. Do one repetition to each corner jump.

It is likely that you will need to practice stages 1 and 2 for several training sessions before you try to move on to stage 3. If you are not planning to move on to stage 3 in a training session, you can do another repetition of each arc.

X Bend Grid - Progressions
Stage 1
Do one repetition starting from each facilitator.

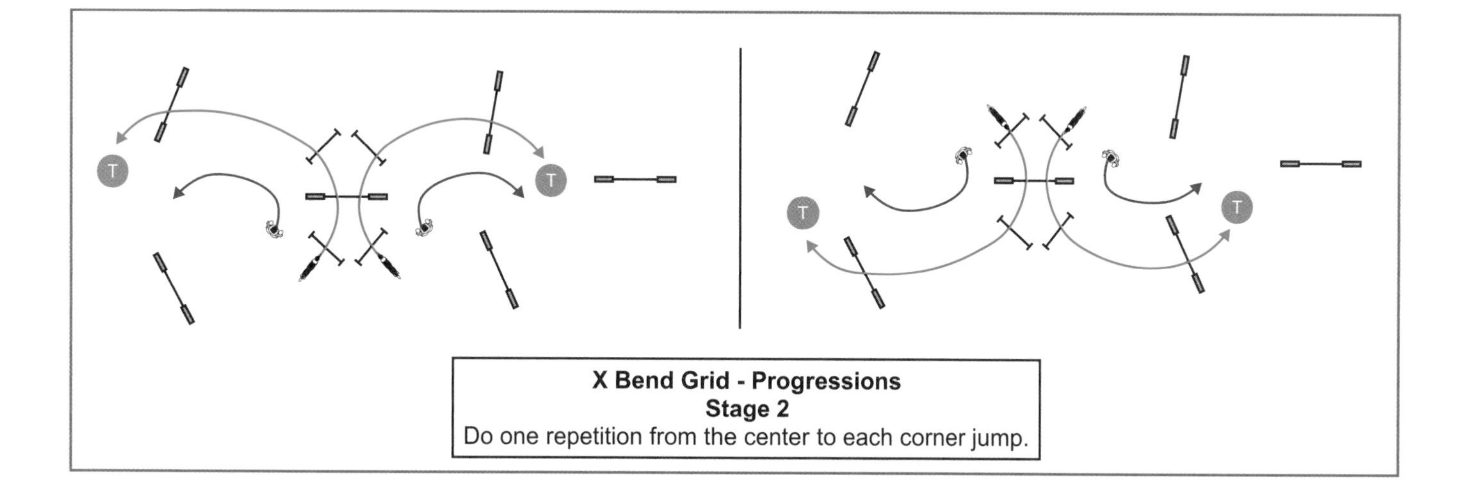

X Bend Grid - Progressions
Stage 2
Do one repetition from the center to each corner jump.

Stage 3

Now your dog will go from tight collection on a bend into extension and then back into tight collection again. Rather than placing the target, carry it with you and drop it at your feet as you break off the exercise. Do the four repetitions shown in the diagram. This is a difficult exercise; be sure not to overdo it.

Problem Solving

Problem: Your dog jumps into the arc and exits going straight over the off-course facilitator jump rather than bending.

Solution: You may have sent your dog into the grid with too much speed. Try starting closer to the step-in facilitator. If your dog repeats the error, he may not be able to physically "hold on" to the bend so he chooses the straight exit, which is easier to perform. Go back to stage 2 and do bend work on an arc a few times before attempting this exercise again. You may have to remove the off-course facilitator jumps until your dog can actually perform the bend.

Problem: When going from extension to collection, your dog fails to get the weight shift necessary to enter the small "X" and he performs the set point in a frightening manner.

Solution: Immediately go back to stage 2 and work the small "X" to the outside jumps. If this does not fix the problem, you are moving too fast with the exercise.

How Much to Practice?

This grid can be included in your dog's maintenance training as one you visit every two or three months. It is a particularly good grid for tuning up your dog prior to competition or for a dog that has become careless with collection.

Proofing

You are proofing your dog as you gradually increase the difficulty of this grid. He must work hard to take the bend rather than the off-course jump.

You can gradually increase your lateral distance from your dog.

Adding Handler Motion

Handler motion is built into this grid. However, you can work on taking a short lead-out and increasing your speed. Remember, though, adding handler motion should only enhance your dog's performance, never degrade it. If the motion is adversely affecting your dog's performance, limit your motion as much as possible and gradually build up your speed.

Adding Handling

There is no change of side in this exercise so crosses are not necessary.

Grid Variations

See X Grid.

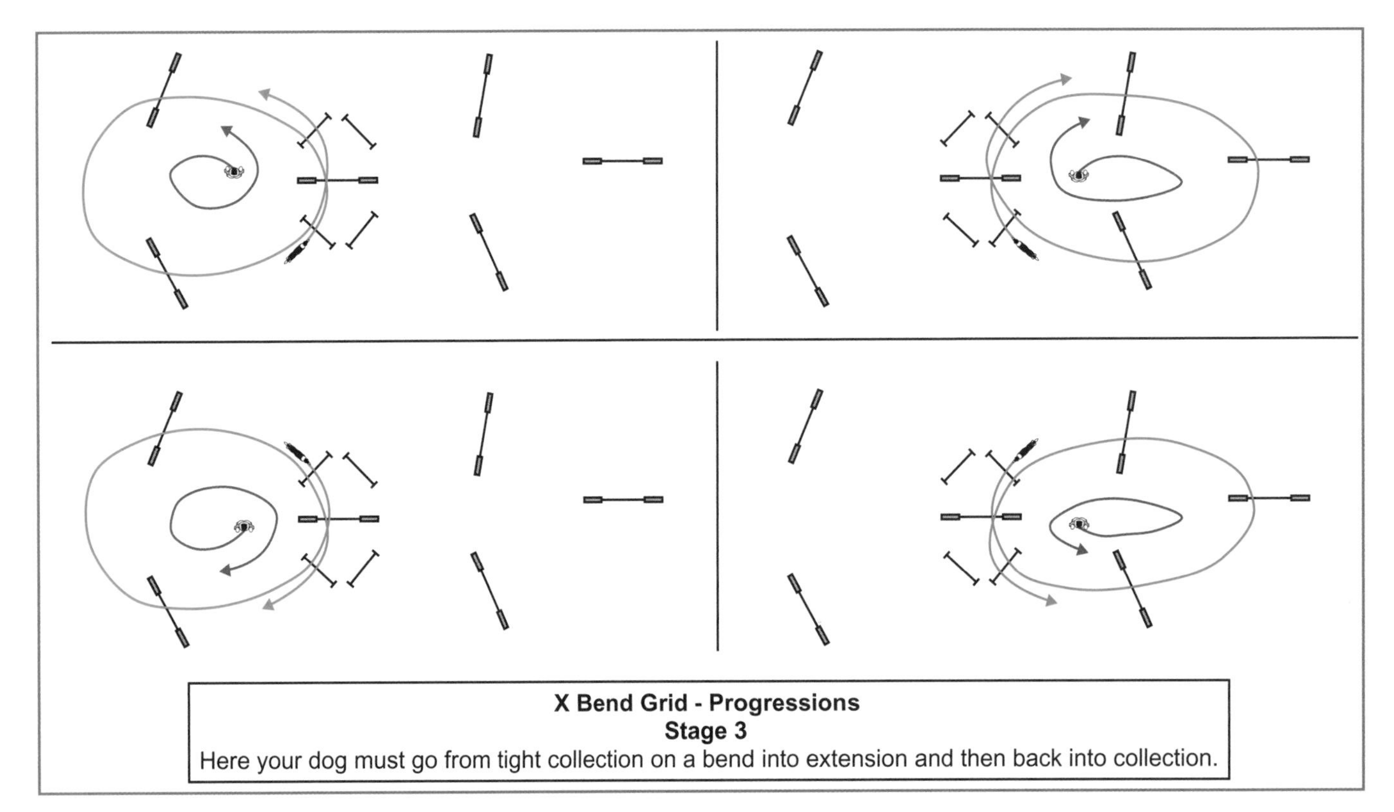

X Bend Grid - Progressions
Stage 3
Here your dog must go from tight collection on a bend into extension and then back into collection.

ZIG-ZAG GRID

Overview

It's quite a test for your dog to find and drive the line in this grid because of the physicality required. That said, while it is a physically difficult grid for dogs to perform, they appear to really like it. When this happens, I always ponder the "why." The dogs cannot give me an answer, but when I see a dog truly enjoy a grid that is difficult, I feel it must provide him with an answer as to just how his body should work while performing the task.

Schooling this line helps dogs understand how best to use their bodies to flatten out their serpentine lines; the flatter the line, the faster the time. This grid is also a mental challenge for your dog to find and drive the line, which most do with ease. It is a plyometric grid for footwork and balance; there is no height involved.

A dog's hind feet are working differently on this line then they do on other plyometric lines. Some dogs will become ever so supple with their spine and make it into a lovely slalom, while other dogs prefer to drive straight through the line. Either is appropriate and it is just a matter of what your dog chooses to offer.

Due to the nature and set up of this grid, there is no way to make it small enough for the tiny dogs. This is not a problem; just expect that small to tiny dogs may stride the line while bigger dogs will bounce the line.

Reference DVD

None.

Setting Up the Grid

Five jumps are required for this grid: three winged jumps and two nonwinged jumps. The jumps are placed as shown in the diagram, always using the winged jumps as jump #1, #3, and #5 and the nonwinged jumps as #2 and #4.

This grid takes some practice to set up. In the interest of fairness to your dog, take the time to give the grid a good look from both ends before asking your dog to perform it. Make sure there is a straight line through the center of the jumps.

The spacing between the jumps is the same for all dogs. Set jump #1 (winged jump) at a slight angle on your center line. Then place jump #2 (nonwinged) with about 12" of space between the standard and the wing of jump #1 to form a wide "V." Continue in this same manner until the line is complete. If you measure from the center of one jump to the center of the next, the spacing should be 6'.

Height is not a part of this grid; the jumps are *never* raised.

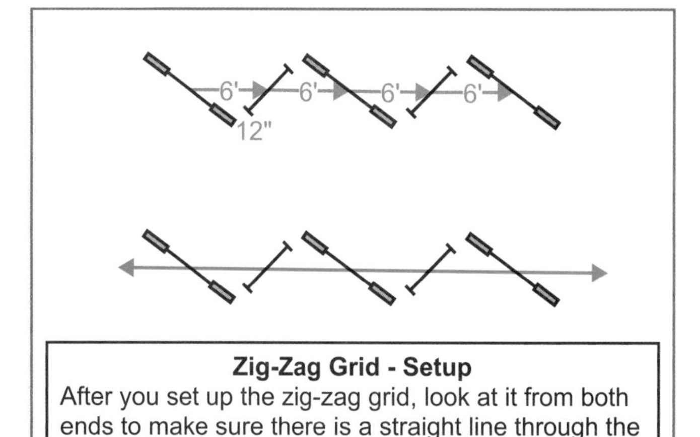

Zig-Zag Grid - Setup
After you set up the zig-zag grid, look at it from both ends to make sure there is a straight line through the middle of the jumps.

Jump Spacing and Height

Use the information below to determine the jump spacing and jump heights for the grid. Although I have used these distances with success at seminars, they are only guidelines and you may need to adjust them for your dog. Spacing between the jumps is measured from the center of one jump to the center of the next.

Big Dogs

- Space the jumps 6' apart and set at a maximum of 16" in height. The height of these jumps never increases during the exercise.

Medium Dogs

- Space the jumps 6' apart and set at a maximum of 16" in height. The height of these jumps never increases during the exercise.

Small Dogs

- Space the jumps 6' apart and set at a maximum of 6"–10" in height. The height of these jumps never increases during the exercise.

Tiny Dogs

- Space the jumps 6' apart and set at a maximum of 4"–6" in height. The height of these jumps never increases during the exercise.

Target

The target moves for each stage of this grid as described in "Progressions."

Dog's Starting Position

- Line up your dog so he is facing the center of the first jump on a slice.
- The distance between your dog and the jump should be half the distance of the first space in the grid, in this case 3'.
- Your dog can be in a sit, stand, or down.
- Your dog should be looking forward at the jump or target before you release him.

If you do not have a start-line stay, have a training partner restrain your dog.

Handler's Position

- Lead out and stand one step ahead of the target and one step laterally off the target. This allows your dog to get to the target without passing the plane of your body.
- Face the direction your dog is traveling, looking over your shoulder to watch him.
- Sometimes stand to the left of the target and sometimes stand to the right to work your dog on both sides.

Progressions

This grid is built up progressively during a training session.

Stage 1

Place the target in front of jump #3, making sure it is clearly visible to your dog from his starting position. Do two repetitions and then repeat from the other side of the grid.

Stage 2

Place the target about 10' after jump #5 *before* you take your dog to the start line. Do two repetitions starting from each side, one with your dog on your left and one with him on your right.

Problem Solving

Problem: Your dog never enters the grid, instead running alongside it to the target.

Solution: Place the target in front of jump #2 so your dog only needs to perform one jump to get his reward. Repeat twice, once from each end of the grid. Repeat stage 1 with the target in front of jump #3.

Problem: Your dog begins the grid well, but then aborts the effort and runs to his target.

Solution: Sometimes just changing the side you are working on will solve this problem for your dog. If that solves the problem, you will want to do more work at stage 1 on the weaker side before trying the entire grid again on that side.

If changing sides does not work and your dog still pulls out of the line, return to stage 1. Once your dog is jumping #1–#3, move the target so it is in front of jump #4. After doing this sequence once or twice, move the target so it is in front of jump #5. Finally, place the target on the landing side of jump #5.

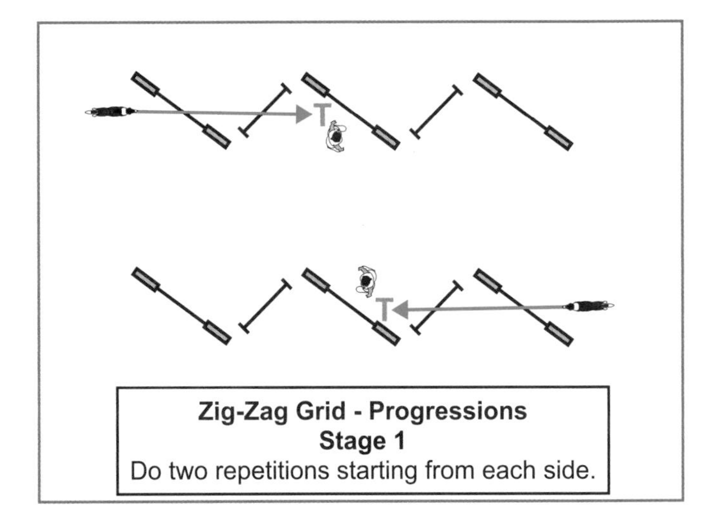

Zig-Zag Grid - Progressions
Stage 1
Do two repetitions starting from each side.

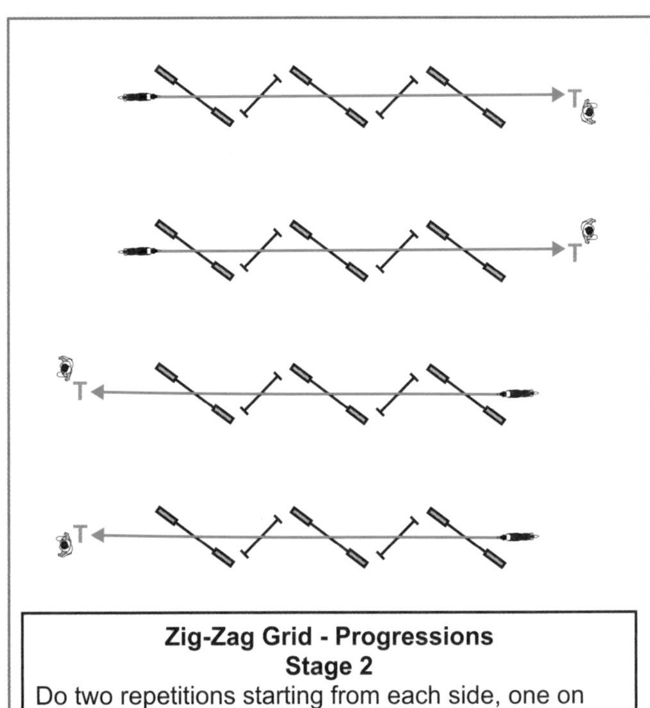

Zig-Zag Grid - Progressions
Stage 2
Do two repetitions starting from each side, one on your left and one on your right.

How Much to Practice?

This grid can be included in your dog's maintenance training as one of the plyometric grids you use. It is also a good grid for tuning up your dog prior to competition to see if your dog can easily find and drive his line.

Proofing

Because of the difficulty of this grid, the only proofing I would do is to straighten the angles of the jump slightly to see if your dog can still recognize and drive the line with ease.

Please note that this grid is never intended to become a straight line.

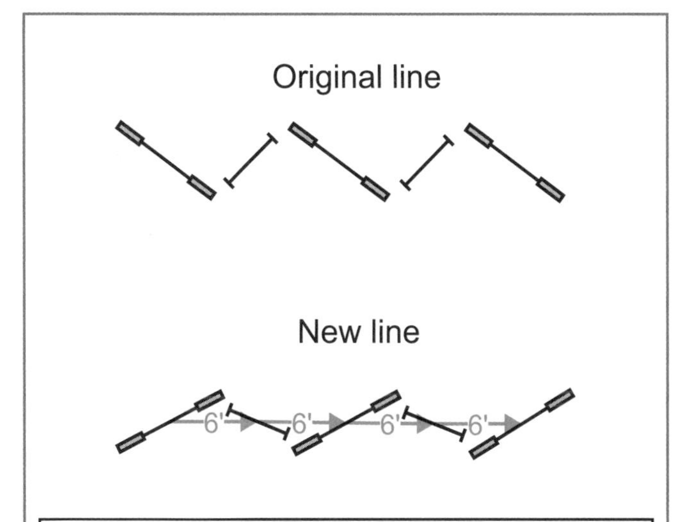

Zig-Zag Grid - Proofing
To proof the grid you can straighten the angle of the jumps slightly to see if your dog can find the line.

Adding Handler Motion

The initial training of this grid is done with you motionless and neutral, allowing your dog to focus on the difficult jumping task. Do not be in a rush to add motion to the exercise. Remember, adding handler motion should only enhance your dog's performance, never degrade it. If the motion is adversely affecting your dog's performance, limit your motion as much as possible and gradually build up your speed.

When you are ready to introduce handler motion:

1. Lead out to jump #3. Release your dog, and move forward at a walk. Your dog should complete the grid correctly and continue driving forward toward to the target. As you walk, your dog will pass you so it's a good idea to have a trained "Go On" cue that you can give as your dog catches up with you.
2. Lead out to jump #3, release your dog, and move forward at a jog.
3. Lead out to jump #3, release your dog, and move forward at a run.
4. Run with your dog from the start or take a short lead-out.

Adding Handling

There is no change of side in this exercise so crosses are not necessary.

Grid Variations

None.

I have worked with Susan Salo for the past 11 years training 7 of my own dogs and several of my students' dogs. The gifts I've received by working with Susan through a multitude of grids have been invaluable. All of the dogs have shown marked improvement in their confidence and efficiency while performing. I, on the other hand, have learned that jumping is a complex task that cannot be taken for granted and is influenced (both positively and negatively) by my position and movement. The grids Susan presents offer a methodical approach to teaching dogs the various mechanical skills required to jump in a consistent and balanced form. At the same time, they provide an opportunity to learn how to adjust my handling based on how much "help" a particular dog may need from me for a given performance. Susan's grids have become a routine part of my agility training. The dogs love doing them as much as I do! I can't thank her enough.

—Katie Oilschlager, Agility competitor, instructor at Susan Garrett's Say Yes Dog Training, owner of Think Pawsitive Dog Training, LLC

APPENDIX 1: TYPES OF GRIDS

Bend Work/Lead Change Grids

- Bend work foundation grid
- Circle grid
- Circle to extension grid
- Circle to figure-8 grid
- Figure-8 grid
- Lead change grid
- Oval to figure-8 grid
- S grid
- X grid
- X bend grid

Collection to Extension Work

- Adjustable stride #1
- Adjustable stride #2
- Circle to extension grid
- Jumps and tunnels grid
- X grid
- X bend grid

Extension to Collection Work

- Jumps and tunnels grid
- X grid
- X bend grid

Foundation Grids

- Adjustable stride grid #1
- Bend work foundation grid
- Ladder grid #1
- Progressive grid
- Set point exercise

Handling Grids

- Circle to extension grid
- Circle to figure-8 grid
- Figure-8 grid
- Lead change grid
- Oval to figure-8 grid
- S grid
- Serpentine grid

Plyometric/Bounce Grids

- Circle grid
- Figure-8 grid
- Ladder grid #1
- Ladder grid #2
- Progressive grid
- Straight-line stride grid
- Zig-zag grid

Stride Grids

- Adjustable stride #1
- Adjustable stride #2
- Straight-line stride grid

Maximum collection is an odd-looking moment in the dog's motion as his hind feet pass his shoulders. This moment determines how far the dog's shoulders can reach forward. As this dog attains maximum collection, his back, neck, and head are creating angle of elevation.

APPENDIX 2: SAMPLE LESSON PLANS

On the last day of every seminar I teach, everyone wants to go home with a specific lesson plan for continuing with the work I have introduced. Unfortunately, I cannot offer this unless I am working regularly with a dog. Each dog is an individual with specific needs, but more importantly, it would be a grave error to commit any dog to a training plan because *your dog's needs continue to evolve and change over time.* You must continuously assess your dog's jumping skills throughout his agility career, and your training plan must change to accommodate your dog's needs at any point in time.

It is with great trepidation that I offer a few lesson plans here to assist dogs with their ongoing jumping needs and education. While I have put much thought into this portion of the book, the information is intentionally generic and must be tailored to the needs of the individual dog at any specific time. Therefore, do not feel that you cannot mix and match lesson plans to suit the needs of your dog, as it is my sincere wish that each of you will begin to identify those needs and have this resource as a guide to offer help to your dog.

All dogs' needs will change. Even brilliant jumping dogs may go for extended periods with little maintenance work for their jumping skills, but then have times when they need more maintenance or a "tune-up" in a particular area. Other dogs need weekly work to keep their skills sharp and their confidence high. To my mind this is a private matter between dog and handler. At the finish of a brilliant run, no one will ever ask you, "How much work did that take?" Likely you will simply hear, "Great run," and at that moment I hope you look down, smile at your dog, and reply "Yes, it was," and leave it at that. The work involved is always a secret, if you will, between horse and rider or handler and dog. If we do our job well enough, no one else needs to know about or witness our animal's shortcomings.

The more you trial and train, the more you will undoubtedly need to reinforce good jumping biomechanics. With that thought in mind, that is a lot of jumps for any dog to perform, so a solid conditioning program needs to be of the utmost importance in your dog's daily life. Your dog needs to carry an appropriate muscle mass for his size and body type. He needs to have top nutrition and hydration offered. If your dog is not properly conditioned and maintained, he will begin to burn muscle as he becomes depleted, which of course is not optimum for performance enhancement. To avoid stress and reduce the possibility of injury, always be aware of the surface you are working your dog on, and watch how hard your dog is having to work to get the job done on that surface.

When following any lesson plan, the outcome needed for your dog is *success.* It is critical for you to be able to recognize when a good place to stop has arrived for *your* dog, even if you have not finished working through "the plan." These lesson plans are outlines only! For many dogs doing two to four repetitions of one or two skills is enough for a session. We want your dog to build success on success; many dogs have never known what that feels like. Go slowly, but not so slow as to bore your dog. Keep your sessions short and happy, and build a solid foundation. Think of it this way: when you do gridwork, you are making deposits into your dog's savings account, and with each trial or seminar, you are making a withdrawal. If you don't put money back into the bank, your dog will end up bankrupt. Take the time to build a hefty savings account for your dog and monitor the withdrawals carefully.

"I am the instructor. You are the trainer." —Unknown

Lesson Plan: Dogs with Little or No Jump Education

This foundation lesson plan is for a dog with little or no jump education or an older dog that needs to go back to gain education.

Week 1: Introduce the set point exercise and ladder grid #1.

- Introduce the set point exercise with a single jump and then do it with a double.
- Work on the set point for three days and then go to every other day for the remainder of the week.
- During the same session, change between the single jump and the double frequently.
- When your dog begins the every-other-day rotation, introduce ladder grid #1.
- Set up the ladder grid alongside the set point exercise and rotate your dog back and forth between the two grids, rather than doing the set point to completion and then the ladder grid to completion.

As the days progress, check to see if your dog's *first* jumping effort demonstrates ease of motion and looks good in terms of body organization. This is a good time to go back and refer to the photos and explanation in "Anatomy of the Jump." If it takes your dog three, four, or five repetitions before his jumping effort look effortless, then he is still struggling with the process. You can move on to introduce new grids, but continue to allow time for practicing set point work.

When your dog begins the every-other-day rotation, add in the ladder grid and allow for five or six repetitions in each session. At this time it is advisable to rotate your dog between the two exercises rather than doing set point to completion and then the ladder grid to completion.

Week 2: Introduce the adjustable stride grid #1.

- Every other day continue with the set point exercise and ladder grid #1, rotating back and forth between the two grids.
- Introduce the adjustable grid with a single winged jump, doing it at least twice during the week. In the second training session, change out the winged jump for another type of jump (double, panel, tire, etc.).
- Offer a change of jump on the second session.

When doing the adjustable stride grid, pay attention to whether your dog is comfortable moving up to each new distance. He should be recognizing that the jump has moved. If your dog is struggling, offer very small increments of change until he is comfortable with the exercise, which may take a while depending on the mindset of your dog. The more operant your dog, the quicker he understands this exercise.

If your dog is struggling with the adjustable stride grid, end the training session with one or two set points to rebuild confidence, which should always be protected.

Week 3: Introduce the bend work foundation grid.

- Introduce the bend work foundation grid. Work on it every other day during this week.
- Continue with the set point exercise, but use it as a form of warm-up for the other gridwork you will be doing in a session. Be sure to alternate which jump you use as the set point jump.
- End each training session with the ladder grid #1.

Week 4: Introduce the progressive grid.

- Practice gridwork every other day.
- On the first day of work, do the set point exercise as a warm-up and introduce the progressive grid.
- On the second day of work, pick two grids your dog has been doing well and that he seems to enjoy. Rotate your dog through the two grids three times, stop, and go play with your dog or take a walk—no more training.
- On the third day of jump work, introduce the set point exercise on the slice. Then select one grid that was a problem for your dog in the prior work and follow the steps for working through that grid. Finish the session with the progressive grid and make it fun.

After four weeks of consistent work, you should begin to be able to identify your dog's strengths and weaknesses (at that point in time).

Remember that training is pressure to our dogs. Using this methodology of inserting a few of the less successful exercises into the pattern of the grids your dog does well allows you to build your dog's confidence as you improve his weak areas.

Week 5: Introduce the S grid.

- Practice gridwork every other day.
- On the first day of work, do the set point exercise as a warm-up and introduce the S grid. Finish the training session with the ladder grid #1.

- On the second day of work, do the set point exercise as a warm-up and offer the progressive grid.
- On the third day of work, introduce the set point on a bend. Finish the training session with a grid your dog does well and enjoys.

Week 6: Introduce the figure-8 grid.

- Practice gridwork every other day
- Introduce the figure-8 grid, practicing every other day. It will take more than one training session to build this grid to completion. End each session with either the set point exercise or ladder grid #1 to relieve stress and allow your dog to fly through a grid that is better known to him. Again, you are keeping a balance of applying pressure with the training and then releasing it.

As you will note, there is more handler motion required as you progress through the grids. Make certain this is a smooth process for your dog. Remember to ask yourself, "When I begin to move, does my dog's performance change?" If the answer is yes, is it changing for the better or does it become worse? If your answer is the latter, slow down the motion you are providing until your dog can settle into his work.

Week 7: Review the grids your dog has learned so far.

Practice gridwork every other day.

This week you are going to work through all of the exercises your dog has learned thus far. Set up two different grids in each training session. Do no more than three repetitions of each grid.

My friend Anne Stocum uses the phrase, "Roughly right is good enough." I love this quote because it allows people to not feel compelled to always have perfection. Perfection in anything is elusive; we feel little tastes of it and want more, which is what keeps all of us striving for it. Just don't make the poor dog pay the price! If during this week a grid needs more fine tuning, put it on the list for week 8.

Week 8: Go back to the grids that were problematic last week.

- Practice gridwork every other day.
- This week is dedicated to putting a bit more work into any grids that your dog had trouble with in week 7. Finish or begin each session with the set point exercise. Mix in either ladder grid #1 or the progressive grid as necessary to relieve pressure from working on one of your dog's weaker grids.

Week 9: Introduce the circle to figure-8 grid and the zig-zag grid.

- Practice gridwork every other day.
- On the first and second days of work, warm up with set point work, and then introduce the circle to figure-8 grid. It will take you at least two sessions to begin to get a good flow of motion from your dog.
- On the third day of work, warm up with set point work and introduce the zig-zag grid.

Week 10: Introduce the circle grid.

- Practice gridwork every other day.
- Pick one grid your dog performs with ease and joy. Work that grid for a few repetitions and then introduce the circle grid.

Lesson Plan: Puppies

Starting young puppies is one of my absolute favorite parts of teaching; they are so very willing and happy to learn new things. I enjoy watching them gain confidence and understanding of task, and am constantly amazed at how quickly they "get it" compared to older dogs that have not been encouraged to think independently.

Young dogs do not yet possess their full muscle mass, so they cannot count on strength alone to accomplish the tasks required of them. This means they quickly learn to use some finesse to accomplish the jumping tasks instead of brute force. I see many older dogs without adequate training that use or misuse strength as a substitute for mechanical skill; whereas a dog that learns skills at an early age is a better problem solver and has a greater sense of body awareness.

This 15-week-old puppy) has already mastered a lovely set point and is organizing his body exceptionally well for flight. The head is down and the back is round and soft; the feet are close together, demonstrating good understanding of the mechanical aspects of the task.

This is an excellent example of a young dog moving confidently through a baby dog grid. Note that the dog's head is down and his focus is forward and on task, allowing for a soft spine and fluid motion. Each stride regulator is meant to be the center of the dog's stride, which this young dog is doing very well. The stride regulators become a road map as to where the dog places his feet.

Dogs that have started their careers with this jumping program are amazing in their intelligence at finding the correct path, even if their handler is slightly out of position. Since they have been schooled through many different patterns since puppyhood, they can identify these patterns in a course and know what they have to do with their body to perform them successfully. They move towards jumps full of confidence and without rushing. They use their bodies in a way that makes it look truly effortless. It still gives me goose bumps to watch these dogs as they quickly and decisively make choices. They make jumping look so easy, while many other dogs struggle with the task. Is it that some agility dogs are just more gifted and athletic? I truly think not. By following a training process that imparts an understanding of jumping, these dogs enjoy a body that has been encouraged to be supple, athletic, and relatively ambidextrous.

At a recent seminar I had a very young Kelpie puppy, 14 weeks old, with a very experienced handler. On day one of the seminar the young dog would choose to go around most jump bumps put before him; yet by day three, this same puppy was completing a line of five stride regulators for a total of 30' of distance driving to his toy. The puppy was terribly proud of his accomplishment and had grown in confidence within only three short sessions of work.

Exactly when I start a young dog is dependent on each dog's mindset and coordination. But, as a general rule, I start teaching puppies these skills between four and six months of age. Dogs at this age have not completely developed their neurological pathways yet, nor have their growth plates closed; while I am encouraging you to begin this education, there are cautionary guidelines:

- Each dog is an individual and needs to be treated as such; some are ready for this training at four months and some are not.
- Training sessions need to be very short in duration.
- Restrained recalls are a wonderful motivational tool, but for jumping foundation work, balance at the start line is important. If you don't have a stay and need someone to restrain your puppy to work on these exercises, they should hold your dog unemotionally and not try to get him excited or allow him to pull toward you, which will shift his weight to his front.
- Puppies do not jump any height. Stride regulators/ jump bumps are used for training at this point.

Following these guidelines, puppies between four and six months of age can do all of the foundation grids as well as most of the other grids in this workbook. I do not have puppies work on going from extension into tight collection, so I would not do stage 3 of either the X grid or X

The first photo shows a set point exercise for a puppy. I use both 4" and 8" PVC cut into 4' or 5' lengths (or whatever length will fit between your jump standards when the PVC is placed on the ground). The pieces of PVC are then cut in half lengthwise so each piece makes two stride regulators. The second photo demonstrates the setup for teaching a young dog a diagonal line or slice. The last photo demonstrates the setup for the puppy version of beginning bend work.

© JEANINE MCANANEY

This is the progressive grid set up for puppies.

bend grid with a young dog. Please refer to the *Puppy Jumping* DVD for more information.

Each grid is a question to the young dog, a puzzle for him to solve if you will.. Your dog needs to learn to read the task ahead and not simply focus on the handler, which can make for an insecure dog on course. Every time a dog turns his head to "check in" with the handler, he is asking a question, "Where am I to go?" Our goal in his jumping training is to teach him to look ahead at the job he must perform in each grid and focus on the tasks. This is why the importance of the target at the end of the grid cannot be overstated; it is essential to encourage your dog to look at the job at hand and drive to a target. I do prefer a toy but if a dog will not interact with a toy and food must be used, the food must then be placed on something highly visible. When a toy is used, do remember to actually "play" with the puppy once he has made contact with the toy!

When my training partner and I started working with our young pups (they were the same age), we would meet once a month to introduce new concepts to the puppies, do one or two exercises with three or four repetitions each, and then be done to "play." There are so many foundation skills to be put in place with puppies that you do not need to stress any particular area of learning. If you do it correctly, it is all simply a fun game to play with your puppy while he is learning valuable problem-solving skills.

Above all else, each session with your young dog is about building a solid relationship, so remember to make each and every session a fun experience for your dog. If he is having a great time, so will you!

Following is one training plan you could follow with your young dog. But I cannot overemphasize the importance of constantly assessing your puppy and determining what he is or is not ready for. Puppies go through many phases as they grow physically and mentally. If your dog is going through an awkward gangly stage, then skip your jump training during this period. If he is going through a phase in which he is having trouble focusing, then skip your jump training during this period. If your dog is struggling with a particular grid, let it go and wait another month to reintroduce it to him.

Month 1: Introduce the set point exercise and the ladder grid #1.

- Do one or two training sessions this month.
- Introduce the set point exercise and ladder grid #1, using jump bumps between the standards rather than bars. Do no more than three or four repetitions of each grid.
- End the session with lots of play!

Month 2: Introduce the set point exercise on a bend and on a slice.

- Do one or two training sessions this month.
- Set up the set point exercise on a bend, the set point exercise on a slice, and the ladder grid #1 using jump bumps rather than bars between the standards. Do no more than three or four repetitions of each grid, but rotate back and forth between the grids rather than doing each grid multiple times in a row.
- End the session with lots of play!

Month 3: Introduce the adjustable stride grid #1.

- Do one or two training sessions this month.
- Warm up with the set point exercise, but change the appearance of the wings you are using with the jump bump. Introduce the adjustable stride grid #1 using jump bumps rather than bars between the standards. Do only three or four repetitions. Finish with one or two repetitions of the set point or the ladder grid #1.
- End the session with lots of play!

Month 4: Introduce the bend work foundation grid.

- Do one or two training sessions this month.
- Warm up with the set point exercise, but change the appearance of the wings you are using with the jump bump. Introduce the bend work foundation grid using jump bumps rather than bars between the standards. Do only three or four repetitions. Finish with one or two repetitions of the set point or the ladder grid #1.
- End the session with lots of play!

Month 5: Introduce the progressive grid.

- Do one or two training sessions this month.
- Set up the set point exercise (again changing the appearance of the wings you are using with the jump bump) and the progressive grid using jump bumps rather than bars between the standards. Do only three or four repetitions of each grid, but rotate back and forth between the grids rather than doing each grid multiple times in a row.
- End the session with lots of play!

Month 6: Introduce the S grid.

- Do no more than one training session every two weeks.
- Do the set point exercise on a bend as a warm-up. Introduce the S grid using jump bumps rather than bars between the standards. Do only three or four repetitions. Finish with one or two repetitions of the set point, ladder grid #1, or the progressive grid.
- End the session with lots of play!

Month 7: Review.

- Do no more than one training session every two weeks.
- Set up two or three of the grids that you have learned. Do only three or four repetitions, but rotate back and forth between the grids rather than doing each grid multiple times in a row.
- End the session with lots of play!

Month 8: Introduce the figure-8 grid.

- Do no more than one training session every two weeks.
- Warm up with the set point exercise, but change the appearance of the wings you are using with the jump bump. It will take more than one training session to build the figure-8 grid to completion. End each session with either the set point exercise, ladder grid #1, or the progressive grid.
- End the session with lots of play!

Month 9: Introduce the zig-zag grid.

- Do no more than one training session every two weeks.
- Warm up with the set point exercise, but change the appearance of the wings you are using with the jump bump. Introduce the zig-zag grid using jump bumps between the standards rather than bars. Do only three or four repetitions. Finish with one or two repetitions of the set point.
- End the session with lots of play!

Month 10: Introduce the circle to figure-8 grid.

- Do no more than one training session every two weeks.
- Warm up with the set point exercise, but change the appearance of the wings you are using with the jump bump. Introduce the circle grid using jump bumps rather than bars between the standards. Do only three or four repetitions. Finish with one or two repetitions of the set point, ladder grid #1, or the progressive grid.

End the session with lots of play!

Lesson Plan: Young Dogs Transitioning from Jump Bumps to Jumps or Just Attaining Full Jump Height

First, a word about young dogs: while doing jump grids, your dog must understand that execution of task is his job and must be taken seriously. For a young, high-drive

© JEANINE MCANANEY

Once a young dog begins to have a good understanding of the task at hand, I am always changing the appearance of jumps to ensure that he learns to drive to whatever is in front of him. Presenting jumps (at this point still with bumps rather than bars) in different ways at an early age encourages his problem-solving skills and will make for a brave dog that is not easily over faced by jumps that do not look "normal." I do not use this jump setup to create height, but rather to teach dogs to read the effort required of them. To a young dog, this setup appears to be bigger and more imposing than just a jump bump. In fact, many young dogs will opt to go around or under the slanted bars. If this happens, I make the center space bigger and more inviting to the dog. Over several repetitions, I gradually close the gap. The poles must never be crossed to create height and must always be presented behind the large stride regulator (8" PVC). Therefore, the dog can only go through the exercise in one direction.

dog, this means he must sometimes sacrifice speed until he learns to use his body in the appropriate manner. If you have a young dog that can get "spun up" to an almost out-of-control state, I advise against attempting to school jumping when his brain is absent.

If this sounds like your dog, I suggest giving him a good run and play session before you begin a gridwork session. You need to take off "the edge" so he can settle, think, and offer an appropriate performance. Like small children, many young dogs can hold things together for only short periods in the beginning. If you commit to a routine for getting your dog ready to think, it will take less and less time to work off the edge, and your dog will understand that when you place him on the start line, it is business time.

The information included here assumes that you have worked through puppy jump grids as described in the lesson plan for puppies and that you have been training your handling foundation and the other obstacles separately.

Transitioning from Jump Bumps

When a puppy is about 10 months old, you can introduce a set point jump with a low jump bar as illustrated in the photo. The bar should not be placed any higher than the height of your dog's elbow. You can use a bar presented this way on any jump that is supposed to have height in a grid.

Work through the lesson plan for dogs with little or no jump education, introducing bars on the jumps and using facilitator jumps instead of the jump bumps you were using in the puppy grids.

The timing of when you raise the bars on jumps in a grid that are intended to have height depends on your dog's physical and mental readiness.

Beginning Course Work

As you progress to beginning course work where you are handling sequences, keep the sequences short and have a set point grid set up in your training area. If a bar comes down, break off the sequence—don't continue on! Offer your dog the chance to "rebalance" by doing a couple of set points to his target. Then go back and let your dog try the sequence again. While punishing knocked bars is not appropriate, running on once a jumping mistake has occurred is also not a good way to create an understanding of task. I always have a set point at the ready when training my dogs, so they can be reminded of good balance and execution of task as necessary.

As you begin to add more obstacles to the sequences, balance that work by doing some gridwork during the same session. For example, start your training session with a couple of set points. Move on to your sequence/handling training exercise, and then finish the training session with ladder grid #1 or ladder grid #2 to keep your dog's footwork competent and balanced.

Your goal is to keep your dog's jumping skills solid and confident while moving steadily toward your end goal. There will be setbacks, as there are with any type of dog training, yet they should be brief and not of the type that will erode your dog's confidence or long-term understanding.

When a puppy is about 10 months of age, I introduce a jump bar. I place a large jump bump (8" PVC) between the wings, which by now the puppy is already familiar with. The jump bump is just in front of the bar as shown. This ensures the young dog will make a nice, round arc and not touch the bar.

One Gridwork Session a Week!

Ideally your weekly training plan includes at least one session that is dedicated just to gridwork, allowing your dog to focus on his jumping in exercises that don't include handling.

I recommend starting each gridwork session with a couple of set points. Remember to keep changing the jump you use for the set point or make it look different (add flower pots in front of the wings, for example).

During a session with a young dog, I like to mix it up between a plyometric grid and one that requires a good deal of thought from your dog. For example, I might do the zig-zag grid (a plyometric grid) coupled with the serpentine grid, or I might do the straight-line stride grid coupled with ladder grid #2 (a plyometric grid).

If you have a dog that needs to build more confidence, do only one repetition of the thinking grid and then do a repetition of the plyometric grid before going back to the more difficult grid. This dog's last effort in a jump training session should be a grid he thoroughly enjoys. You always want to quit before your dog stops wanting to work. For some less confident dogs, this may be as few as four to six total repetitions total in a session (not of each grid!). You are not just building your dog's jumping skills at this time, you are being sensitive to the needs of your partner so you can strengthen your partnership and build confidence.

Here's some additional information about specific grids to keep in mind with young dogs:

X grid: This is a difficult grid, but it's an important one for overly confident but less-than-thoughtful young dogs because it will keep them challenged mentally. If your dog does not care to collect after extension, do the grid from extension *into* collection, stopping at his target after the center portion. Do not allow your dog to open up again and complete the grid (extension to collection to extension) for at least one or two additional training sessions.

Figure-8 grid: This grid builds in some handler motion and is excellent for developing speed and enthusiasm in less confident dogs.

Circle to figure-8 grid: This is another grid that is useful for less than confident dogs. They will build confidence if you balance the work carefully and know when to end a training session.

Ladder grid #1, ladder grid #2, and zig-zag grid: These grids are usually a great deal of fun for dogs. However, because your dog must bounce, they require a good deal of strength. If your dog is not willing to move with enough speed to bounce, do not offer these grids until you build more enthusiasm. See the problem solving information for each grid that discusses how to backchain the grids.

Ending a Gridwork Session

End each session with a grid your dog finds "easy" and enjoyable. However, it is important that the last jumping effort does not always include handler motion. Once handlers begin running more in gridwork, they dislike leaving themselves out of the game. But to keep the balance between enthusiasm and good execution from your dog, there needs to be a balance between putting pressure on your dog's performance with handler motion and allowing execution of task in a thoughtful manner with no pressure.

Lesson Plan: Maintenance Program

This is a lesson plan for maintenance work with a dog that is not having problems with any of his jumping skill sets. Because I am on the road teaching a great deal, this is the program I use most often to keep my dogs jumping clean and to maintain their athleticism. Even the most skilled athletes need to revisit the basics often, so foundation grids are an important part of maintenance jump work. Even if you're handling at the Masters level, you need to occasionally offer your dog the chance to focus on his jumping and work quietly to his target on the ground when you aren't in motion.

- *Adjustable stride grid #1:* Offer this grid to your dog once a month. It only requires seven repetitions, four moving the jump out and three more moving the jump back to the starting distance. I love offering my dogs this grid when I am traveling because there are usually jumps that look different from the ones they see at home and in my geographic area. It's an excellent opportunity to check their response to jumps that appear very different.
- *Set point exercise:* I do the set point exercise each day while traveling, but I only do two or three repetitions with a dog that is not having any jumping problems. I use the opportunity of being in new places to practice set points with jumps my dogs haven't seen before. You can also make the set point exercise part of your agility handling training ses-

sions by doing two or three set points before your training session as a warm-up and two or three at the end as a cool down.

- *Ladder grid #1 or #2 and progressive grid:* During the week I do one session where I offer my dogs a ladder grid along with the progressive grid. We do two or three repetitions of each grid.
- *Bend work:* Bend work is an important skill set to include in your maintenance training. I like to mix up which grid I use for maintenance bend work:
  - *S grid:* This grid is one my favorites because it presents problems for the best of dogs from time to time. The grid inspires speed and sometimes the dogs are caught off guard reading the upcoming lead change and they add extra steps.
  - *Circle to figure-8 grid and figure-8 grid:* Both of these grids allow your dog to get up to full speed while he practices bend work.
  - *Jumps and tunnels:* This is another favorite of mine for offering speed to the dogs and keeping them highly motivated.
  - *At least one grid your dog hasn't seen for a while:* Although foundation skills are a critical part of regular maintenance work, once a month you want to select one or two grids that your dog either has never seen before or hasn't schooled through for some time. Just remember that when you select a difficult grid, be sure to end with something your dog finds easy and fun. It may be another month until you tune him up again and you do not want to leave your dog feeling unsuccessful.

Using Gridwork to Recharge Your Dog's Enthusiasm

Today's courses require that we frequently "crank down" on our dogs with control and then open them up again, which puts tremendous pressure on them. Dogs can have trouble finding a sense of flow and rhythm in this type of course. Some dogs may find too many courses of this nature demotivating. Monthly maintenance gridwork can provide the perfect opportunity to recharge your dog's enthusiasm.

Set up three grids: two that your dog really enjoys doing and one that they find more difficult. Start with a couple of repetitions of a fun grid, then move on to one or two repetitions of the more difficult grid, and then move back to a fun grid. Always end the session by doing a grid he likes. Beginning with what your dog knows and likes, and ending with something that can fire him up, allows your dog to have fun while honing skills.

Lesson Plan: Tuning Up for an Important Competition

Before you start a jumping "tune-up" program prior to an important competition, you need to consider the fitness of your dog. Think about how many jumps a day your dog will be performing to accomplish the tune-up plus how many jumps per day he will be performing during the competition. As a horsewoman first and foremost, I am constantly shocked at how few agility people do the math. One day of competing at a USDAA trial or at a handling seminar is at least 100 jumps for your dog. Dogs only have so many jumps in them before their bodies begin to show the wear and tear of repetitive stress. Everywhere I go I preach to people, who I am certain are sick of hearing it, that the agility dog needs to be extremely fit to withstand all the stresses this sport will put on him. The core strength required of the animal to produce that many jumps, let alone to produce them well, is enormous.

With this in mind, I begin a jumping tune-up at least three weeks out from a big competition to make certain my dog is fit enough and will peak at a good time. The ladder grid is an important part of the tune-up. While many people do not grasp the importance of the plyometric grids, I will say again, it is the dog's footwork that carries him to each and every obstacle. The low ladder grids are, to my mind, an essential part of offering your dog information about how to come forward and approach jumps. Your dog should be able to produce and sustain good speed, balance, and footwork through these grids.

I also recommend coming back to this lesson plan after a big competition. As Annie Pyle remarked to me after the 2014 AKC Nationals, going back to the gridwork after a big competition basically hits your dog's reset button for performance.

Week 1: Do three gridwork sessions this week.

- For each session, do the set point exercise using different jumps along with ladder grid #1. You can rotate your dog back and forth between the two grids, rather than doing the set point to completion and then the ladder grid to completion. Do five or six repetitions of the ladder grid and three or four set points.

- For the second session, add the adjustable stride grid #1 as a third grid to work. Because your dog is already well-schooled in gridwork and this is just a tune-up effort, the first effort your dog offers should demonstrate confidence and good form. If this is the case, then do only seven repetitions of this grid.
- For the third session, add a bend work grid (your choice) as a third grid to work.

Week 2: Do three gridwork sessions this week.

- For each session set up ladder grid #2 to continue building core strength. If you want to do a different plyometric grid, set up the zig-zag grid instead and assess how easily your dog finds and drives his line.
- For the first session, set up the circle to figure-8 grid or the oval to figure-8 grid to test your timing and your dog's striding to jumps while you are in motion and handling. Set three or four of the jumps at a height that is 2" higher than your dog's normal jump height. This helps keep your dog looking at the jumps and assessing each task more carefully. Do one or two set points before beginning the grid and then one or two set points on completion of the grid.
- For the second session, set up the circle to extension grid. Set three or four of the jumps at a height that is 2" higher than your dog's normal jump height. Do one or two set points before beginning the grid and then one or two set points on completion of the grid.

  Be aware of whether your dog's footwork is clean, particularly to the change of direction obstacle. Is your dog adding strides to perform the lead change? Is he responding in a timely way to your handling information? Is he redirecting back to looking for work immediately once information is given or does he get stuck on you after those transitions? If your dog is having trouble redirecting back to work, take a step back. Slow down your motion and use your target on the ground several times. Then break off the session with a couple of set points. Revisit this grid in a day or two.
- For the third session, repeat one of the handling grids from the prior sessions.

This is not the time to feel pressure to perform many repetitions of any gridwork that does not serve your dog. If you think your dog requires more work, do the week one grids again.

Week 3: Do three gridwork sessions this week.

- Begin and end each session with both the set point exercise and ladder grid #1.
- For the first session, set up the adjustable stride grid #2.
- For the second session, set up the X grid or X bend grid along with the Jumps and Tunnels grid. Set three or four of the jumps at a height that is 2" higher than your dog's normal jump height. Do one or two set points before beginning the grid and then one or two set points on completion of the grid. The X grid is a difficult grid, so offer the Jumps and Tunnel exercise to end the session and take off some pressure.

  For the X grid, pay close attention to how well your dog extends when going from the center X to the jumps at a distance as well as how well he collects when going from the outside jumps into the X. This exercise will help your dog practice the quick weight shift he needs for performing jumps as well as entering weave poles and contacts. If your dog struggles with clean, quick lead changes in the air, select any of the lead change grids in place of the X grid, and work on tuning up that skill set.

  While doing the X grid, use as little motion as you can while still giving your dog the information he needs. To me the question should always be, "How little help does my dog need from me to get this done?" I am not recommending that you be a lazy handler, but if your dog has a high level of knowledge then handling is more of a supporting role than a dominant role wherever possible.
- For the third session, set up the figure-8 grid. This grid allows for more handler motion and gets maximum speed from your dog, while still saving his legs from too much jumping and pounding before a big competition.

Things to Remember During This Time

- It is your job to know when your dog has done enough and to break off sessions at a good point rather than continuing to drill your dog until things begin to go bad. Most dogs at this level only require a check of their skill sets before going into a competition. Your dog already knows his job and you know yours. This is not the time to drill endlessly, looking for perfection in every detail. And, it is not the time to play catch-up on jumping skills you may have been neglecting.

- During these three weeks, it is important to provide your dog with plenty of good aerobic exercise that allows him to stretch out. Run or swim your dog as much as possible, but remember that three weeks out from a big competition is too late in the game to be making major changes or doing work that has simply been put off for too long.
- I like to give my dogs two to four days off from agility and jumping training prior to a big competition, but the exact number of days off depends on your dog. During this break, your dog should still get plenty of normal exercise; it is just a short break from training so he arrives at the trial fresh and ready to play.

A Note About This Lesson Plan

This lesson plan is a good general plan for dogs that are not having any major problems with their jumping. If your dog is struggling with some of the skills, it is your job to customize a tune-up training plan for him. While I cannot provide a specific tune-up plan for your dog, I can share a few guidelines to keep in mind while tuning up your dog for a big competition:

- If you have a high-drive young dog that goes into "speed mode" and ceases to be mindful of how to execute his job, select the more complex grids (X grid, zig-zag grid, circle to extension grid) or any of the grids that offer a good deal of collection into extension. With this type of dog, I focus on working them primarily from extension into collection to make certain he is being mindful of the job he must perform. The mind-body connection is crucial for this dog's success. It is your job as his teammate to use these grids to remind him of how to focus and use his body properly. The reward for these dogs is to allow them to perform the grid from collection into extension. However, I would not allow them too many repetitions of that performance before competition.
- If you have a less motivated dog, select grids that allow your dog to get into rhythm and flow (circle to figure-8 grid, serpentine grid, jumps and tunnels grid, adjustable stride grid #1 or #2, figure-8 grid, etc.) With these dogs, I would work almost entirely on your dog going from collection *into extension* to build up his confidence and drive toward jumps. Save the complex problems for the trial. Focusing on difficult grids during this time will take a toll on a less motivated dog and begin to slow him down as he overthinks. You want to allow your dog speed in his preparation and have him brimming with confidence before the trial.

I hope you will begin to get a sense of "which grid, when" for your dog to ensure he continues to offer the highest level of performance with the most enthusiasm possible. Have fun with the process and enjoy your dog's brilliance. Remind him often just how clever he is. Our dogs will perform heroics for us in the ring in an effort to save us from our mistakes!

Lesson Plan: Dogs That Take Off Too Early

I am always struck by just how emotional this topic is for agility enthusiasts. People who I work with regularly have emailed or called me because someone commented at a trial that their dog left early for a jump. In a panic they ask, as if it is a contagious disease, "Is my dog going to do this all the time now?" I have seen far too many participants in my jumping seminars come to tears over this topic as they look for a solution to make agility fun for themselves and their dogs once again. They are desperate for a glimmer of hope or the chance of a fix for their problem.

I read Linda Mecklenburg's article on early takeoff in *Clean Run* many times and with great interest. I thought the article was brilliant and, most importantly, gave the handlers of these dogs the chance to not blame themselves for the problem, and perhaps shed fewer tears. Although I dislike labels for animals or people, to work on solving the problem we have to refer to it by some name—and taking off early for the jump is what these dogs are doing.

Pain, Structure, or Confidence

Dogs that have physical pain, dogs that have certain structural characteristics (very straight shoulders, high-set neck, lack of slope from the point of the croup to the tail set) that make it difficult for them to get their shoulders out of the way as they load their weight back onto their hips for takeoff, and dogs that have a confidence problem, often *appear* to be taking off early because they stutter step, measure the jumps, or both. They are not taking off early, but rather they are trying to delay their takeoff and get closer to the jump. They often lower themselves as they attempt to buy some time.

Training the mechanical skills needed for jumping by using gridwork, and properly treating the dog in the case of an injury, can resolve the dog's jumping problem.

Vision

Dogs that consistently take off early have a long takeoff distance from the jump and a short landing distance. Usually the dog is actually beginning his descent *before* he reaches the bar. He will shorten or omit his final stride in order to take off early.

The group of people who are currently doing research with dogs that demonstrate early takeoffs believe that the dogs have a vision errors or a combination of errors. For most of these dogs, CERF tests come back normal and retinoscopy often doesn't indicate problems. There are now human pediatric optometrists helping with the research. In addition to finding near- and far-sightedness problems, they are finding dogs with astigmatism and depth perception problems. Many more dogs need to be tested, both dogs that jump "normally" and dogs that take off early, and a great deal more research is needed to understand the significance of the findings, but progress is slowly being made.

Every dog that has come to me with this problem has had their eyes checked and has been given a clean bill of health. But I always trust the dogs; they give us all the information we seek. Sadly, until the research provides an answer, the dogs that suffer from this problem are truly suffering. Early takeoff takes a huge toll on the confidence of these dogs, yet they continue to try to play the game with us as best they can. All we can do is be of as much help to our dogs as possible.

Some General Guidelines and Tips

Thanks to those dogs I work with that continue to do their very best as they struggle with this problem, I can give handlers some general guidelines and advice.

- Indoor venues with poor lighting will greatly exacerbate the problem. Indoor trials on dirt not only tend to have poor lighting, but there's usually poor contrast between the jumps and the dirt flooring. The situation is even more difficult if the venue has walls that offer no contrast. You should take these factors into consideration when entering your dog in a trial.
- Poor outdoor lighting (such as lots of glare) and busy backgrounds can greatly exacerbate the problem and should be a consideration.
- Bending lines offer these dogs the best opportunity to excel. A long, straight line of jumps in a row can cause the problem to show itself. This is never the time for handler convenience, meaning you cannot run off and leave your dog until he has fully assessed the line and offers to move toward the jumps. You cannot hurry your dog at these times and you cannot get too far ahead of him. The farther ahead of your dog you get, the more pressure he feels and the worse the problem can become.
- Exiting from a dark tunnel or chute into the light is another place on course that is difficult for dogs, and handlers need to be mindful of their dogs and wait for them.
- Lowering your dog's jump height should be considered. Your dog is really trying; this is not a behavior he chooses to offer. Many of these dogs are more comfortable at a lower height.

I do not believe these dogs can be "cured" until a medical intervention is discovered, but I do think they can be managed if you choose to do the work—these dogs are high-maintenance jumpers and will be throughout their agility careers. Trialing and seminars cause these dogs to "spend" a lot of their confidence, so you need to be mindful of this and constantly make deposits into your dog's savings account by using gridwork.

These dogs never reach a point where you can slack off for long periods of time and have a competent jumping performance remain intact.

Retraining for Confidence

A great deal of retraining from the ground up is necessary to rebuild your dog's confidence and allow him to develop a bit of a different stride to aid him with his takeoff. In the horse world (always my point of reference) there are wonderful amateur horses that have learned how to "pat the ground" in a subtle way to buy themselves some flexibility for their takeoff spot. The horses do this in an upright manner, never dropping their shoulders toward the ground as dogs do. I have seen a few dogs perform this maneuver in an upright position with success. When I first saw a dog offer the behavior, I was amazed and a bit shocked, but once dogs figure out how to do it, it becomes the way that they power themselves up for the lines of jumps ahead of them on course. They use their shoulders in a different way than they did in the months before retraining. These dogs are not "fixed," but they are being managed for their problem and still enjoy the sport.

I recommend starting your retraining by following the lesson plan for young dogs transitioning from jump bumps to jumps or just attaining full jump height. As you work through the grids, keep the following in mind:

- Initially, do all of the grids with no handler motion. You will lead out to a target and recall your dog. The target is an important piece of this work.
- Remember that your motion puts pressure on your dog and the goal here is to allow him a chance to become comfortable reading and responding to lines of jumps. If you increase the speed of your motion before your dog is comfortable, he will revert to his previous jumping style. A second set of eyes or a video camera is invaluable for evaluating how your dog is responding to your motion and determining whether you have gone too far, too fast.
- It is a good idea to keep the jump height low while initially working through these exercises. Once your dog has found a comfortable stride and is showing good jumping form, you can then add height in small doses for the exercises where height is appropriate. Always be certain your dog's performance remains consistent and that he does not immediately revert to the old jumping behavior.
- Your rewards must be of the highest value because it is stressful for these dogs to address the problem.

Regular Maintenance

It is impossible to give you a specific schedule for maintaining a dog that takes off early. Each dog is very different and you will need to determine whether he needs to practice gridwork several times a week, every other week, etc. It is a careful juggling act to see how many jumps and how long a time your dog can hold up a good solid jumping performance. Here are some guidelines for how to focus your practice.

- Dogs that take off early need to visit the ladder grids frequently to ensure they come forward in a positive manner to meet the jumps. These dogs should be doing ladder grids prior to each and every competition and again after each competition. You could set up either ladder grid #1 or #2 along with the progressive grid and alternate back and forth.
- Set points should be worked as part of every gridwork training session.
- I would offer this group of dogs the adjustable stride grid #2 and primarily work the bending lines. I would have the dog do the straight-on jump only once or twice per session, carefully monitoring the dog's response to the straight-on jump. I would also keep the distance used on the more conservative side to keep the dog driving forward.
- Work on bend work regularly, selecting any of the bend work grids. Limit the straight line work as much as possible.
- The adjustable stride grid #1 can be offered, but I suggest you bend the line of jumps slightly so it's a curve rather than a straight line.

I am not suggesting these dogs cannot perform jumps with a straight-on approach, but knowing straight-on jumps often cause concern for these dogs, I limit how many times they have to perform them. You can save those situations for classes and trials, then come and regroup your dog by practicing the drills that build his confidence.

The severity of the problem varies greatly from dog to dog. Offer help and be understanding of how hard your dog is trying. It is difficult enough to perform jumps, let alone if your dog has trouble seeing them! A dear friend once told me that these dogs come to us as working dogs—to *not* work them is simply not an option. It is our job to manage and determine what they can perform and then manage them carefully, enjoying what they offer along the way.

Olympic diver Greg Louganis once reminded me that he needed to achieve over 100 flawless repetitions to perfect each dive he performed. Just imagine how many repetitions he did that were not perfect to achieve his end goal of Olympic gold.

APPENDIX 3: JUMPS FROM A DOG'S PERSPECTIVE

When I teach a foundation jumping seminar, I try to educate the participants about jumping from the dog's point of view. This requires handlers to learn to look at courses from the dog's vantage point and not generalize their own viewpoint of a jump here, a tunnel there, and another jump over there. The dog sees each and every jump as a separate entity because from the dog's point of view, each jump is different than the last. For example, see the jumps in **Figures 1 and 2.** Both jumps are doubles, yet each jump presents a very different picture to the dog. Most people find this quite fascinating since they have not considered these differences before. I always think of my horse training experience first; therefore, I look at the picture the animal sees and consider its effect on the animal and how it may affect the performance of a particular obstacle.

Hierarchy: Rating Jump Bars

First we need to look at the jump bars themselves. In **Figure 3** you can see several bars on the jump. I have rated the bars from top to bottom in order of dominance, meaning how quickly your dog's eye is drawn to it. If you look quickly at the photo you will see the top bar with its bold striping is the first one that catches your eye. The second pole with the red spiral stripe is the next most prominent, followed by the pole with blue vertical stripes. The least dominant pole is the faint lavender-colored one on the bottom.

So what does this mean to the dog? Consider the rate of speed your dog is moving on course, then consider what is in your dog's line of sight in addition to the jump. Is there a favorite obstacle just before or immediately after the jump? If this is the case, perhaps there is a tunnel following a jump, the dog is far better served if that jump was set with the most prominent bar in the photo (black and yellow striping) as opposed to the least prominent bar (lavender-striped pole) so it is clearly visible to a fast-moving dog that needs information very quickly.

Light Conditions and Similarity

You must also consider the time of day and how much light is shining on the jump. Because the cones and rods in a dog's eyes work differently than those in the human eye, the dog's visual acuity can be conflicted when bright light makes an already unimportant-looking jump bar almost invisible. I am not suggesting you get on your hands and knees to see what is in the dog's line of sight for every jump and how the light is hitting it, just that you become aware of these factors which can strongly affect your dog's performance.

You also need to consider whether all the jumps in your training arena look similar. Many trainers prefer the jumps with a fixed ground bar because of the ease with which they can be moved around. This preference, however, can cause problems with regard to the dog's understanding of jumping.

Several years ago I was teaching a seminar at a facility that had only a couple freestanding wings (no attached ground bar); the rest of their jumps all had a ground bar. When I used the freestanding wings in a grid, every dog added strides before those jumps. They added strides because the jumps with the freestanding wings had less definition than the ones they were used to. The appropriate place for takeoff was less clear to the dogs, causing the extra stride. The next time I returned to this facility there were at least 20 new jumps, all of which had no ground bar. But one of the dogs that had learned agility only using the jumps with the ground bars (arguably one of the best small dogs in the world), continued to struggle with doubles that had no ground bar for years.

Dogs, like horses, should be schooled with all the different jumps they will encounter in the ring. This training should be in a comfortable environment so the dog can work through any issues and meet all the jumps coming forward without patting the ground, measuring, or otherwise trying to buy himself time to figure out where an appropriate takeoff place might be.

If you look at **Figures 4 and 5**, you will see two doubles (oxers). Both are without ground bars and present an uncluttered picture to the dog of the task required. I have a hard time with the fact that in the agility world, doubles are set with one or two angled bars under the back bar of the spread. See **Figure 6**. I think this is very misleading to dogs since it draws their focus down toward the ground instead of up to the top bar, which is where they need to focus.

When you look quickly at the two doubles in Figures 4 and 5, they appear to be just two doubles. Now think about what you learned earlier with regard to jump bars. If you place a dominant bar in the front and the least important-looking bar at the back of this double, which bar do you think the dog will lock onto? The one on the front of the jump! So the placement of the bars themselves can be of crucial importance.

In the world of equine show jumping, course building has risen to the level of an art. Deciding just where on the course a specific jump should be placed to maximize its difficulty in a technical course is paramount.

At a glance these jumps may look the same, but to dogs they're quite different. Which bar will the dog lock onto in each example?

Doubles set with one or two angled bars under the back bar of the spread are very misleading to dogs. This type of setup draws the dog's focus down toward the ground instead of up to the top bar, which is where they need to focus.

Homemade Jumps Redux

When I first began agility, I, like many others, had quite a few homemade jumps. After I took the sport seriously (it is a very addictive game) I purchased new, well-made equipment and put away my homemade obstacles. I have since returned many of them to my training field to use for the purpose of training the dogs I work with to come forward boldly to whatever jump is put before them. In **Figure 7** you can see a very busy and bright panel jump. Many young dogs opt to go around this jump the first time they see it and need a few repetitions of jumping it before they are comfortable.

In **Figure 8** you can see the flower box I use as a ground line on a single jump or as the center of a large double. This jump also causes many seasoned competitors to add strides or go around it altogether the first time they see it.

In **Figure 9** you see a very busy and imposing jump that has a solid-appearing picket fence underneath and a jump bar on top. This jump is also challenging to dogs. The picket fence catches and traps their eye and often they see the top bar late unless they are well-schooled early on to take the entire picture into their view.

Serving Your Dog a Varied Menu

You must provide your dog training time with all the obstacles he will ever see in the ring, and then some, while schooling them at home in a safe and comfortable environment. You don't want your dog to be taken aback by a strange-looking jump during the one or two classes per year that *really* count.

If all your jumps are the same, if all your poles are the same, you are not doing your dog a service. You really do need to mix it up and have a few different types of jumps and poles so that there will be no surprises in the ring, where it counts the most.

7

8

9

APPENDIX 4: THE VALUE OF PLYOMETRIC EXERCISES

The foundation jump work is largely based on plyometric exercises which are defined as jumping and bounding movements that involve rapid eccentric (i.e., lengthening) and concentric (i.e., shortening) muscle actions. This type of training enhances explosive muscular performance. Fred Wilt (1920-1994), a highly respected track and field coach from the United States, first introduced the term plyometrics in 1975. The word can be broken into parts from its Latin roots: "plio" meaning "more" and "metric" meaning "measure," thus implying measurable increases.

The neural stretch receptors are muscle spindles found within the belly of a muscle. As a muscle stretches, the spindles send a message to the spinal cord to inhibit or control how much further the muscle can stretch. In essence, the muscle spindles are stretch-control regulators that communicate directly to the spinal cord about how much stretch is happening within the muscle and the speed of that stretch. The muscle's coil, like a spring—as in when the dog loads his weight onto his hindquarter as he prepares for a jump—is absorbing the energy required for the coil's release—as in when the dog actually lifts off the ground to jump.

The low ladder grids and the other plyometric grids have two major ways to influence the forced increase in production of the required muscles: 1) Increase the speed at which motor units can be recruited, and 2) Increase the number of motor units activated during a given contraction—essentially what plyometric training accomplishes.

These exercises are widely used with well-documented success for all athletes that require explosive and quick motion, including our agility dogs. The ladder grid #1 has been a staple of my foundation jumping program right from the beginning. Unfortunately though, this grid is dismissed by many agility handlers as a nonessential portion of the dog's athletic training, mainly due to the fact them thinking that "any dog can jump, therefore why would one need to dedicate time to training it?" Fair enough, but the difference is night and day. A dog jumping fallen branches and ditches while running free in the woods can navigate these obstacles with great ease, because: 1) He has total focus forward on his path, and 2) because of this focus, his body responds quickly and appropriately. This is not, however, the dog we run with for agility.

An agility dog rarely has the luxury of total focus on a task. He must divide his focus between the task (obstacle performance) and handler information. And we must all admit that this information is often late, and we are often in the dog's path obscuring his sight of the obstacle until it's too late for the dog to respond in the manner we would like. Yet, many handlers feel it appropriate to withhold reward or even punish the dog for a dropped bar. My question is simply, "How can we hold our dogs to a higher level of performance than we are capable of producing?" Dogs that have worked on their low ladder grids have better balance and footwork, which allows them to be more resilient to the many errors we will make as handlers. Dogs that have not practiced their speed, balance, and footwork are slower to respond when things do not go just right.

I am very passionate about giving the dog the opportunity to practice the skill set we heavily rely on for agility in

a quiet, nonstressful way. And I believe that all jumping goes back to the stride the dog produces. Is that stride strong? Does it take the dog purposely forward to meet the jumps? Does the dog drive forward to an appropriate takeoff place given the rate of speed at which we are running? Does the dog exude confidence when approaching a jump? If we provide our dog with the opportunity to practice speed, balance, and footwork, the answer to all of these questions can be "yes." This is where the low ladder grids are crucial because they set up the dog to find this skill set and offer it willingly. Dogs with a solid foundation genuinely enjoy jumping hurdles, and what is better than truly enjoying your work?

In the years since beginning this work it has become evident that dogs with a good jumping foundation also have greater mental acuity than dogs who do not. What I mean by this is that they have better problem-solving skills. Since each type of grid is a new or different question to the dogs, they have learned from an early age to figure these out as they move, meaning they think quickly on their feet without taking extra pats of the ground as they assess the task. This is a major accomplishment when you consider agility is a timed event and speed is an integral part of the dog's job.

For my part, the dog earns his way to full jump height once he proves he can handle this part of the job cleanly. Then and only then does the dog also earn the right to do it faster. This is where the proofing part comes into play and taking a hard look at the impact of our motion on the dog. Slowing the dog down to execute his task with precision is never meant as a punishment to the dog; it is simply that most handlers rush into running with their dogs prior to the dog's understanding of the mechanical effort required to do the task with precision.

When I started working with dogs, it was clear to me that most (if not all) dogs will fix a mistake on their own if given the chance to repeat the exercise; therefore, they clearly do not like the feeling of making errors. Back in those early days handlers were not allowed to run with their dogs (and still are not for foundation jumping) and the dogs made very few mistakes. That has not changed. I hear at many seminars the dogs are jumping much better than they normally do; the reason being the jump work is set up for the dog to find success. We can then begin the process of duplicating that success with speed and handler motion. Everyone knows that dogs can jump; however, jumping 20 obstacles at full speed while multi-tasking brings that task to a new level of difficulty that requires time and training for success to be successfully duplicated.

Ease of motion is what we see when watching any athletic task that is well performed. We understand when watching great athletes that this is trained, practiced behavior. It does not occur quickly for most and continued practice is required to maintain that level of performance. Should it be different for our dogs?

APPENDIX 5: THE V-BOUNCE APPARATUS

These construction plans are adapted from a design by Anne Ibach.

Tools Needed

- PVC cutter or hacksaw
- Measuring tape
- Marker pen or pencil

Materials and Cutting

- 4 – 10' lengths of 3/4" Schedule 40 PVC pipe:
  - Out of two of the 10' PVC pipes, cut four 5' lengths.
  - Out of one 10' PVC pipe, cut two 4' lengths (the remainder is waste)
- Out of the last 10' PVC pipe, cut:
  - Eight 11" lengths
  - Eight 4" lengths
  - 8 – 3/4" 90° Schedule 40 PVC elbows
  - 4 – 3/4" 45° Schedule 40 PVC elbows
  - 4 – 3/4" PVC Schedule 40 tees
- 8 – 3/4" PVC Schedule 40 end caps

Assembly

Assemble the the materials according to the diagram.

You'll make two of these units.

Gluing

(Optional) If you want to glue some of the joints, *only glue what is shown within the dotted lines in the diagram.* The joints outside the dotted lines need to be adjustable to enable the apparatus to be used for dogs of different sizes.

Notes

When you begin training you will use only one V, placed in front of the jump. The legs that form the second V will be removed, and each unit will look like this.

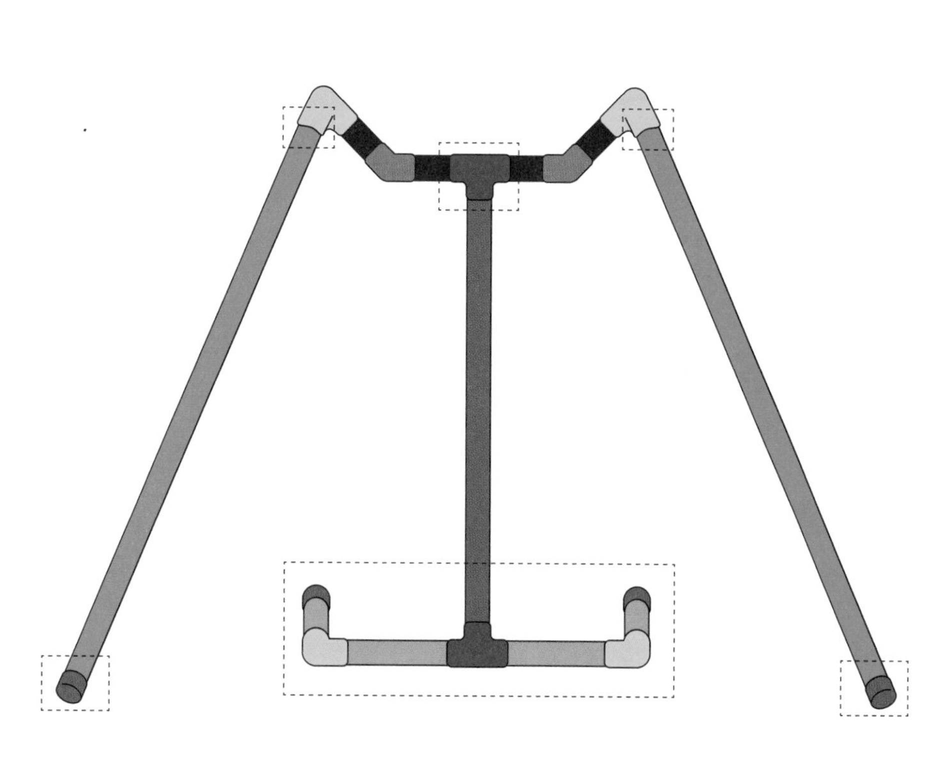

The two units are shown fully assembled with Vs at front and back, and a jump placed between them.

One leg has been removed from each unit and there is a V only at the front of the jump.

ABOUT THE AUTHOR

Susan Salo has over 35 years of experience in the world of equestrian show jumping. A lifelong horsewoman, she has ridden for many years with some of the nation's most noted horsemen including Gene Lewis, George Morris, and the late Jimmy Williams. Susan has competed throughout the United States and Canada. Turning professional, she moved to the East Coast and spent 16 years in New Hampshire and Virginia helping clients achieve their goals.

Susan brings her extensive experience of combining speed with efficient jumping to the sport of dog agility. She offers a unique perspective and knowledge of the mechanical aspects of jumping, which when properly applied, can create muscle memory and balance for the canine athlete. Not to be confused with an agility handling seminar, her jumping lessons and workshops focus entirely on the dog and building better jumping skills and instilling more confidence and speed. Training with Susan is an opportunity for you to develop your "eye" for jumping form and witness your dog learning about balance, striding, and scope until jumping becomes effortless for him.

Susan trains both horses and dogs at her residence in Northern California where she lives with her Jack Russell Terriers, Patrick and Story.

This is Susan's first book. She has published five DVDs on jumping skills:

- *Foundation Jumping*
- *Puppy Jumping*
- *Advanced Jumping*
- *Tuning Up for Competition*
- *Proofing Jump Work with Motion*

Susan Salo
PUPPY
Jumping
Susan Salo
FOUNDATION
Jumping
Susan Salo
ADVANCED
Jumping
Susan Salo
TUNING UP FOR
Competition

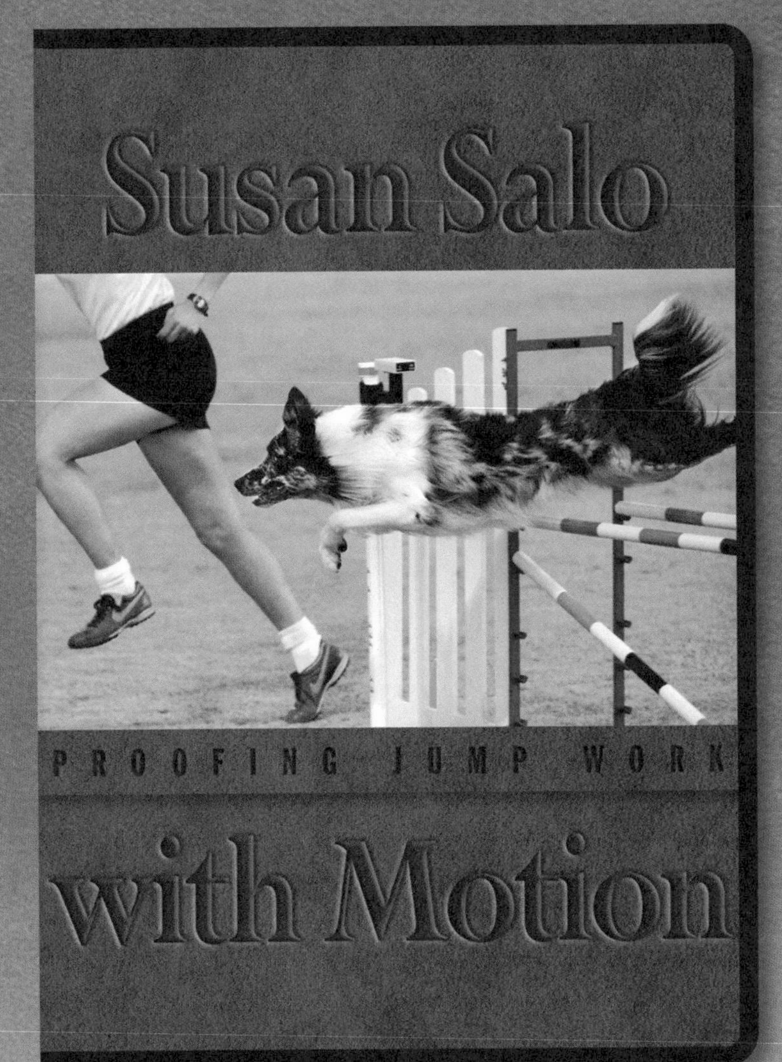
Susan Salo
PROOFING JUMP WORK
with Motion